The Human Population

A **SCIENTIFIC** *Book*
AMERICAN

The Human Population

W. H. FREEMAN AND COMPANY
San Francisco

Library of Congress Cataloging in Publication Data

Main entry under title:

The Human population.

"A Scientific American book."
"The chapters of this book first appeared in the
September 1974 issue of Scientific American."
    1.   Population—Addresses, essays, lectures.
    2.   Underdeveloped areas—Population—Addresses, essays,
lectures. I. Scientific American.
HB871.H87   301.31   74-19465
ISBN 0-7167-0515-X
ISBN 0-7167-0514-1 pbk.

The eleven chapters in this book originally appeared
as articles in the September 1974 issue of *Scientific
American*.

Printed in the United States of America

9 8 7 6 5 4 3 2 1

Contents

Foreword

The world population is growing and at an increasing rate. This is a familiar story. According to a widely held apprehension, we are fated to multiply like bacteria in a culture until we overwhelm the earth's resources. The authors of this book reckon with a different prospect. In the future, men will look back upon this period as a brief episode of rapid population growth that terminated a long history of near-zero growth during which high birth rates offset high death rates; population growth will have returned to the near-zero rate, but then low death rates will have been balanced by low birth rates. To comprehend present population trends it is necessary not only to count heads but also to recognize that the human condition is undergoing historic transformation.

The possibility that mankind may yet make rational accommodation of its numbers to the resources of this planet is presaged in the populations of the industrial or "developed" countries. These populations, a fourth of the world total, constitute a biological novelty never seen until the present century. With increasingly equal numbers of individuals, boys and girls and then men and women, in every age group into the sixth decade of life, substantially all of their members enjoy good health and expect to live out a complete human biography. These populations have reduced (or are reducing) their birthrates to the same low levels as their death rates: they are approaching zero growth. With their passage through the "demographic transition" have come radical changes in the nature of the family and in the role of women.

By contrast, the populations of the agricultural or "underdeveloped" nations exhibit the familiar structure observed in the populations of most organisms. With median ages as low as 20 or less, the young vastly outnumber the old. The expectancy of life in these countries is typically "nasty, brutish and short." Females are outnumbered by the males from about the age of 15 onward. This was the human condition everywhere until the present epoch.

Death rates in the underdeveloped countries are falling, however, in consequence of the introduction of the most portable technologies of the developed countries. Birth rates in many underdeveloped countries have begun to fall, as well, signifying that these populations also are moving into the demographic transition. Because death rates are falling faster, population growth has accelerated in some countries to doubling times of less than 25 years. The populations of the developed countries experienced a corresponding (but smaller) surge of growth as their economic development got underway.

It is apparent that economic development—a consequence of industrial revolution—is accompanied by a biological revolution. People voluntarily reduce their fertility as they experience improvements in their circumstances and, among other things, are assured of surviving offspring. Fertility rates in the developed countries continue to oscillate, however, for reasons that are not understood. The ultimate arrival at zero growth may, therefore, depend upon fine tuning from applied demography.

The question mark on the immediate future is the rate at which the underdeveloped countries will proceed with their industrial revolutions. Most are supplied with the necessary material resources (few are as so ill-favored as Japan!) and with the most precious resource of all: manpower. What they lack is the technology that has secured the material existence of the peoples of the developed countries. It may be that wider understanding of the true nature of the celebrated "population explosion," plus common humanity, will revive the flow of technical and economic assistance from the rich nations to the poor.

The chapters of this book first appeared in the September 1974 issue of SCIENTIFIC AMERICAN, the twenty-fifth in the series of single-topic issues published annually by the magazine. To our colleagues at W. H. Freeman and Company, the book-publishing affiliate of SCIENTIFIC AMERICAN, we declare herewith our appreciation for the enterprise that has made this issue so speedily available in book form.

THE EDITORS*

September 1974

1

The Human Population

The Human Population

RONALD FREEDMAN and BERNARD BERELSON

The articles presented in this book point out, among other things, that rapid population growth cannot last long. The question is: Will population level off because of high death rates or low birth rates?

The rate of growth that currently characterizes the human population as a whole is a temporary deviation from the annual growth rates that prevailed during most of man's history and must prevail again in the future. Today's situation is unique in mankind's experience: the highest growth rate in human history (about 2 percent per year) from the highest base in absolute numbers (nearly four billion). The world is currently adding nearly 80 million people per year, about as many as the population of the eighth-largest country (Bangladesh).

Over the millenniums until very recent times the human population increased at a very low rate. From the time of the agricultural and urban revolution about 5,000 years ago the population increase probably never reached as much as .1 percent a year for any long period until the late 17th century. As Ansley J. Coale shows elsewhere in this book [see "The History of the Human Population," page 15], the acceleration of world population growth was particularly pro-

nounced in countries that are among the most highly developed today: the European countries and the lands Europeans settled overseas. That growth was the product of the decline in their death rates, prolonged over three centuries and most marked from about 1800 on, and the lag in the parallel decline in their birth rates. Now the population is engaged in what can truly be called a vital revolution. We happen to live in the crucial transitional generations. Earlier the high fertility of mankind was balanced by high mortality. Currently, however, death rates have been falling almost everywhere. The birth rate has also been falling in many nations and communities, but this trend has come along later and more slowly. The population has therefore been increasing, and up to now at an increasing rate. In the 1970's the rate of increase has slightly exceeded 2 percent per year. That means a doubling time of less than 35 years, and the number currently being doubled is a very large one. Projection of such growth for very long into the future produces a world popula-

tion larger than the most optimistic estimates of the planet's carrying capacity. In the long run near-zero growth will have to be restored—either by lower birth rates or by higher death rates.

Moreover, the world is demographically divided. The developed countries are now close to replacement levels of reproduction (although there is no certainty that they will remain there). The underdeveloped countries are growing very fast: mortality is falling more or less rapidly, but fertility is changing very little, except in a few small countries. The differing age structures of the two kinds of population contribute their own problems.

The possibility that growth may be halted and the population stabilized by the control of fertility is illustrated by the recent demographic history of the developed countries: some 30 nations, as classified by the appropriate agencies of the United Nations, that share in the material abundance of industrialization. Decline in the death rates of these countries has given their populations life expectancies that approach or exceed 70 years. The age structure of these populations, trending toward roughly equal numbers in every age cohort up to the sixth decade [see top illustration on pages 10 and 11], constitutes a biological novelty not seen before in human populations. Fertility rates in many developed countries have declined close enough to their

HUMAN POPULATION OF SOME 5,000 YEARS AGO depicted itself in the rock paintings on the opposite page. The paintings are in the Tassili, a remote mountainous region of the Sahara on the southern border of Algeria. The running human figures carrying bows are hunters, but these people were probably pastoral nomads. The large animal in the center is a bull. At that time the Sahara was not as dry as it is today, and it may have been the scene of the human migrations that attended the introduction of animal husbandry and agriculture. The photograph was made by L. L. Cavalli-Sforza of Stanford University, the author of one of the articles in this issue ("The Genetics of Human Populations," page 41).

death rates to produce near-zero rates of growth, given a little time. Confidence about the ultimate stabilization of these populations must be qualified, however, by recollection of the upsurge in their birth rates during the 1940's and 1950's (familiar to U.S. citizens as the "baby boom" of the years that followed World War II) that temporarily reversed the trend of the preceding century. These vital trends originally put in their appearance with the onset of the scientific-industrial revolution and the popularization of material well-being that has made the countries of the European peoples the developed countries of today. The same trends are observed in the Japanese population from the time of the Meiji restoration in 1868, which launched that country's industrial revolution.

As early as the 1930's what has become known as the demographic transition culminated, in many of those countries, in the convergence of birth and death rates that brought their growth down close to zero. Since there is no accepted explanation for the subsequent surge and decline of their fertility rates, no one can say with assurance that something similar will not happen again. In any case the demographic future of this portion of the human population is now a function of movement in its birth rates. Further decline in mortality (even to zero!) would have little effect on growth; almost everyone in the developed world now lives past the childbearing years, and saving the lives of older people does not affect the growth rate of a population to any degree. With modern contraceptive technology widely available and in use in most developed countries, their birth rates may be said to be under voluntary control. It can be anticipated, as Charles F. Westoff observes [see "The Populations of the Developed Countries," page 69], that human fertility in these novel circumstances will oscillate in response to cultural and economic pulls and pressures, not yet securely understood. The conjugal family of industrial civilization [see "The Family in Developed Countries," by Norman B. Ryder, page 81] is typically a small family. And the true liberation of women from the commitment of their lives to childbearing [see "The Changing Status of Women in Developed Countries," by Judith Blake, page 91] sets another kind of inertia against return to high levels of fertility.

Even so, some of these populations still retain considerable potential for growth. Higher birth rates in the recent past mean large proportions of couples

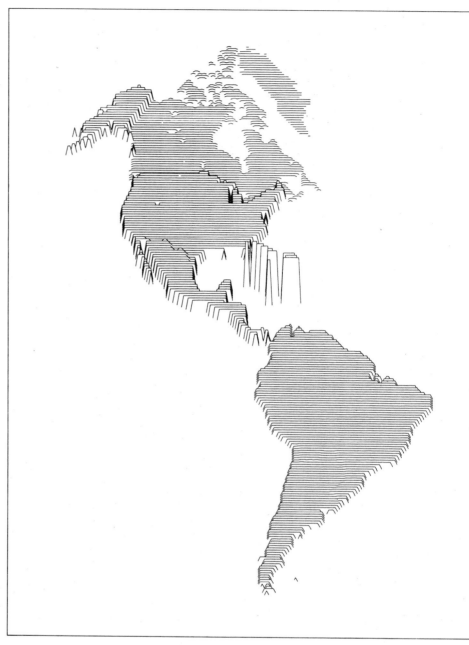

DENSITY OF POPULATION in various regions of the world as of 1971 is shown by the peaks and plateaus of these maps prepared for SCIENTIFIC AMERICAN by the Laboratory for Computer Graphics and Spatial Analysis and the University Mapping Service of Harvard

who must live through their reproductive years before zero growth will be achieved. Thus even if the country's fertility persists at a replacement level, the U.S. will not reach zero growth for 50 or 60 years, at which time its population will be 40 percent larger.

The principal impetus to world population growth comes today from the underdeveloped countries where nearly three-fourths of mankind dwell. Death rates in those countries have been falling over the past 25 years toward the low levels of the developed countries. Birth rates, however, remain twice as high as they are in the developed countries. The

result is a population increase averaging 2.5 percent and in many countries exceeding 3 percent.

The populations of such countries are now growing faster than those of the developed countries grew during the phase of rapid population growth of the European peoples [see "The Populations of the Underdeveloped Countries," by Paul Demeny, page 105]. Mortality rates in such countries are converging toward those of the developed countries, although there is still some way to go, particularly when age structures are taken into account. (The crude death rates of the underdeveloped countries run about 14 per 1,000 population, as against

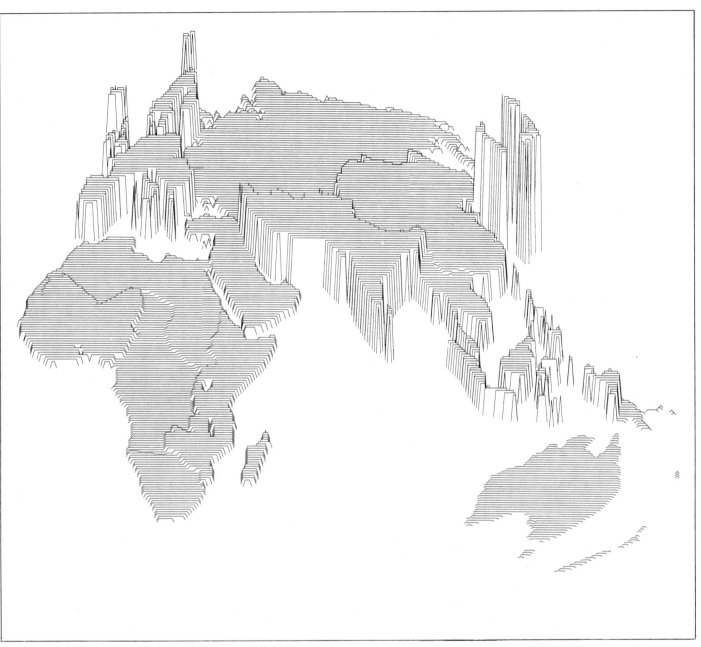

University. Most of the areas are not individual countries but modified United Nations regions. The tallest peaks are for Japan, which has a population density of 283 per square kilometer. The lowest plateau is for Greenland, which has a population density of virtually zero. The maps should be compared with the maps on the next two pages, which show energy consumption for the same regions.

about nine per 1,000 in the developed countries.) In some countries further decline in mortality may come slowly without further improvement in nutrition, living standards and public health services. The large gaps between the underdeveloped and the developed countries remain in fertility, represented by an overall crude birth rate of 39 per 1,000 population compared with 17 per 1,000. Some large countries such as Nigeria, Bangladesh and Pakistan have crude birth rates that are three times higher than those of the U.S.

Accordingly it is almost inevitable that the world's population will grow to between 6.5 billion and 8.5 billion in the next 75 years, with nearly all the growth in the underdeveloped countries. As Tomas Frejka of the Population Council has shown, employing a computer model of the world population that incorporates data on age structure, the population would grow to 6.3 billion even if reproduction rates in all countries could be brought down to replacement levels as early as 1980 [see "The Prospects for a Stationary World Population," by Tomas Frejka; SCIENTIFIC AMERICAN Offprint 683]. Arrival at the replacement rate by the end of the century, a more plausible but by no means certain event, would yield a world population of 8.2 billion in 2050. More than 90 percent of the additional four-plus billion would be in the underdeveloped countries. The world would know an India of 1.4 billion population, a Brazil of 266 million, a Bangladesh of 240 million, a Nigeria of 198 million. China is the big unknown in world statistics; in spite of reports of a decline in the country's fertility rate, a population of more than a billion is probable in the next decades.

Thus short of a catastrophic rise in death rates a population increase of major dimensions is in store. Stabilization of the world population may not occur this side of the 10-to-15-billion range, and eight billion seems to be a minimum.

Whatever mankind can do to moderate such trends, it must clearly accommodate to growth. Over the next few decades roughly everything must be doubled just in order to stay even. Roger Revelle [see "Food and Population," page 119] considers that the projected demand—amplified as it must be by the appetites of the developed countries and by the development of the underdeveloped countries—still does not exceed the earth's resources.

Concurrent with such profound change in the facts of life and death and in the structure of populations, the living generations have been experiencing equally revolutionary changes in the family, the community and the state, in technology and the use of resources, in economic relationships and in man's impact on the environment. These changes in the condition of man can be signalized by the observation that the human population is in migration from the agricultural village to the industrial and commercial city [see "The Migrations of Human Populations," by Kingsley Davis, page 53]. Everywhere cities are growing faster than countries. In the developed countries the majority of the inhabitants are already resettled into great networks of metropolitan centers with dependent hinterlands. Although most people in the underdeveloped countries still live in villages, their cities are growing too, in spite of grossly inadequate facilities and relatively little opportunity for employment. Such high rates of population growth prevail in rural areas that this migration still does not diminish the rural population or even slow its growth by much.

Most of the world's people now live in countries with programs or policies to change fertility levels and growth rates, but efforts either to increase or to decrease birth rates appear to have had mixed results. If population growth is to be halted and stabilized by fertility control, then the faster fertility is reduced, the smaller the eventually stationary population will be. The governments of most underdeveloped countries sponsor family-planning programs, usually but not always with the explicit goal of reducing the number of births. In some smaller countries, notably Taiwan and South Korea, birth rates have fallen to a substantial degree because of birth control practiced by couples served by such programs. Whether this would have happened without the programs is still a debated question and one technically difficult to resolve. These same countries have also made substantial progress in

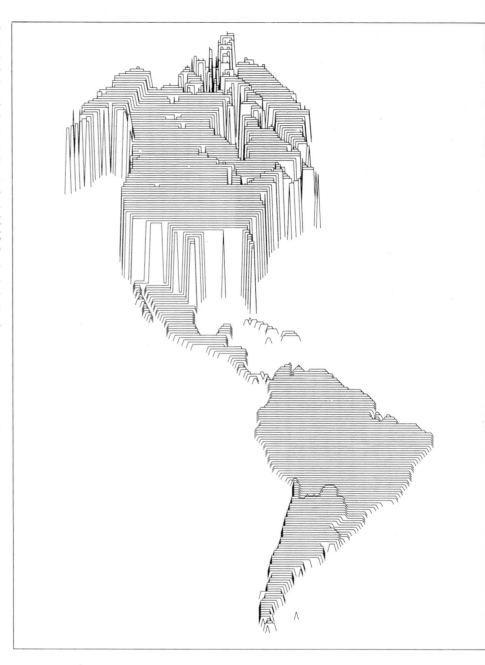

ENERGY CONSUMPTION, a measure of the standard of living, is shown for the same regions as of 1968, the most recent year for which data were available. In many places the topography is the inverse of that in the population maps on the preceding two pages. The

other ways toward the fulfillment of aspirations for economic development and "modernization."

Government policies with respect to fertility in developed countries, whether implicit in welfare programs or explicit in the promotion of large families, tend to be pronatalist. There is no evidence, however, that such policies have been notably successful in deflecting the downward trend in birth rates in those countries more than temporarily. It may be expected that when the underdeveloped countries have changed all those characteristics that distinguish the traditional society from the modern one, they too will be developed, and one re-

sult will be the reduction of their fertility.

As the other contributors to this issue give evidence, there is substantial agreement about the demographic trends and conditions that set the terms of public policy. The making of policy, however, involves ideology as well as the demographic and social facts. It may seem strange that some people question the validity and definition of "the population problem" at this late date, but there are at least two recent developments of considerable importance. The first is a growing scientific sophistication about the consequences of population growth, as the simpler answers of 10 to 15 years ago

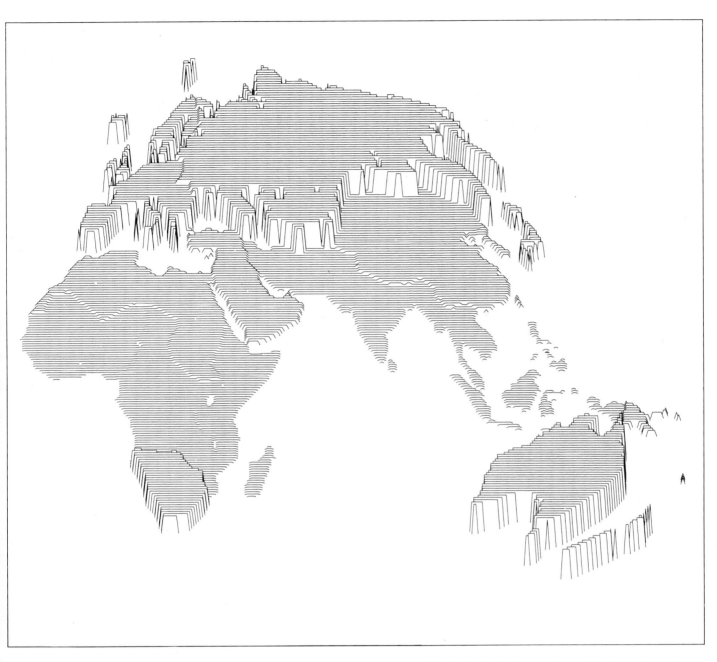

units of energy consumption are the equivalent of kilograms of coal burned per capita. The highest plateau is the U.S., with a figure of 10,331; the lowest is western Africa, with 51. The world average is 1,733. Individuals who participated in the making of maps were Allan Schmidt, David Sheehan, Nicholas Chrisman, Geoffrey Dutton, Howard Fisher, Herbert Heidt and Eliza McClennen.

give way to more qualified and more complex ones. The second is a broadening of the definition of the problem to include not only economics but also the terrestrial environment, to regard population growth not only as a burden on the development of underdeveloped countries but also as a multiplier of the stresses on the resources and the environment of developed countries.

On the economic side the bible of the early 1960's was Ansley Coale and Edgar M. Hoover's *Population Growth and Economic Development in Low-Income Countries,* an estimate of how much high growth rates would retard development. In one underdeveloped country

after another rapid population growth appears to increase the difficulty of working with limited human and material resources to solve the problems of food supply, of urban and rural unemployment, of providing minimal social services. The predominant view still is that rapid population growth is such a serious hindrance to development that the reduction of fertility rates will greatly enhance the possibility of social and economic progress. There is, however, another view. In the early 1970's a UN symposium preparatory to the 1974 World Population Conference, with experts from around the world in attendance, concluded that "a preoccupa-

tion with population should not divert attention from critical issues in the world development process.... Population growth is not always an obstacle to development [although] very high rates of population growth are usually an obstacle to development."

Today such analysis is questioned with regard to the handling of discount rates and the extent to which savings by low-income individuals contribute to capital investment. Moreover, the advantages of population growth are asserted: stimuli to harder work and agricultural innovation, and larger markets to foster the substitution of imports. Such questions have led some to the fundamental position that it is not population growth that matters but the proper organization of society, the redistribution of income and the rectification of social injustice. Does population growth seriously threaten economic development or is it only a marginal issue? Today qualified experts can be found on both sides of the debate.

In the recent concern with the environmental aspect of population the tables are turned: in one scenario the problem is not the problem of countries such as India but the problem of countries such as the U.S.; the solution calls not for fewer babies there but for less consumption here. The debate has swung between extremes, with one position being stigmatized as doomsaying and the other as technological optimism.

One can distinguish at least three general positions on the population problem. There is population as crisis, so grave that catastrophe is near unless drastic steps are taken to stop world population growth now. There is population as a multiplier and intensifier of other social problems, not "everything" but a substantial something; an example is the 1972 report of the U.S. Commission on Population Growth and the American Future. Then there is population as a nonproblem (or even a false problem with imperialist overtones), the real

problem being development or how to bring about a socialist organization of society or redistribute income or improve the status of women or rectify social injustice or promote technological change, with the population problem being automatically taken care of as a by-product. In short, the very nature of the population problem—what the real consequences of population growth are and what growth really means for human life—is under closer scrutiny and disputation today than it was a decade ago.

It was inevitable that the increased interest in population during the 1960's would move the subject into the political arena. Indeed, that was demanded by the emergence of government population policies. As a result population issues are now caught up in broader and deeper political tensions, both domestic and international: tensions concerning natural resources, food, energy, medical care, neocolonialism, the terms of international trade, the provision of assistance for development and the relative merits of socialist and nonsocialist forms of government.

Any strong international trend, and population-related actions were such a trend in the 1960's, is likely to generate a countertrend. Now, for better or worse, there is a kind of political backlash at work in many parts of the world with which workers in the field of population

problems must contend in addition to the problems themselves. Any effort to limit this sensitive topic to scholarly and professional discussion was doomed to failure; after all, if a policy is to be recommended by a government, it by definition becomes a political matter.

A key controversy centers on the strategy for reducing fertility rates in the underdeveloped countries. In the public forum such consideration has tended to focus on the alternatives of economic development and family planning. It is an unrewarding polarization. Political leaders are pushed by events to treat population and development policies as being integrally related rather than as alternatives.

Development, which requires extensive social change, impinges at every point on factors that sustain high fertility in the underdeveloped countries. Poverty so extreme, widespread and persistent holds people in despairing resistance to change. The high rate of infant mortality makes the next infant a desirable hedge against high mortality rates. In many countries the preference for sons presses fertility still further against that other lottery of sex determination. The economic value of children in these circumstances contrasts with the dependency of youth in the developed countries: they help to make the family's living; they are

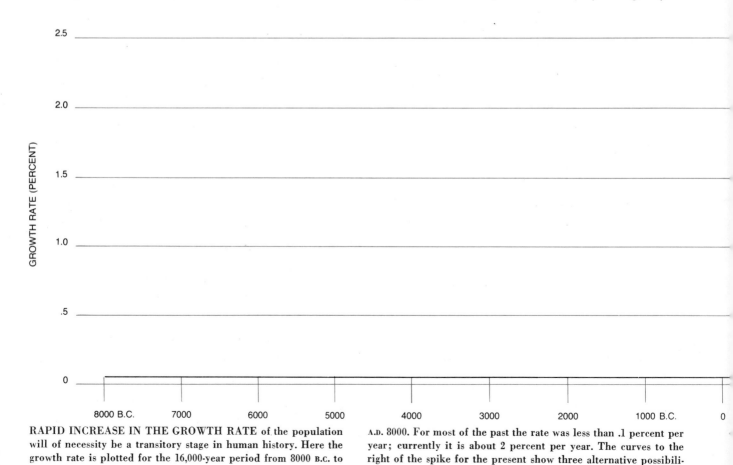

RAPID INCREASE IN THE GROWTH RATE of the population will of necessity be a transitory stage in human history. Here the growth rate is plotted for the 16,000-year period from 8000 B.C. to A.D. 8000. For most of the past the rate was less than .1 percent per year; currently it is about 2 percent per year. The curves to the right of the spike for the present show three alternative possibili-

the support of their parents in illness and old age, and their value is affirmed in social and religious life. Women are held in inferior status by the dedication of their life role to that of mother, wife and worker in the family enterprise. Illiteracy reinforces social isolation and traditional behavior; lack of education confines the range of choice and the time horizon of decisions about life. Village life limits the exchange of goods, ideas and people; it also limits the complexity of technology and the division of labor.

All aspects of this pattern of underdevelopment do not prevail everywhere, and various countries have arrived at different states of change in these characteristics. Many countries differ in important ways from their European precursors at a similar stage in the transformation, exhibiting a much more rapid decline in mortality, a greater access to advanced technology and an aspiration to quickly reach demonstrated goals that were attained only slowly by the first arrivals. These differences may facilitate reduction in fertility, along with development in general, in some countries. Modernization is proving to be slow and difficult, however, in many countries; if decline in fertility must wait out the process of social transformation, it will be some time in coming. In the last article in this issue Gunnar Myrdal reminds us that the task of technology

transfer requires action by the developed as well as the underdeveloped countries [see "The Transfer of Technology to Underdeveloped Countries," page 131].

Fertility control may not require the total transformation of the old order in the underdeveloped countries. Recent research on the demographic transition in Europe finds that decline in fertility did not "automatically" follow on attainment of this or that bench mark in urbanization, industrialization, literacy or decline in mortality. In our time major declines in mortality have occurred with little social or economic development. Educational levels have been raised rapidly in Sri Lanka and in the state of Kerala in India; this has been attended by some decline in fertility, although there has been little economic change.

Beyond general development, which is pursued on its own nondemographic grounds, family-planning programs have been organized in many countries as direct action on the problem of population growth. Such effort has found its own justification, furthermore, on humanitarian and medical grounds, even though its success in fertility control is debated. The effort also commends itself because it is relatively cheap; it spreads the word and so contributes to modernization and it provides access to contraceptive services as progress in development increases motivation. Here again the developed

countries have a role to play. As Sheldon J. Segal shows [see "The Physiology of Human Reproduction," page 29], the existing technology of contraception may have serious limitations in the physical circumstances of the traditional village and in the slums of the new cities of the poor; the "ideal contraceptive" is still awaited in the underdeveloped countries as it is in the developed ones and may have a more decisive historic role in the former, allowing fertility control in less favorable physical circumstances and at lower levels of motivation.

Against this background what can governments do to change fertility rates? It can be said there are five courses of action: persuade, manipulate services, change incentives, transform social institutions, coerce. Family-planning programs provide services and persuasion, and some countries restrict access to modern means of fertility control; development, of course, changes social institutions. In Singapore some incentives are being tried: no paid maternity leave beyond two children, and similar scaling of obstetrical delivery fees and income-tax deductions; Taiwan offers a positive incentive in the form of educational bonds for parents who stop at three children. If community pressure backed up by a one-party political apparatus counts as "coercion," then China may be the first

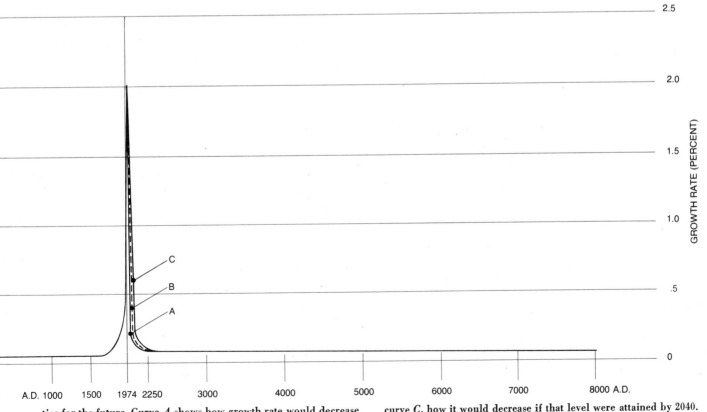

ties for the future. Curve *A* shows how growth rate would decrease if replacement level of fertility were attained by the year 2000; curve *B*, how it would decrease if that level were attained by 2020; curve *C*, how it would decrease if that level were attained by 2040. In other words, except for the extended present, population growth rates have been and are likely to be within a very narrow range.

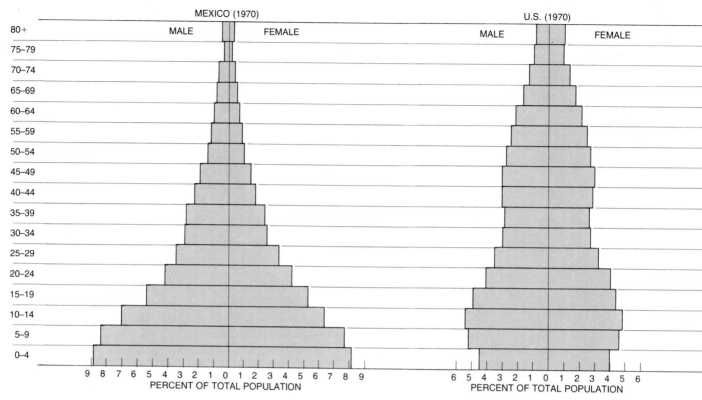

MEXICO (1970)   U.S. (1970)

AGE STRUCTURE OF POPULATIONS is profoundly affected by changing fertility. In a country such as Mexico with a recent his-

tory of high fertility the age structure is pyramidal. In a country such as Sweden with a recent history of low fertility the structure

country to employ all five ways of fertility control specified here; reports from some cities and communes indicate that China's fertility rate is indeed falling. India, in 1952, was the first country in the world to proclaim a population policy designed to lower birth rates through a family-planning program. It has conducted a vigorous campaign of persuasion under the symbol of the "Red Triangle"; it has tried to provide services on a massive basis, with spotty success; it has used monetary incentives, for example, to promote vasectomy; it has made some progress in the development and the transformation of social institutions. The government of Bangladesh, an even harder-pressed country, has reckoned openly with the possibility of such coercive measures as limitation on ration cards and compulsory sterilization for parents who have had more than two children.

Finally, serious issues present themselves under the heading of the control of human mobility. Today both internal and international migration is predominantly in the rural-to-urban direction: from the countryside to the city, from the farms of one nation to the factories of another. In most places this trend presents causes for concern: urban congestion, unemployment, environmental deterioration, problems of housing and

sanitation and transportation, lack of social services, political unrest and difficulties of acculturation.

International migrations are usually controllable: the valve of immigration can be opened or closed. A few countries want more immigrants (Israel and Australia are examples), but even they want only a certain kind. The industrial countries of continental Europe want more laborers from the Mediterranean countries but only on a temporary basis: the unemployed are exportable each way. In some tragic situations minority groups are forced out in order to make the remaining population more homogeneous. In the U.S. the Commission on Population Growth and the American Future urged that the substantial illegal immigration be stopped.

Internal migration to the cities is more difficult to affect. Among the many examples of what has been tried to limit the growth of large urban centers are regional development (Greece and Finland), decentralization of government activities (the Netherlands), relocation of the capital (Brazil and Tanzania), support of new towns (Japan and Britain), damping of wage differentials between urban and rural areas (Zambia), reorientation of education toward agricultural interests (Indonesia and Tanzania), subsidies for industrial location (France,

Sweden and Togo), rural land reclamation (Kenya) and even a "citizenship tax" on living in the city (Seoul in South Korea).

The effect of such efforts, although difficult to measure, has not been striking, and the further modernization of agriculture will intensify the pressures. The cities can only be expected to grow even more, with all the problems that implies. Again there is the (reported) counterexample of China, where as a matter of national policy migration to the cities is stringently controlled and many people are actually exported for various periods from the cities back to the land.

If the task is to reduce population growth in the world as a whole, and hence in most individual countries, at a rate substantially higher than the one that would otherwise obtain, the prospect is uncertain. Reasons for pessimism are not hard to find. First, high fertility itself is greatly resistant to change. It has been ratified by the experience of centuries, and for most people in the world it is institutionally interwoven with the entire cultural fabric. Beyond that the demographic momentum built into the age structure of populations is profound and long-lasting. If one were looking for a promising arena in which to demon-

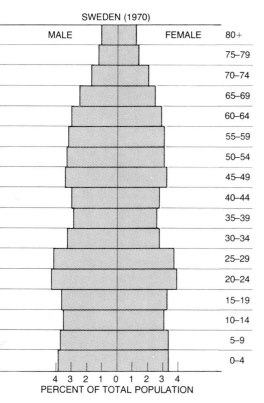

SWEDEN (1970)

MALE   FEMALE

80+
75–79
70–74
65–69
60–64
55–59
50–54
45–49
40–44
35–39
30–34
25–29
20–24
15–19
10–14
5–9
0–4

4 3 2 1 0 1 2 3 4
PERCENT OF TOTAL POPULATION

is quite rectangular up to age 60. The U.S. age structure lies between the two extremes.

strate the possibilities of social engineering, one would not choose population.

Second, the means of intervention may not be available. Coercion is not generally acceptable. The modernizing of social institutions is a goal almost everywhere, but progress is disappointing, and in any case it is hardly achievable in the immediate future. Family planning can claim some limited successes, but there is no proved formula for the mass adoption of birth control in an underdeveloped country. Hence intervention comes up against real limits of social and government policy.

Third, population issues are themselves changing. On the one hand they have become politicized, with all that implies in the way of disputation, compromise and absorption into political issues. On the other hand, the technical bases of population issues have shifted in recent years; as we come to know more we seem to end up knowing less, at least insofar as effective direct action is concerned. The population problem is more problematic now. The threshold factors required for the reduction of fertility are more in dispute; the value of family planning is called into question with alternatives being advanced that are hard to attain quickly, such as social revolution or the redistribution of income or the correction of social injustice.

Nevertheless, the effort continues. The present is a period of taking stock and reformulating programs. Growing recognition of the difficulty of population problems, together with the great pressures exerted in many countries by food shortages and a wide range of unmet demands for a better life, are forcing many governments to reconsider their entire strategy for development, in part to accommodate population growth and to control it. After all, policy to limit fertility is a very recent effort to deal with a very difficult problem. Successes in some countries and the possibility that there has been a major advance in China provide some practical encouragement.

Most countries are committed to consideration if not to action. Indeed, 1974 is World Population Year, by proclamation of the UN. Representatives of most of the world's governments have just met under UN auspices to discuss population problems and to consider a "World Plan of Action." Such a meeting would have been unthinkable as recently as 15 years ago, when even such matters as family-planning programs were defined as being outside the area of legitimate government action. Population issues, the preserve of a small group of specialized scholars a few decades ago, are now discussed everywhere and are being acted on in countries involving most of the world's people.

Not all population measures are successful. How could they be? Neither are measures on other great social problems. As has been said, some problems do not have solutions, only consequences. There is now, however, an unprecedentedly widespread recognition that the world is going to have to accommodate several billion more people in the coming decades, that the curve of growth takes a long time to level off and that the earlier it begins to level off, the better.

AREA	PEOPLE (MILLIONS)	CRUDE BIRTH RATE (PER 1,000 POPULATION PER YEAR)	CRUDE DEATH RATE (PER 1,000 POPULATION PER YEAR)	ANNUAL RATE OF NATURAL INCREASE (PERCENT)
WORLD	3,860	33	13	2.0
DEVELOPED COUNTRIES	1,120	17	9	0.8
UNDERDEVELOPED COUNTRIES	2,740	39	14	2.5
AFRICA	375	46	19	2.7
ASIA (EXCEPT JAPAN)	2,100	38	14	2.4
LATIN AMERICA (TROPICAL)	265	38	8	3.0
U.S.	210	15	9	0.6
JAPAN	108	19	7	1.2
EUROPE	472	16	11	0.5
U.S.S.R.	250	18	8	1.0
OTHERS: CANADA, AUSTRALIA, NEW ZEALAND, LATIN AMERICA (TEMPERATE)	80	22	8	1.4

CURRENT OVERALL STATUS of the human population and its major subdivisions is given by these numbers. The figures are for 1973, the most recent year for which data and estimates are available. The maps and charts in this article are based on UN sources.

2

The History of
the Human Population

The History of the Human Population

ANSLEY J. COALE

Until some 200 years ago the size of the human population remained fairly stable because high birth rates were balanced by high death rates. The great demographic transition came when death rates fell

In designating 1974 World Population Year the United Nations has given expression to worldwide interest in the rapid rate of population increase and to apprehension about the consequences of continued rapid growth. Much less attention is given to the growth of the population in the past, to the process by which a few thousand wanderers a million years ago became billions of residents of cities, towns and villages today. An understanding of this process is essential if one would evaluate the present circumstances and future prospects of the human population.

Any numerical description of the development of the human population cannot avoid conjecture, simply because there has never been a census of all the people in the world. Even today there are national populations that have not been enumerated, and where censuses have been taken they are not always reliable. Recent censuses of the U.S., for example, have undercounted the population by between 2 and 3 percent; some other censuses, such as the one taken in Nigeria in 1963, are evidently gross overcounts. Moreover, in many instances the extent of the error cannot be estimated with any precision.

If the size of the population today is imperfectly known, that of the past is even more uncertain. The first series of censuses taken at regular intervals of no more than 10 years was begun by Sweden in 1750; the U.S. has made decennial enumerations since 1790, as have France and England since 1800. The census became common in the more developed countries only in the 19th century, and it has spread slowly to other parts of the world. India's population has been enumerated at decennial intervals since 1871, and a number of Latin American populations have been counted, mostly at irregular intervals, since late in the 19th century. The first comprehensive census of Russia was conducted in 1897, and only four more have been made since then. The population of most of tropical Africa remained uncounted until after World War II. A conspicuous source of uncertainty in the population of the world today is the poorly known size of the population of China, where the most recent enumeration was made in 1953 and was of untested accuracy.

As one considers earlier periods the margin of error increases. The earliest date for which the global population can be calculated with an uncertainty of only, say, 20 percent is the middle of the 18th century. The next-earliest time for which useful data are available is the beginning of the Christian era, when Rome collected information bearing on the number of people in various parts of the empire. At about the same time imperial records provide some data on the population of China, and historians have made a tenuous estimate of the population of India in that period. By employing this information and by making a crude allowance for the number of people in other regions one can estimate the population of the world at the time of Augustus within a factor of two.

For still earlier periods the population must be estimated indirectly from calculations of the number of people who could subsist under the social and technological institutions presumed to prevail at the time. Anthropologists and historians have estimated, for example, that before the introduction of agriculture the world could have supported a hunting-and-gathering culture of between five and 10 million people.

From guesses such as these for the earlier periods and from somewhat more reliable data for more recent times a general outline of the growth of the human population can be constructed [*see illustrations on next page*]. Perhaps the most uncertain figure of all in these calculations is the size of the initial population, when man first appeared about a million years ago. As the human species gradually became distinct from its hominid predecessors there was presumably an original gene pool of some thousands or hundreds of thousands of individuals. The next date at which the population

RUBBING OF A GRAVESTONE records the death of a mother and her child in 18th-century Massachusetts. The inscription reads (with emended punctuation and orthography): "In Memory of Mrs. Naomi, Wife of Mr. Ritchard, Woolworth, who died August 22d, 1760, aged 39 Years; also Joseph, their Son, died the Same Day aged 6 days." It is probable that both mother and son died as a result of some crisis attendant on childbirth, in the case of the mother perhaps from puerperal fever. Such deaths were very common throughout most of man's history; the high death rate they contributed to demanded that the birth rate also be high merely to sustain the population. A decline in the death rate, which had an important effect on the survival of infants and children, began in most parts of Europe and America in the decades following the events recorded on this gravestone. The figures at the top of the stone are a scythe and an hourglass, traditional symbols of mortality; a crowing cock, which probably represents an admonition to vigilance, and an object whose identity is uncertain but that may be a candle with snuffer, another commonplace figure in the imagery of death. The stone is at Longmeadow, Mass., and has been attributed to Aaron Bliss. The rubbing is reproduced from *Early New England Gravestone Rubbings*, by Edmund Vincent Gillon, Jr., published by Dover Publications, Inc. Surveys of gravestones are among the methods by which demographers measure historical populations.

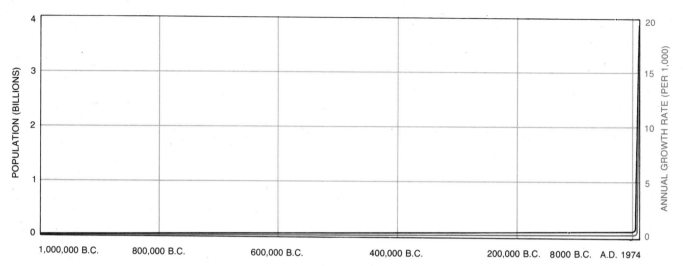

OVERVIEW OF THE HUMAN POPULATION, from the emergence of man about a million years ago to the present, emphasizes the dichotomous nature of man's history. At this level of detail the growth curve approximates one where the size of the population (*black*) and the annual rate of increase (*color*) are constant for almost the entire period, then rise vertically in the most recent years.

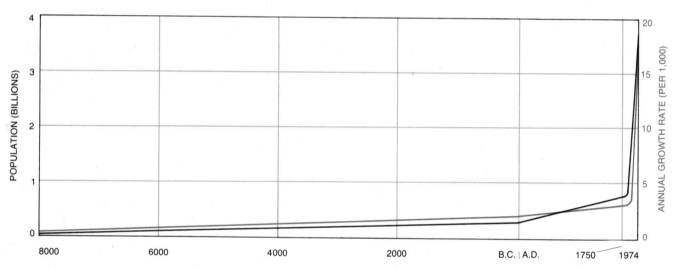

INTRODUCTION OF AGRICULTURE some 10,000 years ago marks the beginning of a period that represents about 1 percent of that considered in the illustration at the top of the page. Even in this much briefer time span, however, the rate of population increase was modest throughout most of the period, and the gain during the past few centuries again appears to be almost vertical.

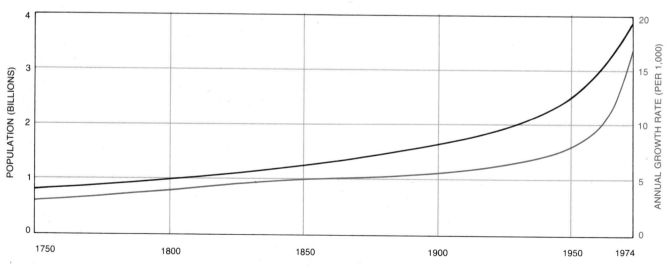

PERIOD SINCE 1750 is characterized by rapid and rapidly accelerating growth in the size of the world population. This period represents only about .02 percent of man's history, yet 80 percent of the increase in human numbers has occurred during it. Moreover, within this period the rate of increase has climbed most dramatically in very recent times: it has doubled in the past 25 years.

can be estimated is at the initiation of agriculture and the domestication of animals, which is generally believed to have begun about 8000 B.C. The median of several estimates of the ultimate size of the hunting-and-gathering cultures that preceded the introduction of agriculture is eight million. Thus whatever the size of the initial human population, the rate of growth during man's first 990,000 years (about 99 percent of his history) was exceedingly small. Even if one assumed that in the beginning the population was two—Adam and Eve—the annual rate of increase during this first long interval was only about 15 additional persons per million of population.

After the establishment of agriculture the growth of the population accelerated somewhat. The eight million of 8000 B.C. became by A.D. 1 about 300 million (the midpoint of a range of informed guesses of from 200 million to 400 million). This increase represents an annual growth rate of 360 per million, or, as it is usually expressed, .36 per 1,000.

From A.D. 1 to 1750 the population increased by about 500 million to some 800 million (the median of a range estimated by John D. Durand of the University of Pennsylvania). It was at this time that the extraordinary modern acceleration of population growth began. The average annual growth rate from A.D. 1 to 1750 was .56 per 1,000; from 1750 to 1800 it was 4.4 per 1,000, bringing the population at the end of this 50-year interval to about a billion. By 1850 there were 1.3 billion people in the world, and by 1900 there were 1.7 billion, yielding growth rates in the respective 50-year intervals of 5.2 and 5.4 per 1,000. (These totals too are based on estimates made by Durand.)

By 1950, according to the UN, the world population was 2.5 billion, indicating an annual growth rate during the first half of the 20th century of 7.9 per 1,000. From 1950 to 1974 the growth rate more than doubled, to 17.1 per 1,000, producing the present world population of 3.9 billion. The median value of several projections made by the UN in 1973 indicates that by 2000 the population will be 6.4 billion, an increase that implies an annual growth rate during the next 25 years of 19 per 1,000.

It is evident even from this brief description that the history of the population can be readily divided into two periods: a very long era of slow growth and a very brief period of rapid growth. An understanding of the development of the population during these two phases

can be derived from a few simple mathematical relations involving the absolute size of the population, the growth rate and the factors that determine the growth rate.

Persistent growth at any proportionate rate produces ever increasing increments of growth, and the total, even at a relatively modest rate of increase, surpasses any designated finite limit in a surprisingly short time. An increasing population doubles in size during an interval equal to 693 divided by the annual rate of increase, expressed in additional persons per 1,000 population [*see illustration on page 20*]. Thus in the period from A.D. 1 to 1750, when the growth rate was .56 per 1,000, the population doubled about every 1,200 years; in the next few decades, when a growth rate of about 20 per 1,000 is anticipated, the population will double in 34.7 years.

The cumulative effect of a small number of doublings is a surprise to common sense. One well-known illustration of this phenomenon is the legend of the king who offered his daughter in marriage to anyone who could supply a grain of wheat for the first square of a chessboard, two grains for the second square and so on. To comply with this request for all 64 squares would require a mountain of grain many times larger than today's worldwide wheat production.

In accordance with the same law of geometric progression, the human population has reached its present size through comparatively few doublings. Even if we again assume that humanity began with a hypothetical Adam and Eve, the population has doubled only 31 times, or an average of about once every 30,000 years. This is another way of saying that the peopling of the world has been accomplished with a very low rate of increase, when that rate is averaged over the entire history of the species. The average annual rate is about .02 additional persons per 1,000. Even when only the more rapid growth of the past 2,000 years is considered, the average rate is modest. Since A.D. 1 the population has doubled no more than four times, or about once every 500 years, which implies an annual rate of 1.4 persons per 1,000.

In the context of these long-term averages the rate of growth today seems all the more extraordinary, yet the source of this exceptional proliferation is in the conventional mathematics of geometric series. The population of the world increases to the extent that births exceed deaths; the growth rate is the difference between the birth rate and the death

rate. Another way of stating the relation is that the average rate of increase, over a long period, is dependent on the ratio of the sizes of successive generations. This ratio is approximately equal to the average number of daughters born to women who pass through the span of fertile years multiplied by the proportion of women surviving to the mean age of childbearing. This product specifies the average number of daughters born during the lifetime of a newborn female, after making allowance for those women whose biological fertility is abnormal and for those who die before reaching the age of childbearing. When the product is 1—signifying one daughter per woman, under the prevailing conditions of fertility and mortality—successive generations are the same average size. When the product is 2, the population doubles with each generation, or about every 28 years.

The fertility of a population can also be measured by the number of offspring, both sons and daughters, born per woman during a lifetime of childbearing; this number is called the total fertility rate. Mortality is summarized by the average age at death, or the average duration of life, which is expressed as the expectation of life at birth. In 1973 the total fertility rate of American women was 1.94; the expectation of life at birth was 75 years. Thus women experiencing 1973 birth rates at each age would bear an average of 1.94 children, and women experiencing 1973 death rates at each age would have an average duration of life of 75 years.

When the average life span is short, the proportion of women surviving to the mean age of reproduction is small. In fact, among populations for which there are adequate data there is a close relation between these two numbers, and we can with some confidence estimate the proportion of women surviving to become mothers from the average duration of life. Another predictable characteristic of the human population is the ratio of male births to female births; for any large sample it is always about 1.05 to 1.

Because of these constant relations in the population it is possible to calculate all the combinations of female life expectancy and total fertility that will yield any specified growth rate. Of particular interest are the conditions producing zero population growth, since during most of the past million years the population has approached zero growth [*see illustration on page 19*]. In a static population the average duration of life is the reciprocal of the birth rate. Expressed another way, in a population of constant size the birth rate is the number of births per person-year lived and the average duration of life is the number of person-years lived per birth.

There are many combinations of fertility and mortality that will just maintain a population at fixed size. Consider a static population in which the average duration of female life is 70 years. Given this mortality rate, the proportion of women surviving to the mean age of childbearing is 93.8 percent. Because the size of the population is to remain constant the average number of daughters born per woman must be 1/.938, or 1.066; since there are 1.05 male births for each female birth, the total fertility rate must be 2.05 × 1.066, or 2.19. The birth rate in such a population is 1/70, or 14.3 per 1,000 population.

If the average duration of female life is 20 years, as it probably was at times during the premodern period, then 31.6 percent of the women survive to the mean age of childbearing and those who live to the age of menopause have an average of 6.5 children; the birth rate under these circumstances is 50 per 1,000. (It should be pointed out that there is no inconsistency in the survival of many women to menopause in a population in which the average age at death is 20 years. When the death rate is high, the average age at death is not at all a typical age at death. When the life expectancy in a static population is 20 years, for example, about half the deaths occur before age five, about a fourth occur after age 50, and only about 6.5 percent occur in the 10-year span centered on the mean age at death.)

The importance of these relations is that they express the possible combinations of fertility and mortality that must have characterized the human population during each era of its history. If some other combination of fertility and mortality had been maintained for more than a few generations (as has happened during the past two centuries), the population would have expanded or contracted dramatically.

These combinations also determine the most extreme fertility and mortality rates possible in a static population. One limit is set by the minimum feasible mortality. When the average life expectancy is 75 years, 97.3 percent of all women survive to the mean age of reproduction, and it is necessary for them to have only 2.1 children to maintain the population; this represents a birth rate of 13.3 per 1,000. Any further reduction in mortality might raise the average duration of life to 80 years or more, but it would not significantly change the proportion of women surviving to childbearing age, nor would it much reduce the number of births per woman required to maintain the population. The other limit is imposed by fertility. When the life expectancy falls to 15 years, only 23.9 percent of all women live to have children, and those who do must have an average of 8.6 in order to prevent a decline in population. Although it is certainly biologically possible for a woman to bear more than eight or nine children, no sizable populations have been observed with

CENSUS TALLY SHEET from the first enumeration of the U.S. population was employed in one of the earliest attempts to keep a current and regularly revised account of the size and distribution of a national population. Sweden, in 1750, was the first nation to institute a periodic census; the U.S. followed in 1790, when this schedule for a New York City neighborhood was filled out. The columns record the number of free white males 16 years old and older, free white males under 16 years old, free white females, other free persons and slaves. In the bottom half of the column appears the name of Alexander Hamilton.

WOMEN SURVIVING TO MEAN AGE OF CHILDBEARING (PERCENT)

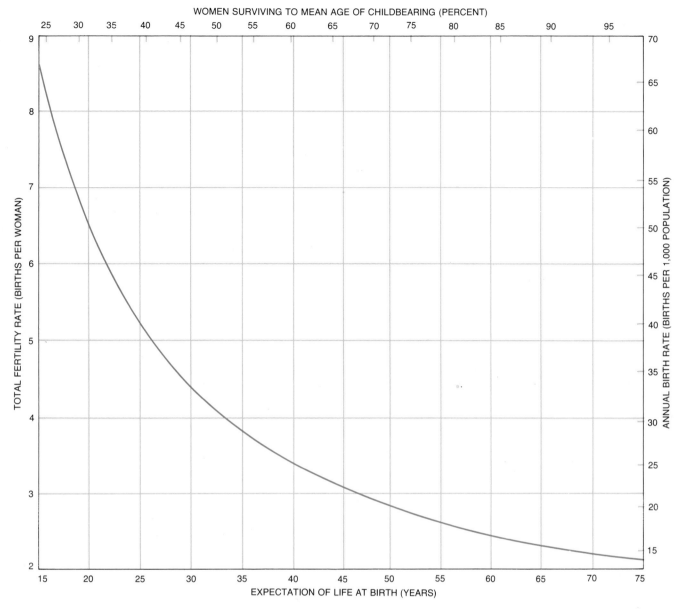

POPULATION IN EQUILIBRIUM can be maintained at constant size by many combinations of fertility and mortality. The total fertility rate is the number of children born per woman to a hypothetical group of women subject in each year of their lives to annual birth rates prevailing at a specified moment. Analogously, the expectation of life at birth is the average life span of a hypothetical group of people subject at each age to the death rates prevailing at a specified time. When the population is neither growing nor declining, two other demographic measures can be derived from these data: the birth rate and the proportion of women surviving to the mean age of childbearing. Some combination of these rates that approximates the conditions of zero growth must have prevailed during most of man's history. If the birth rate was 50 per 1,000, for example, then the average life span must have been 20 years, about a third of all women must have lived to childbearing age and those who survived must have had an average of 6.5 children.

total fertility much higher than eight births per woman.

Accurate records of human fertility and mortality are even more meager than records of numbers of people. Today fewer than half of the world population live in areas where vital statistics are reliably recorded; in most of Asia, almost all of Africa and much of Latin America, for example, the registration of births and deaths is inadequate. Precise information about fertility and mortality is therefore limited to the recent experience of the more developed countries, beginning in the 18th century in Scandinavia, the 19th century in most of the rest of Europe and the 20th century in Japan and the U.S. Much has been inferred about the present vital rates of underdeveloped countries from the age composition recorded in censuses, from the rate of population increase between censuses and from retrospective information collected in censuses and demographic surveys. For past populations, however, valid data on births and deaths are very rarely available, and they must therefore be derived by analyzing the forces that affect fertility and mortality.

Differences in fertility can be attributed to two factors: the differential exposure of women of childbearing age to the risk of childbirth through cohabitation with a sexual partner, and differences in the rate at which conceptions and live births occur among women who are cohabiting. In many populations the only socially sanctioned cohabitation is that between married couples, and thus the laws and customs governing the formation and dissolution of marriages influence fertility. A conspicuous example is the pattern of late marriage common until a generation ago in many Western European nations. For many years before World War II in Germany, Scandinavia, the Low Countries and Britain the average age of first marriage for women

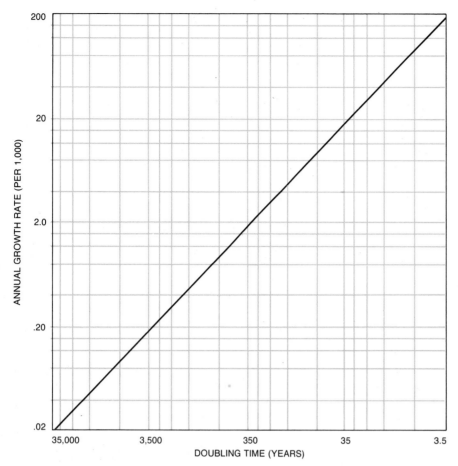

DOUBLING TIME for a population is calculated by dividing the annual growth rate, in additional persons per 1,000 population, into the number 693. Until about 10,000 years ago the growth rate was .02 or less, and at least 35,000 years were required for the population to double. The rate today approaches 20 per 1,000, and the population could double in the next 35 years. Sustained growth has extreme consequences: 10 doublings, which would require 350 years at the present rate, would produce a population of more than four trillion.

was between 24 and 28, and from 1 to 30 percent remained unmarried at age 50. As a result the proportion of women of reproductive age who by being married were exposed to the risk of childbearing was less than half, and in some cases, such as Ireland, was as low as a third.

A much different nuptial custom that may also reduce fertility is common in areas of Asia and North Africa. Women are married at age 17 or 18, but the average age of the married male population is often eight or nine years greater than that of the married women. The fertility of some of the women is probably reduced by marriage to much older men, often widowers. Marriages are made by arrangement with the bride's parents, in many cases requiring the payment of a bride price, and older men are more likely to have the property or the prestige needed to claim the more desirable young women. Still another social influence on fertility is found in India, where Hinduism forbids the remarriage of widows. Although the prohibition has not always been scrupulously observed, it has

doubtless reduced Indian fertility below what it might otherwise have been.

Among cohabiting couples fertility is obviously influenced by whether or not measures are employed to avoid having children. Louis Henry of the Institut National d'Études Démographiques has defined "natural fertility" as the fertility of couples who do not modify their behavior according to the number of children already born. Natural fertility thus defined is far from uniform: it is affected by custom, health and nutrition. Breast-feeding, for example, prolongs the period of postpartum amenorrhea and thereby postpones the resumption of ovulation following childbirth. In some populations low fertility can be attributed to pathological sterility associated with widespread gonorrheal infection. Finally, fertility may be influenced by diet, as has been suggested by the work of Rose E. Frisch and her colleagues at Harvard University. Age at menarche appears to be determined at least in part by the fat content of the body and is hence related to diet. Furthermore, among women past

the age of menarche a sufficient reduction in weight relative to height causes amenorrhea. In populations with meager diets fertility may therefore be depressed. Because of the severe caloric drain of pregnancy and breast-feeding, it is probable that nursing prolongs amenorrhea more effectively in populations where the average body fat is near the threshold needed for a regular reproductive cycle.

The most conspicuous source of differences in fertility among cohabiting couples today is the deliberate control of fertility by contraception and induced abortion. In some modern societies very low fertility rates have been obtained: the total fertility rate has fallen as low as 1.5 (in Czechoslovakia in 1930, in Austria in 1937 and in West Germany in 1973).

The prevalence of birth-control practices is known from the direct evidence of fertility surveys for only a few populations, and for those only during the past two or three decades. (The International Statistical Institute has begun a World Fertility Survey that should illuminate present practices but not those of the past.) Indications that fertility was deliberately controlled in past societies must be inferred from such clues as the cessation of childbearing earlier among women who married early than among those who married late. Evidence of this kind, together with the observation of a large reduction in the fertility of all married women, indicates that birth control was common in the 17th century among such groups as the bourgeoisie of Geneva and the peers of France. Norman Himes, in his *Medical History of Contraception*, has shown that prescriptions for the avoidance of birth, ranging from magical and wholly ineffective procedures to quite practical techniques, have been known in many societies at least since classical Greek times. A doctoral dissertation at Harvard University by Basim Musallam has demonstrated that *coitus interruptus*, a contraceptive method that compares in effectiveness with the condom and the diaphragm, was common enough in the medieval Islamic world to be the subject of explicit provisions in seven prominent schools of law. On the other hand, analysis of parish registers in western Europe from the 17th and 18th centuries and observations in less developed countries today suggest that effective birth-control practices are not common in most rural, premodern societies.

Large fluctuations in fertility, and in mortality as well, are not inconsistent with the long period of near-zero growth that characterizes most of the history of the population. Although the arithmetic of growth leaves no room for a rate of increase very different from zero in the long run, short-term variations were probably frequent and of considerable extent. In actuality the population that from our perspective appears to have been almost static for hundreds of thousands of years may well have experienced brief periods of rapid growth, during which it expanded severalfold, and then suffered catastrophic setbacks. The preagricultural population, for example, must have been vulnerable to changes in climate, such as periods of glaciation, and to the disappearance of species of prey. Once the cultivation of crops had become established the population could have been periodically decimated by epidemics and by the destruction of crops through drought, disease or insect infestation. Moreover, at all times the population has been subject to reduction by man's own violence through individual depredation and organized warfare.

Because earlier populations never expanded to fill the world with numbers comparable to the billions of the 20th century, we must conclude that sustained high fertility was always accompanied by high average mortality. Similarly, sustained low fertility must have been compensated for by low mortality; any societies that persisted in low fertility while mortality remained high must have vanished.

In the conventional outline of human prehistory it is assumed that at each earlier date the average duration of life was shorter, on the principle that early man faced greater hazards than his descendants. It is commonly supposed, for example, that hunters and gatherers had higher mortality than settled agriculturists. The greater population attained by the agriculturists is correctly attributed to an enhanced supply of food, but the appealing inference that reduced mortality was responsible for this acceleration of growth is not necessarily justified.

The advent of agriculture produced only a small increment in the growth rate; if this increment had been caused by a decline in mortality, the change in the average life expectancy would have been hardly noticeable. If in the hunting-and-gathering society the average number of births per woman was 6.5, for example, the average duration of life must have been 20 years. If the fertility of the early cultivators remained the same as that of their predecessors, then the in-

crease in the life span required to produce the observed acceleration of growth is merely .2 year. The increase in life expectancy, from 20 to 20.2 years, would not have been perceptible.

If one assumes that preagricultural man had substantially higher mortality than the early cultivators, it must also be assumed that the hunters and gatherers had much higher fertility. If the earlier culture had an average age at death of 15 instead of 20, for example, then its fertility must have been 8.6 births per woman rather than 6.5. Such a change is not inconceivable; the complete reorganization of life represented

by the adoption of agriculture could certainly be expected to influence both fertility and mortality. There is reason to suspect, however, that both vital rates increased rather than decreased [*see illustration on next page*].

Both disease and unpredictable famine might have increased the death rate of the first cultivators. Village life, by bringing comparatively large numbers into proximity, may have provided a basis for the transmission of pathogens and may have created reservoirs of endemic disease. Moreover, the greater density of agricultural populations may have led to greater contamination of food, soil and

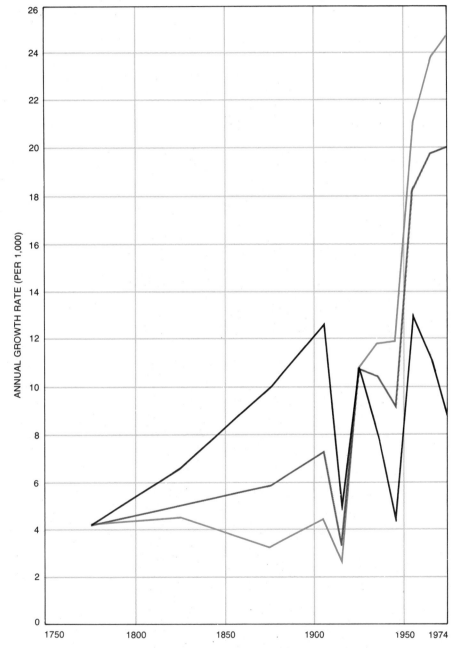

DEVELOPED AND UNDERDEVELOPED NATIONS have different population histories. From the 18th century until after World War I the growth rate in the developed countries (*black*) exceeded that in the underdeveloped ones (*color*). Since the 1920's growth in underdeveloped regions has predominated, and since 1950 the gap has become large. Future trends (*black and color*) will be determined largely by events in the underdeveloped nations.

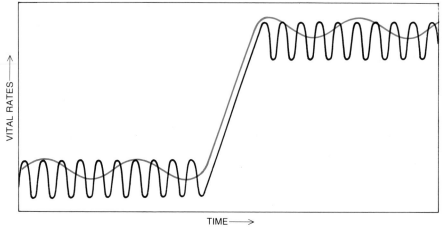

NEOLITHIC REVOLUTION had demographic consequences whose net effect was a slight increase in the rate of population growth. One reconstruction of these events suggests that the death rate (*black*) increased as a result of greater susceptibility to disease in village life, and perhaps also because agriculture is vulnerable to climatic crises. If the death rate did increase, then it is certain that the birth rate (*color*) also rose, and by a slightly greater margin. Both vital rates must have fluctuated from year to year, the death rate somewhat more than the birth rate. Even after the transition difference between the rates was small.

water. Greater density and the more or less total reliance on crops may also have made agriculturists extremely vulnerable to crop failure, whereas the hunting-and-gathering culture may have been more resistant to adversity.

If mortality did increase on the introduction of agriculture, then it is certain that fertility also rose, and by a slightly larger margin. The supposition that both vital rates did increase is supported by observations of the fertility rates of contemporary peoples who maintain themselves by hunting and gathering, such as the Kung tribe of the Kalahari Desert in southwestern Africa. Nancy Howell of the University of Toronto, analyzing observations made by her and by her colleague Richard Borshay Lee, has found that Kung women have long intervals between births and moderate overall fertility. A possible explanation, suggested by the work of Rose Frisch, is that the Kung diet yields a body composition low enough in fat to cause irregular ovulation. Interbirth intervals may be further prolonged by protracted breast-feeding combined with low body weight. If such conditions were common among preagricultural societies, the cultivation of crops could have increased fertility by increasing body weight and possibly by promoting the earlier weaning of infants so that mothers could work in the fields.

Unfortunately these speculations on the demographic events that may have accompanied the Neolithic revolution cannot be adequately tested by direct evidence. Until relatively recent times the only available indicators of mortality rates were tombstone inscriptions and

the age-related characteristics of skeletons. Because the sample of deaths obtained in these ways may not be representative, it is not possible to reliably estimate for early periods such statistics as the average duration of life.

The accelerated growth in the world population that began in the 18th century is more readily understood if the areas classified by the UN as "more developed" and "less developed" are considered separately.

A general description, if not a full explanation, of the changing rates of increase in the more developed areas since the 18th century is provided by what demographers call the demographic transition. The changes in fertility and mortality that constitute the demographic transition are in general expected to accompany a nation's progression from a largely rural, agrarian and at least partly illiterate society to a primarily urban, industrial and literate one. Virtually all the populations classified by the UN as more developed have undergone demographic changes of this kind, although the timing and extent of the changes vary considerably.

The demographic experience common to all the more developed countries includes a major reduction in both fertility and mortality at some time during the past 200 years. In the 18th century the average duration of life was no more than 35 years, and in many of the nations that are now counted among the more developed it must have been much less. Today, almost without exception, the average life expectancy in these nations is 70 years or more. Two hundred

years ago the number of births per woman ranged from more than 7.5 in some of the now more developed areas, such as the American colonies and probably Russia, to no more than 4.5 in Sweden and probably in England and Wales. In 1973 only Ireland among the more developed countries had a fertility rate that would produce more than three children per woman, and in most of the wealthier nations total fertility was below 2.5. Thus virtually all the more developed nations have, during the past two centuries, doubled the average life expectancy and halved the total fertility rate.

If the decline in fertility and mortality had been simultaneous, the growth in the population of the developed countries since 1750 might have been modest. Indeed, that was the experience of France, where the birth rate as well as the death rate began to decline before the end of the 18th century. As a consequence the increase in the French population was much less than that of most other European nations. The combined population of the developed countries experienced extraordinary growth after 1750, however, a growth that accelerated until early in the 20th century. The reason for the increase in numbers is that the decline in mortality has in almost all cases preceded the decline in fertility, often by many years [*see illustration on opposite page*].

The decline in fertility in the U.S., as in France, began early; it appears to have been under way by the beginning of the 19th century. Because of early marriage, however, fertility in the U.S. had been very high, so that the excess of births over deaths was still quite large. In most of the other more developed countries the birth rate did not begin to fall until late in the 19th century or early in the 20th.

Another universal feature of the transition is a change in the stability of the vital rates. In the premodern era the high birth rate was relatively constant, but the death rate fluctuated from year to year, reflecting the effects of epidemics and variations in the food supply. In those countries that have completed the demographic transition this pattern is reversed: the death rate remains constant but fertility varies considerably.

The causes of the event that began the demographic transition—the decline in mortality in the late 18th century—are a matter of controversy to social and medical historians. According to one school of thought, until the middle of the 19th century medical innovations in England could not account for the reduction of the English death rate; the principal factor proposed instead is an improvement in the average diet. Others argue that protection from smallpox through inoculation with cowpox serum, a procedure introduced late in the 18th century, was sufficient to markedly reduce the death rate. They propose that the further decline in mortality in the early 19th century may have been brought about by improvements in personal hygiene.

A third hypothesis is that before the 18th century fortuitous periods of low mortality were not exceptional, but that they were followed by periods of very severe mortality caused by major epidemics. According to this view, the late 18th century was a normal period of respite, and improved conditions early in the 19th century averted the next cycle of epidemics, which would other-

wise have produced a recurrence of high mortality rates.

Whatever the cause of the initial decline in the death rate, there is no doubt that subsequent improvements in sanitation, public health and medicine made possible further reductions during the 19th century; indeed, the process continues today. It is equally clear that the reduction in mortality was dependent on the increased availability of food and other material resources. This rise in living standards was in turn brought about by the extension of cultivation, particularly in the Western Hemisphere, by increased productivity in both agriculture and industry and by the development of efficient trade and transportation.

The decline in the birth rate that eventually followed the decline in the death rate in the more developed countries was, with the exception of late-19th-cen-

tury Ireland, almost entirely a decline in the fertility of married couples and can be attributed directly to the practice of contraception and abortion. The reduction in fertility was not a result of the invention of new contraceptive techniques, however. Among selected Americans married before 1910, English couples interviewed in the 1930's and couples surveyed in France and several eastern European nations after World War II, the principal method of birth control was *coitus interruptus,* a technique that had always been available. The birth rate declined because the perceived benefits and liabilities of having more children had changed, and perhaps also because the couples' view of the propriety of preventing births had been modified.

Reduced fertility can be considered one of the consequences of the charac-

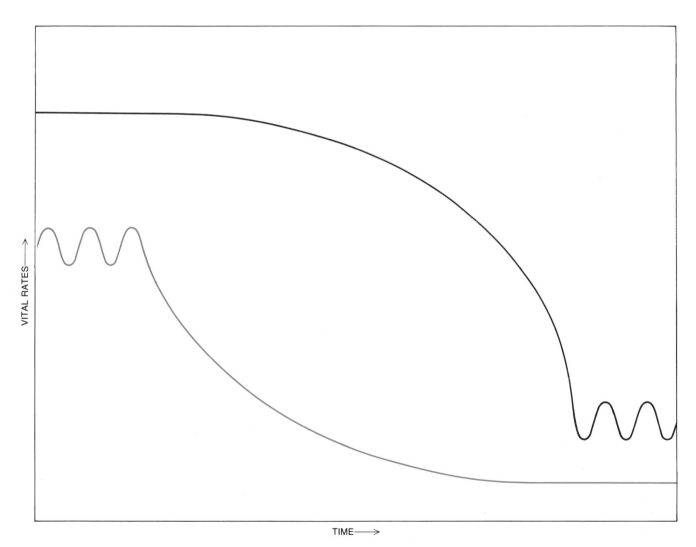

TIME⟶

THE DEMOGRAPHIC TRANSITION, represented schematically here, is the central event in the recent history of the human population. It begins with a decline in the death rate (*black*), precipitated by advances in medicine (particularly in public health), nutrition or both. Some years later the birth rate (*color*) also declines, primarily because of changes in the perceived value of having children. Before the transition the birth rate is constant but the death rate varies; afterward the death rate is constant but the birth rate fluctuates. The demographic transition usually accompanies the modernization of nations; it began in Europe and the U.S. late in the 18th century and early in the 19th, but in the underdeveloped nations it began only much later, often in the 20th century. In the developed countries the transition is now substantially complete, but in much of the rest of the world only mortality has been reduced; the fertility rate remains high. In the interim between the drop in mortality and fertility population has increased rapidly.

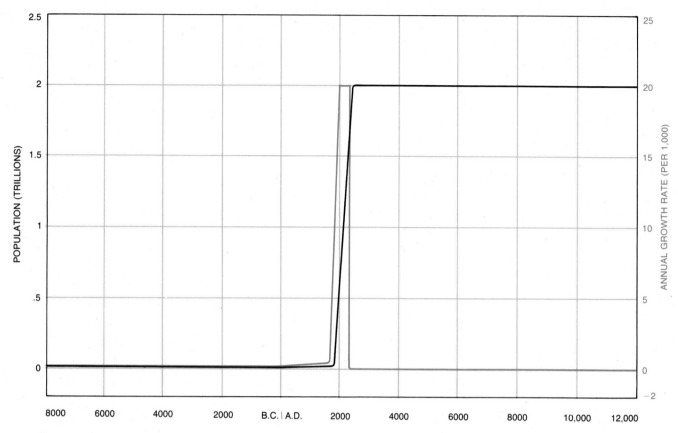

RETURN TO NEAR-ZERO GROWTH does not necessarily imply a low future population. If the rate of increase (*color*) were to remain at its present level until the year 2300, then immediately drop to zero, the average growth rate over the next 10,000 years would be as low as it has been during the past 10,000. Population, however (*black*), would reach two trillion, 500 times the present one.

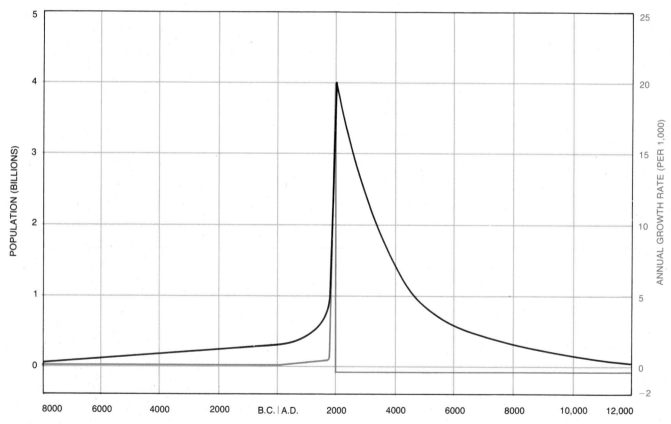

IMMEDIATE REDUCTION of the growth rate to —.2 would result in a slow decline, eventually returning the world population to its level of 10,000 years ago: about eight million, or 1/500th of the present population. Under these circumstances too the rate of change in the size of the population during the next 10,000 years would differ from zero no more than it did during the past 10,000.

teristics by which the more developed countries are defined. In an urban, industrial society the family is no longer the main locus of economic activity, nor are children the expected means of support in old age. In an agrarian, preindustrial society, on the other hand, the family is a basic economic unit and sons are a form of social security. Moreover, in the less developed countries the costs of raising and educating a child are minimal; indeed, a child may contribute to the welfare of the family from an early age. In the industrial society child labor is prohibited, education is compulsory and it often extends through adolescence. These conditions conspire to discourage couples in the more developed countries from having large families, whereas in long-established agrarian societies social norms supporting childbearing tend to be perpetuated.

In the less developed countries the estimated rate of population growth was virtually zero until about 200 years ago, when a moderate rate of increase, about four per 1,000, was apparently induced by a reduction in mortality [*see illustration on page 21*]. The cause of this reduced death rate is uncertain. Durand has suggested that the interchange of staple foods between regions that had previously been isolated might have contributed to population growth in Asia and in Europe as well. In particular the introduction of the potato into Europe and of maize and the sweet potato into China have been cited as possible contributing factors.

Since the aggregate population of the less developed countries includes many large areas that have not been reliably enumerated, a description of the historical course of population growth in these countries is subject to much uncertainty. A slight reduction in the average rate of increase in the latter half of the 19th century, for example, can be attributed entirely to an estimated zero rate of growth in China, and that estimate is based on uncertain data. There is no doubt, however, that in the poorer nations rapid growth began in the 1920's, 1930's and 1940's, and that since World War II the population increase has accelerated dramatically.

The enormous recent growth of the populations of the less developed nations can be interpreted in terms of the demographic transition, but some parts of the process have been more rapid and more extreme than they were in the industrial nations; moreover, the transition is not yet complete, and its future course can-

not be predicted. Mortality has dropped precipitously, but fertility has so far remained unchanged or declined only moderately. In the combined populations of the less developed countries the number of births per woman is about 5.5, and the average duration of life is more than 50 years, yielding an annual growth rate of about 25 per 1,000. Since World War II mortality in the less developed countries has fallen much more quickly than it did in 19th-century Europe, largely because modern technology, and particularly medical technology, can be imported more rapidly today than it could be discovered and developed 100 years ago. Insecticides, antibiotics and public health measures that were unknown during the European demographic transition are now commonplace in the less developed countries.

According to estimates prepared by the UN, the average duration of life in the less developed areas has risen from 32 to 50 years during the past three decades, an increase of 56 percent. During the same period the birth rate is estimated to have declined by no more than 7 to 8 percent. The actual fall in fertility is in fact even less, by about 4 percent, since demographic changes have reduced the proportion of women in the childbearing years. (Although the fertility of the less developed countries as a group remains very high, there are some countries where the birth rate has fallen significantly—by from 25 to 50 percent— and very rapidly. They include Hong Kong, Singapore, Taiwan, South Korea, West Malaysia, Barbados, Chile, Cuba, Jamaica, Trinidad and Tobago, Puerto Rico and Mauritius. According to reports from travelers, there has also been a decline in fertility in China, particularly in the cities.)

The present rapid growth in the world population is a result of a high rate of increase in the less developed areas and a moderate rate in the rest of the world. According to projections prepared by the UN, more than 90 percent of the increase in population to be anticipated by 2000 will be contributed by the less developed nations, even though a large reduction in fertility in these countries is expected in the next 25 years. The future course of the world's population depends largely on demographic trends in these countries.

The events of the demographic transition provide no sure way of calculating when or how quickly fertility will decline in the less developed nations. The experience of the industrial world is not

a satisfactory basis for prediction. The history of the Western population during the past 200 years suggests that vital rates normally fall as a concomitant of modernization, but it provides no checklist of advances in literacy, mortality reduction and urbanization that would enable one to estimate when fertility will fall. In the more developed world there are instances of large reductions in fertility in populations that were still rural, mostly illiterate and still subject to moderately high mortality, as in the Garonne valley in southwestern France before 1850. In other instances fertility did not decline until after education was almost universal, the population was mostly urban and agriculture had become the occupation of a small minority, as in England and Wales.

The present rate of world population increase—20 per 1,000—is almost certainly without precedent, and it is hundreds of times greater than the rate that has been the norm for most of man's history. Without doubt this period of growth will be a transitory episode in the history of the population. If the present rate were to be maintained, the population would double approximately every 35 years, it would be multiplied by 1,000 every 350 years and by a million every 700 years. The consequences of sustained growth at this pace are clearly impossible: in less than 700 years there would be one person for every square foot on the surface of the earth; in less than 1,200 years the human population would outweigh the earth; in less than 6,000 years the mass of humanity would form a sphere expanding at the speed of light. Considering more realistic limits for the future, if the present population is not multiplied by a factor greater than 500 and thus does not exceed two trillion, and if it does not fall below the estimated population of preagricultural society, then the rate of increase or decrease during the next 10,000 years must fall as close to zero as it was during the past 10,000 years [*see illustrations on opposite page*].

Arithmetic makes a return to a growth rate near zero inevitable before many generations have passed. What is uncertain is not that the future rate of growth will be about zero but how large the future population will be and what combination of fertility and mortality will sustain it. The possibilities range from more than eight children per woman and a life that lasts an average of 15 years, to slightly more than two children per woman and a life span that surpasses 75 years.

3

The Physiology of
Human Reproduction

The Physiology of Human Reproduction

SHELDON J. SEGAL

*Its complex series of events is organized by molecular messengers.
Advancing knowledge of the system provides humane methods
that enable couples to have the number of children
they choose to have*

The human reproductive process, on which the size and structure of individual families and of the populations of communities, nations and the world ultimately depend, is an orchestration of interrelated behavioral and physiological events and anatomical changes that proceed in perfect sequence and synchrony. At the center of the process are the gonads: the ovaries in the female and the testes in the male. These sex glands have two functions. They produce gametes (eggs and spermatozoa) and they produce the sex hormones. The role of the male ends with fertilization; the female goes on to harbor the fertilized egg in a protective and nutritive setting. The entire process is regulated by a series of chemical substances that issue from the brain and the pituitary gland to influence the gonads and then from the sex glands to order the successive events of egg or sperm development and transport, fertilization, implantation and gestation.

In both the female and the male this remarkable relay of molecular messages [*see illustrations on pages 32 and 33*] begins in specialized nerve cells in the brain. Sensory stimuli from the external environment and/or humoral stimuli from the bloodstream activate these neurons (whose location and pathways are as yet uncharted) and cause them to release small neurotransmitter molecules that reach neurosecretory cells in the hypothalamus at the base of the brain. On receiving the appropriate molecular message (which might signal, for example, a lowered blood level of an ovarian hormone) the hypothalamic cells discharge their stored supply of a gonadotropin-releasing factor, a small polypeptide hormone composed of 10 amino acid subunits. Aggregates of releasing-factor molecules move from the hypothalamic cells into a short local system of small capillaries and veins that carry them only a few centimeters, to the anterior lobe of the pituitary [see "The Hormones of the Hypothalamus," by Roger Guillemin and Roger Burgus; SCIENTIFIC AMERICAN Offprint 1260]. The releasing factor causes the pituitary to discharge its stored supply of two gonadotropins, or gonad-influencing hormones: large glycoproteins called luteinizing hormone (LH) and follicle-stimulating hormone (FSH), which enter the bloodstream and are carried to the sex glands.

In the female the two gonadotropins participate in unison in stimulating ovarian function, but each has a specialized role. FSH is responsible chiefly for causing the maturation of the ovary's Graafian follicles, which contain the oöcytes, or immature eggs, in a multilayered sheath of granulosa cells. In the process the hormone-secreting cells of the follicle are stimulated to produce increasing amounts of estrogens, one of the two kinds of female steroid sex hormone, and the immature egg enclosed in the stimulated follicle is brought to the state of maturation necessary for ovulation. The other gonadotropin, LH, triggers the ovulation process, in which the mature egg leaves the follicle. The empty follicle is transformed into the corpus luteum, a structure that is in effect a temporary secretory organ. LH thereupon stimulates the new luteal cells to produce large amounts of progesterone, the second female sex steroid. (There is probably a role for a third gonadotropic hormone of the pituitary, prolactin, in maintaining the steroid-producing function of the corpus luteum for its usual 14-day life span, but there is some doubt whether this is true in humans.) Because of estrogen's and progesterone's extensive effects on sex behavior and secondary sex characteristics they are usually referred to as the sex steroids, but they also affect other organs, including bone, muscle, blood and the liver, and processes such as carbohydrate and calcium metabolism and water retention.

In the next steps of the molecular relay the steroid hormones act on individual cells of the reproductive organs. The cells that are targets for the sex hormones have unique large molecules in their cytoplasm that bind particular sex steroids. These receptors are highly specific: they are not found in other organs and in the target organs they do not bind other steroids. After binding, the complex of receptor and, say, an estrogen molecule is moved to the nucleus of the cell, where it interacts with the genetic material and changes the pattern of the cell's production of messenger RNA, thus altering the program of protein synthesis. In this manner a nonstimulated cell of the uterus, for example, is converted to the stimulated state.

ADAM AND EVE, the legendary initiators of human reproduction, were depicted by Albrecht Dürer in the illustration on the opposite page, a copper engraving made in 1504. The engraving is celebrated, according to the critic Erwin Panofsky, for the "splendor of a technique that does equal justice to the warm glow of human skin, to the chilly slipperiness of a snake, to the metallic undulations of locks and tresses, to the smooth, shaggy, downy or bristly quality of animals' coats...." Panofsky commented that the engraving is "intentionally a model of human beauty...two classic specimens of the nude human body, as perfect as possible both in proportions and in pose." Although Genesis relates that Adam was formed "of the dust of the ground" and Eve of "one of his ribs," Dürer drew them both with an umbilicus, the mark of placental gestation that characterizes their descendants. The print from which this reproduction is made is in the Museum of Fine Arts in Boston.

Identical molecules play analogous roles in the human male. As in females, integrated processes control both gamete and hormone production by the testis. Although the structures responsible for these two functions (respectively the seminiferous tubules and the Leydig cells) are more independent in the testis than they are in the ovary, they do respond to stimulation by the gonadotropins in a coordinated manner. And so the production, maturation and transport of the sperm and the stimulation of secondary sex characteristics, including the formation of the seminal fluid's normal chemistry, proceed under required hormonal conditions, much as egg production in the female is coordinated with the proper hormonal milieu for the subsequent steps of egg transport and nidation: the implantation of the egg in the uterine lining. The patterns of production of the hypothalamic releasing factor, the pituitary's gonadotropic hormones and the gonadal steroids are noncyclic in the male whereas they are cyclic in the female, but the hypothalamic and pituitary messengers are the same in both sexes. The main gonadal steroid in the male is testosterone.

So much for the general pattern of hormone interactions that serve to integrate the sequence of reproductive events in both sexes. Let me now describe those events in more detail, first in the female and then in the male.

Every month, from the time of sexual maturation, the human female prepares for a possible pregnancy. An egg is produced, the uterine cervix becomes receptive to the passage of spermatozoa, the muscular and secretory capacities of the uterus and the fallopian tubes become conducive to the transport of sperm and egg, and the endometrial lining of the uterus prepares to harbor a fertilized egg. All of this is accomplished by two distinct but cross-linked sequences of events, the ovulatory and the uterine, or menstrual, cycles.

The key event is the monthly development of an egg. As early as about the sixth week of embryonic age some 2,000 amoebalike oögonia, or germ cells, migrate into the human ovary from a specialized region of the yolk sac. In the course of embryonic and fetal development their number increases tremendously through cell division. At birth the two ovaries of the female infant contain nearly 500,000 primary follicles: individual oöcytes, the precursors of eggs, surrounded by a layer of follicle cells. Most of the follicles, however, are destined for spontaneous degeneration, a process that continues during childhood and adolescence and throughout the reproductive years. It is only the occasional egg that actually ovulates and has an opportunity to participate in fertilization—perhaps fewer than 400 in a woman's reproductive years.

From among the scores of thousands of primary follicles, a few start to develop as the circulating FSH levels rise each month a few days before a menstrual period. After about 10 days usually only one follicle continues to flourish and become fully mature, ready to release its egg. At mid-cycle, on approximately the 14th day, ovulation occurs, with the oöcyte bursting from the rupture point in a cascade of follicular cells and fluid. The released egg is swept from the surface of the ovary by the undulating open end of the fallopian tube. At this point the egg still has 46 chromosomes, the normal human complement; the process of reduction division whereby the complement is reduced to 23, to be matched by the 23 chromosomes of the fertilizing spermatozoon, begins during fetal life but is suspended for many years. Now the process is resumed with the expulsion of the first polar body carrying 23 of the chromosomes. The remaining 23 replicate once more, and it is only after a sperm makes contact with the surface of the egg that a second polar body is expelled, again reducing the genetic material by half, so that the union of egg and sperm will produce the normal complement of hereditary material.

Fertilization, once thought to be a simple matter of sperm-egg interaction, is an intricate series of steps that begins when a spermatozoon makes contact with the zona pellucida, a viscous en-

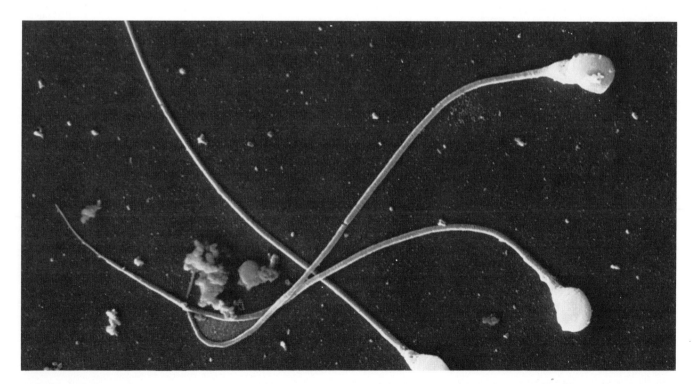

HUMAN SPERMATOZOA are enlarged some 4,000 diameters in this scanning electron micrograph made by David M. Phillips of the Population Council. The sperm were removed from semen by centrifugation and shadowed with platinum. The sperm head consists of densely packed chromatin, the hereditary material, covered by the acrosomal cap containing the enzymes that accomplish the penetration of the egg. Behind the head is a short segment containing mitochondria that supply energy to power the long flagellum.

velope surrounding the egg. By enzymatic action the sperm slices through the zona and makes contact with the surface of the egg. This initiates a series of functional and structural responses. A key event is an immediate blockade against the entry of additional sperm. In fact, without the evolutionary development of a means of preventing polyspermy (the entry of additional sperm) sexual reproduction would not be a successful means of maintaining any species, since polyspermy is almost invariably nonviable. The barriers to polyspermy include changes in the zona pellucida that make it impenetrable and alterations in the egg's surface that preclude the attachment of additional sperm, but the precise nature of the blocks remains unknown. The fertilizing sperm passes through the outer membrane of the egg into the cytoplasm in several stages, in the process both activating the egg to complete its second reduction division and orienting the axis of future development. Even then it is not clear at all that the egg is "fertilized." For about 12 hours the formation within the cytoplasm of distinct egg and sperm pronuclei unfolds. The pronuclei, which are large organelles with a complex structure, move together gradually. Then, following further structural changes, the maternal and paternal hereditary contributions intermingle, and with this event the first cell division of the zygote begins. After 36 hours the single cell has become two. Two days later the fertilized egg may have divided twice more to form a microscopic ball of eight cells. In this condition the egg completes its passage through the fallopian tube and enters the uterus.

Four days after fertilization the egg is a cluster of 32 or 64 cells, which are beginning to divide more rapidly. This stage corresponds to about day 19 or 20 of the menstrual cycle. The cluster of cells remains unattached for one or two days and assumes the form of a signet ring: an inner mass of cells encircled by a single row of aligned trophoblastic, or nourishing, cells. This preembryo state is called the blastocyst. Under the proper conditions the outer ring of cells nestles into the endometrium and begins to form the placenta. The inner cell mass, after several more days of cell divisions and internal rearrangements, becomes a human embryo.

In an integrated manner a second sequence takes place concurrently to ensure the egg a protective and supportive nesting place in the uterus. Early in the four-week menstrual cycle, before

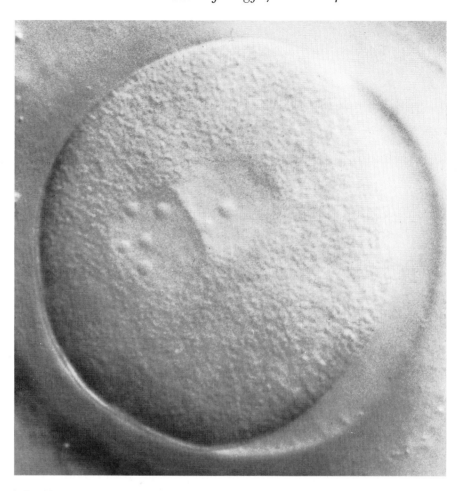

HUMAN EGG is enlarged 1,200 diameters in a photomicrograph made by Pierre Soupart and Larry L. Morgenstern of the Vanderbilt University School of Medicine. Here differential-interference micrography focuses sharply on the equatorial plane of the egg, revealing the female pronucleus and the male pronucleus, derived from the sperm head, in close apposition; nucleoli are visible in each pronucleus. The egg proper is surrounded by the viscous zona pellucida. At this stage, some 20 hours after the sperm's penetration, the hereditary material is replicating within the pronuclear membranes. The membranes will break down as the chromosomes condense and pair up for first division of fertilized egg.

ovulation, the ovary secretes in ever increasing amounts the estrogenic steroids, principally estradiol. These hormones stimulate the endometrium to proliferate and to become much richer in blood vessels. The final surge of estrogen production heralds (and also induces, by means of the hypothalamic recognition of blood estrogen levels) a mid-cycle peak in the LH level. Ovulation follows within 24 hours, and at about this time ovarian steroid production is switched over from a predominance of estrogen to a predominance of progesterone. In response the cells of the endometrium become still more numerous and more corpulent. The endometrial glands grow rapidly in length and thickness and begin to accumulate secretions. The entire endometrial surface, by the 20th day of the cycle, has become a highly vascular, spongy nest ready to accept, protect and nurture a fertilized and dividing egg if one should arrive from the fallopian tube. The tube itself has developed cilia and

increased its flow of glandular fluids for transporting an egg to the uterus.

The uterine lining is now under the remarkable influence of progesterone produced by the corpus luteum. In a nonfertile month the luteal cells begin to reduce their progesterone production about 10 days after ovulation; some four or five days later the level is low enough to result in a sloughing off of the endometrium and menstruation. If an egg is fertilized, the first crisis to be overcome is therefore the avoidance of menstruation. For the pregnancy to survive there must be a source of progesterone to continue the support of the endometrium; without it the blastocyst, or later the new embryo, would pass out with the sloughed-off endometrium and menstrual blood.

The maintenance of progesterone—and indeed the synchrony of maturation, release and fertilization of the egg on the one hand and preparation of the uterus as a proper environment for nida-

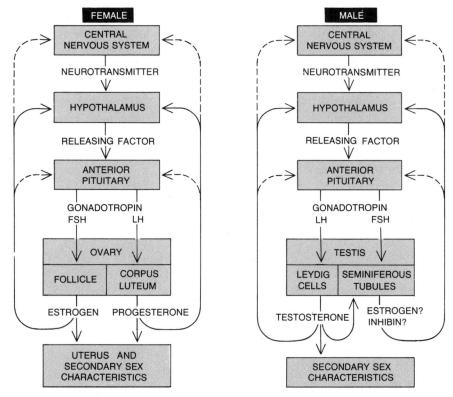

INTERRELATIONS OF ORGANS involved in the reproductive process are shown in this flow diagram. The central nervous system, prompted by external or internal stimuli, causes the hypothalamus to secrete a releasing factor that stimulates the anterior pituitary gland. The pituitary thereupon releases the gonadotropic hormones FSH and LH, which stimulate specific structures in the gonads to secrete the steroid hormones: either estrogen and progesterone or testosterone. The gonadal steroids affect reproductive organs and feed back to the hypothalamus and perhaps to other structures to stimulate and/or inhibit their activity.

tion on the other—is achieved because the hormones involved in each process have such exquisitely integrated and interrelated functions. Consider the implications of the hormonal events of a nonfertile cycle. After ovulation the gonadal steroid hormones feed back at mid-cycle to suppress the pituitary secretion of FSH and LH, and the progressive decline in the concentration of the pituitary gonadotropins in the blood prevents any supplementary ovulations that might interfere with a possible pregnancy. In the absence of a pregnancy, however, a decline in blood steroid concentration in the late luteal phase causes a rise in LH and FSH. In other words, once it is clear that a cycle has been infertile there is an immediate signal to the brain to initiate the events that prepare an egg for release the next month; menstruation intervenes, but the new cycle has already begun. In response to the increase in secretion of FSH and LH follicular maturation proceeds, and with it egg development and increases in gonadal steroid-hormone production. Late in the follicular phase, approaching the period of the maximal rate of follicular enlargement and maximal steroid production, the patterns of FSH and LH di-

verge. FSH secretion declines but LH secretion increases gradually until rising estrogen levels signal the preovulatory surge of both LH and FSH, linking follicular maturation and steroid production to the ovulatory stimulus from the pituitary.

In the case of pregnancy, as I have indicated, avoiding the crisis of menstruation requires an uninterrupted supply of progesterone. The initial source is the corpus luteum, which receives a signal to continue making the steroid. The signal comes from the newly formed blastocyst. Even before nidation the outer cells of the early blastocyst copiously produce a gonadotropic molecule, usually called human chorionic gonadotropin (HCG), that is very similar in function and structure to pituitary LH. The blastocyst's gonadotropin stimulates the maternal corpus luteum to keep on producing progesterone beyond the time of the first expected menstrual period. A second critical point lies ahead, however. The corpus luteum, in spite of maximum stimulation, has a limited life span. Before this time limit is reached, at about the fifth week of gestation, the placenta itself begins to produce sufficient quantities of progesterone to maintain the pregnancy.

To pass the first crisis, in other words, the embryo produces a gonadotropin that stimulates maternal hormonal production; to meet the second crisis the developing embryo itself assumes the required endocrine function, thus becoming self-sufficient in this respect. By five and a half weeks the pregnancy can continue even if the maternal ovaries cease to function or are removed [*see illustration on page 36*].

The noteworthy characteristics of the chain of reproductive events in the female are the restriction of the multiplication phase of oögenesis to the fetal ovary, the dramatic rate of depletion of the oöcytes and the cyclic patterns of pituitary-gonadal interaction. The male reproductive process differs in each of these respects in spite of the similarity of its molecular relay system.

A man produces many billions of spermatozoa in a lifetime, all of which derive from the 1,000 or 2,000 spermatogonia, or germ cells, that migrate into the embryonic testis before the end of the second month of intrauterine life. This process is made possible by the way in which the male germ cells multiply: when the spermatogonia divide, many of the daughter cells are kept in reserve while others undergo further cell divisions and then complete spermatogenesis in the seminiferous tubules. In contrast to the multiplication phase of oögenesis in the ovary, which is confined to a few weeks of fetal life, the multiplication phase of spermatogenesis in the testis begins in the fetal period and continues throughout life. Since there is no significant depletion of the germ-cell stores, there is no gradual loss of gamete-producing function as there is in the ovary; the testis goes on producing millions upon millions of spermatozoa and, in the normal gonad, there always remain additional germ cells to provide the capability of producing millions more. (It is not uncommon, however, for the vascular changes of aging to affect the testis or pituitary and indirectly cause a loss of testicular function.) In the course of spermatogenesis the two important objectives are reduction of the chromosome number from the diploid number (46) of the spermatogonium to the haploid number (23) of the spermatozoon and the preparation of the spermatozoon for its role in fertilization. A complex series of transformations involving both the cytoplasm and the nucleus changes the large, round spermatogonium into streamlined and motile spermatozoa in approximately 74 days.

The testis, like the ovary, must be

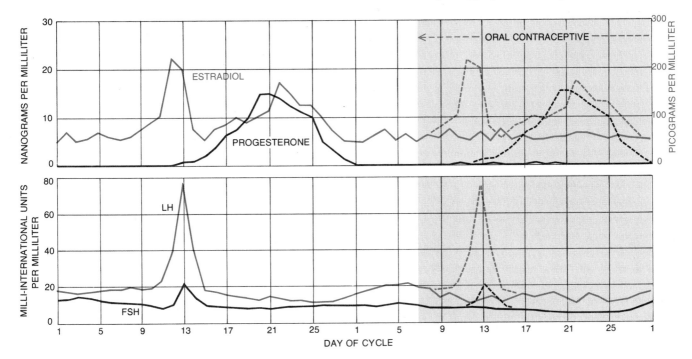

EFFECT OF ORAL CONTRACEPTIVE is to prevent ovulation by interfering with the normal cycle (*left and broken curves at right*). The pill contains synthetic steroids. Released into the circulation, they have a negative-feedback effect that inhibits pituitary secretion of the gonadotropins FSH and LH, which normally induce follicle development, ovulation and the secretion of gonadal steroids. In the absence of endogenous steroids the pill's synthetic steroids act on the endometrium so that a menstrual cycle is simulated.

der various social and cultural circumstances. The process is lengthy and complex, so that any new methods likely to emerge in the near future must now be at some advanced stage of development, with some testing in human subjects already under way. There are a number of such techniques that may be ready for general service within the next three to five years.

Several techniques for contraception in women involve new ways of delivering progestins. One method is injection. Two progestin compounds are being marketed in some countries as injections to be given every three months. They work by suppressing LH release and thereby preventing ovulation. They cause irregular bleeding, however, and there are questions as to their safety and reversibility that need to be resolved. The search goes on for other injectable compounds and inert carriers that will release them slowly and continuously. Progestin can also be released gradually from combination with a polymer that can be implanted under the skin. Subdermal implants—tubes or rods made of a rubberlike polymer into which the synthetic steroids have been introduced—are in an advanced stage of clinical investigation. There are also biodegradable implants; the steroid is incorporated in a polymer made, for example, of the biological molecule lactate, the polylactate is rolled into rods and implanted

under the skin and the hormone is released as the polymer gradually breaks down. Since progestins can be absorbed through the vaginal mucosa, it is also possible to incorporate the steroid in a plastic ring, about the size and shape of the rim of a diaphragm, that a woman can insert easily herself and leave in place a month or longer. This method is at the stage of product development.

A number of new kinds of IUD are under trial. Some of them are simply differently designed inert models but in other cases the IUD is primarily a carrier for an antifertility agent that acts locally in the uterus, either progesterone or a nonsteroid agent such as copper. Copper-carrying IUD's that are available in many countries need to be replaced after about two years; some newer models have a theoretical life span of 25 years. The progesterone-releasing IUD now being tested also has a limitation in effective time span, but its contraceptive effectiveness has been established as about the equal of other available devices.

Another approach is the induction of menstruation. Compounds are being tested that suppress the corpus luteum and thus bring about a menstrual discharge by eliminating the progesterone support the endometrium needs to sustain implantation. No single compound has met the test of effectiveness and safety but many are being synthesized and screened in animals for possible clinical trial. There was some hope that prosta-

glandin, a substance known to affect uterine muscle, could act systematically to suppress the human corpus luteum. Naturally occurring prostaglandins have been tried without success, and now various prostaglandin analogues are being synthesized and tested. Menstruation might alternatively be induced by giving synthetic progestins during the luteal phase of the cycle in doses sufficient to suppress progesterone production but not to maintain the pregnancy. Four synthetic progestins were tested in women and found to reduce luteal function but the effect was counteracted by HCG, which maintained luteal secretion. Nonetheless, the promise of a contraceptive method based on the principle of menstruation induction warrants an investigative effort of the highest priority. Such an approach could solve the problems of safety that appear to be associated with continuous-dosage hormones.

The rhythm method would be quite effective if the time of ovulation could be known precisely. An estrogenic fertility drug that acts through the hypothalamus to induce ovulation has been tested in normally ovulating women as a means of keeping ovulation on schedule. The test was not successful because in successive months of use the interval between drug ingestion and ovulation increased unpredictably. Now that the hypothalamic releasing factor (generally called LRF, for luteinizing-hormone releasing factor) has been isolated and synthesized, the prospect of regularizing ovulation with it has been put to clinical test. The few cases so far reported indicate the procedure may be feasible. A continuing program of synthesis and testing of modified LRF molecules might, on the other hand, find an LRF antagonist: a substance that would counteract LRF's gonadotropin-releasing action.

A "morning after" or "minutes after" pill to be taken after each coital exposure rather than regularly has certain attractions. The synthetic estrogen diethylstilbestrol is now available to reduce the chances of pregnancy following an isolated mid-cycle exposure, but its side effects and disruption of the ovarian cycle make it unacceptable for regular postcoital contraception. Several related compounds have been tested in women without success, and others are available for testing; one is on clinical trial in India. Two synthetic progestins have been tested experimentally but with poor effectiveness and considerable disruption of the bleeding pattern.

Still another possibility for contraception in women is immunization. A woman inoculated with purified human HCG develops antibodies to the hormone; later, when a blastocyst secretes HCG, the antibodies should interfere with the hormone's role in maintaining the corpus luteum so that menstruation takes place even in the event of a fertile cycle. A single inoculation should last indefinitely, but there are several possible ways to counteract the effect if desired. The method is promising and has been tested in a few volunteers, but several problems are still to be resolved.

For millenniums contraception was mainly left up to males. The diaphragm and the pill gave the responsibility (and more control) to females. Now there is revived interest in methods that involve the male, primarily by interfering with sperm production or development or by blocking the path of the sperm.

Progestin given orally can suppress gonadotropin release, and thus sperm formation, while testosterone is supplied to maintain normal secondary sex characteristics. Tests establishing that this combination of results can be achieved constitute a major advance, but the safety and side effects of the method and the specific agents and routes of administration require more investigation. What seems feasible is a biodegradable implant of testosterone that would last at least a year, supplemented by a weekly pill or a semiannual injection of progestin. There is also the possibility of inhibiting gonadotropin release by administering either progestin or testosterone alone by injection every three months. The difficulties are loss of libido from progestin and the danger of metabolic or cardiovascular disorders from the required high dosage of testosterone.

The vas deferens, which is easily accessible, may lend itself to reversible contraception as well as permanent sterilization. Several kinds of removable clip are under clinical study, as are small plastic plugs that can be removed and even a microvalve that can be closed or opened. So far all such devices that have been adequately tested either have failed to close the vas completely or have damaged the tissue. Another possibility is killing spermatozoa or rendering them immotile by putting a foreign body such as a silk filament in the vas without blocking it. The danger in all methods affecting sperm is the occurrence of congenital defects in a fetus that might be generated by a partially damaged sperm.

Judging by the number of leads that are known to be feasible and are being tested it seems likely that some effective new contraceptive methods will be generally available within a few years; it is possible, on the other hand, that all the innovations now being tested will prove to be too unsafe, ineffective or hard to design and produce. The continuous identification of new leads, through basic research providing better understanding of the normal reproductive process, remains critical to the development of better contraceptive techniques.

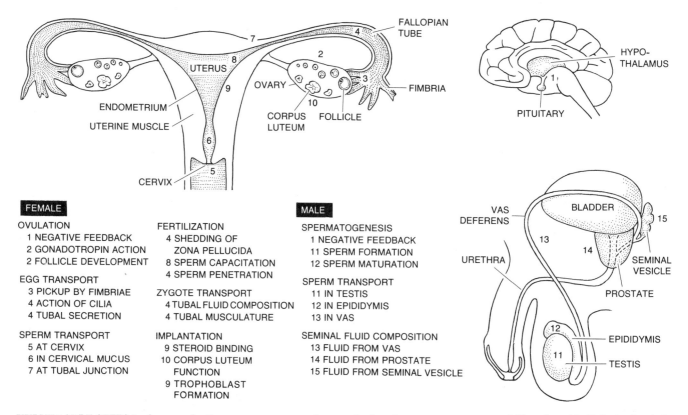

FEMALE

OVULATION
1 NEGATIVE FEEDBACK
2 GONADOTROPIN ACTION
2 FOLLICLE DEVELOPMENT

EGG TRANSPORT
3 PICKUP BY FIMBRIAE
4 ACTION OF CILIA
4 TUBAL SECRETION

SPERM TRANSPORT
5 AT CERVIX
6 IN CERVICAL MUCUS
7 AT TUBAL JUNCTION

FERTILIZATION
4 SHEDDING OF
  ZONA PELLUCIDA
8 SPERM CAPACITATION
4 SPERM PENETRATION

ZYGOTE TRANSPORT
4 TUBAL FLUID COMPOSITION
4 TUBAL MUSCULATURE

IMPLANTATION
9 STEROID BINDING
10 CORPUS LUTEUM
  FUNCTION
9 TROPHOBLAST
  FORMATION

MALE

SPERMATOGENESIS
1 NEGATIVE FEEDBACK
11 SPERM FORMATION
12 SPERM MATURATION

SPERM TRANSPORT
11 IN TESTIS
12 IN EPIDIDYMIS
13 IN VAS

SEMINAL FLUID COMPOSITION
13 FLUID FROM VAS
14 FLUID FROM PROSTATE
15 FLUID FROM SEMINAL VESICLE

VULNERABLE STEPS in the reproductive process suggest points at which contraceptive technology can intervene. One reason more attention has been paid to contraception in women in recent years is that there are so many potentially vulnerable links in the chain of reproductive events in the female. The numbers indicate the site in the male and female reproductive systems of each of listed steps.

4

The Genetics of
Human Populations

The Genetics of Human Populations

L. L. CAVALLI-SFORZA

Since the species Homo sapiens emerged less than 100,000 years ago it has by definition shared a common pool of genes. The differences within a human population are greater than those between populations

In *The Comedy of Errors* Shakespeare makes use of a device that was dear to the hearts of Greek and Roman playwrights. He brings onto the stage identical twins; as he puts it, "the one so like the other, as could not be distinguish'd but by names." To add to the confusion he gives each twin the same name. Moreover, each twin has a servant, and they too are identical twins with the same name. It is no wonder that errors arise. Nature, however, seldom imitates art so closely. Twins are relatively rare, particularly identical ones; they represent only some .3 percent of all births. Therefore not everyone has had the benefit of observing identical twins closely. Those who have done so are usually struck by their remarkable similarity. For all we know, identical twins have identical sets of genes, represented by identical sequences of the paired nucleotides of DNA. They thus provide a tangible and simple proof of the power of inheritance. When in contrast we look at two people selected at random, enough differences are apparent so that the likelihood of confusion between them is remote. Individuality is a familiar property of man; it marks not only facial features and bodily traits but even such details as fingerprints and voice. Indeed, not even identical twins are wholly identical in every respect; it is only that the differences between them are almost always smaller than those between unrelated individuals.

Until recently there existed no precise measure of the full extent of the differences between unrelated individuals. Now, however, the systematic use of electrophoresis as a means of analyzing proteins enables us to make some estimates of this kind. Proteins are simply long chains of amino acids in various sequences. Each type of protein performs a highly specific function in the body. For example, some serve as enzymes that catalyze specific chemical reactions, transforming one compound into another. Other proteins serve for transport; an example is the hemoglobin that carries oxygen from the lungs to the rest of the body. Still others serve other purposes. All the functions of an organism are performed with the assistance of one or another specific protein, and so proteins exist in enormous variety.

Electrophoresis was first used as a technique of genetic analysis by Linus Pauling, Harvey A. Itano, S. J. Singer and I. C. Wells at the California Institute of Technology in 1949. The method basically consists in applying an electric field to a solution of proteins. If two or more proteins present in the solution have different electric charges, they will migrate in the electric field at different rates and thus will separate. The first application of the technique by Pauling and his colleagues clarified the molecular basis of sickle-cell anemia. Electrophoresis showed that the hemoglobin contained in the red blood cells of individuals with the disease is different from normal hemoglobin. It had been known from work done by J. V. Neel of the University of Michigan that the disease, which is particularly frequent among African blacks, is inherited in a precise way. The difference between the hemoglobin found in sickle-cell anemia (called Hb-S) and normal hemoglobin (Hb-A) is due to a single amino acid difference at position 6 on one of the two amino acid chains that make up the hemoglobin molecule [*see top illustration on next page.*]

Since the time of this first study several other workers have used the electrophoresis technique to examine genetic differences among other proteins. For example, many enzymes in human blood have been separated by means of electrophoresis and then stained for purposes of identification. The importance of these methods of genetic analysis cannot be overemphasized. In the great majority of cases differences in the electrophoretic mobility of different enzymes is likely to be a consequence of the substitution of one amino acid for another in the long chain of amino acids that comprises the enzyme molecule. The substitution of one amino acid for another in a protein

"ADORATION OF THE MAGI," painted in 1510 by Hieronymus Bosch (*opposite page*), is an example of postmedieval conceptions of the races of man. By the Middle Ages legends that were based on the mention in the New Testament of "three wise men from the east" who had brought gifts to the newborn King of the Jews had promoted the Magi into kings who ruled the three divisions of mankind: the Asians, the Africans and the Europeans. Long before Bosch artists had begun to portray the supposed King of the Moors, Gaspar, as being dark-skinned and even, as Bosch has done (*left*), with plainly Negroid features. White-haired Balthasar (*kneeling in foreground*) is the king who is usually held to be the ruler of the Europeans. Melchior, with his offering of Arabian frankincense, is supposedly the ruler of the Asians. Some artists have portrayed Melchior with Oriental features rather than as a Middle Easterner. The half-naked man standing in the doorway is an allegorical figure who is evidently intended to represent the Antichrist. Bosch further symbolized the world's burden of evil in the attitude of the shepherds on the roof: they exhibit not reverence but only rustic curiosity. The painting, the central panel of a triptych, is in the Prado.

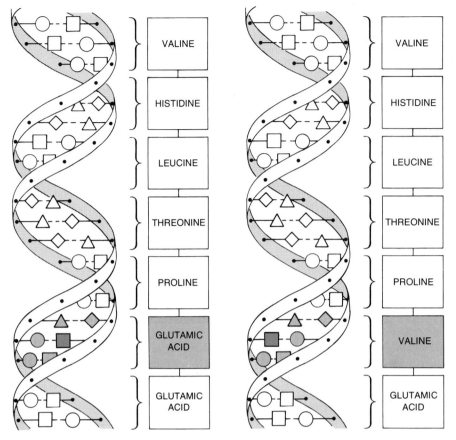

ONE-GENE MUTATION is responsible for the difference between the beta chain of a normal hemoglobin molecule (*left*) and that of hemoglobin S, the variant form responsible for sickle-cell anemia (*right*). Because the middle pair of nucleotides in the sixth nucleotide triplet of the DNA that encodes the beta chain fall in the order thymine-adenine rather than the reverse, the sixth amino acid in the chain is valine (*color*) instead of glutamic acid. The other triplets are shown with arbitrary components; the sequence of amino acids in both beta chains is known, but the sequence of nucleotides in the DNA has not been established.

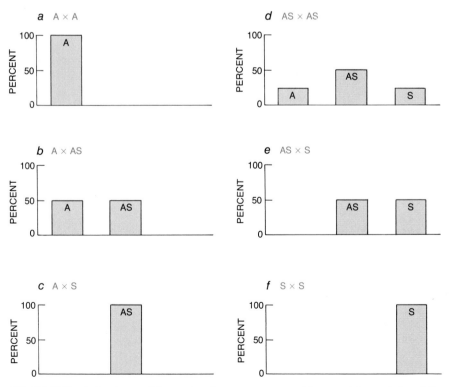

OFFSPRING of the six possible matings between parents with normal hemoglobin (A), those with the sickling trait (AS) and those with sickle-cell anemia (S) are affected as is shown here. The matings (*color*) are $A \times A$, $A \times AS$, $A \times S$, $AS \times AS$, $AS \times S$ and $S \times S$.

molecule is due to the substitution of one nucleotide pair for another in the segment of DNA that is responsible for the synthesis of the protein or of that part of the protein. There are almost no exceptions to the rule that when different individuals show differences in the electrophoretic band or bands that a given enzyme produces, the differences have a simple genetic origin.

The systematic analysis of a large number of enzymes and other proteins has brought a remarkable discovery: a given gene (the DNA segment responsible for the synthesis of a given protein) is by no means identical among the individuals in a population. This observation was made in quantitative terms almost simultaneously by Harry Harris at University College London with respect to man and by Richard C. Lewontin at the University of Chicago with respect to the fruit fly *Drosophila*. When one examines a small sample, say 100 individuals, roughly one in three of the enzymes taken from one of the 100 individuals will show electrophoretic bands that are different from the enzyme bands of some of the remaining 99 individuals. Geneticists customarily call such an enzyme (more precisely, the gene responsible for it) polymorphic. It would be wrong, however, to think that the other two of the three enzymes are invariant from one individual to another. If one analyzes a sample that includes many more than 100 individuals, one finds electrophoretically different forms of nearly every protein studied.

Exactly what these differences mean is far from clear. In many cases there is little evidence that an individual finds it an advantage or a disadvantage to possess a protein in form A rather than in form B or C. There are usually subtle differences in the activity of each form, but all of them are well tolerated by their carriers. As far as we can tell, it often does not seem to matter which form of a polymorphic enzyme we carry, except perhaps in special circumstances. Of course, the differences may seem trivial to us only because we do not know enough about them. For example, we know what function a particular enzyme performs because we identify an enzyme on the basis of which compounds it transforms into which other compounds. The precise importance to the economy of the organism of a specific enzyme, or of small differences in the activities of two slightly different forms of an enzyme, may nonetheless escape us.

In summary, then, electrophoresis analyses have shown that there is an extraordinary diversity among individuals at the biochemical level, that the diversity is genetic in origin and that it must therefore be due to differences in the DNA. We can also estimate what the extent of the differences can be. We get roughly half of our DNA from our father and half from our mother. Let us limit our estimate of differences to the DNA obtained from one parent only. (Apart from the DNA of the sex chromosomes, which accounts for about 5 percent of the total, the DNA received from the father is quite similar to that received from the mother.) If we can count the differences between the father's DNA and the mother's, we shall have some basis for calculating the differences that exist within populations. On the assumption that the differences counted for enzyme-producing genes can be extrapolated to the rest of the genes, the DNA of paternal origin in an average individual differs from the DNA of maternal origin by some 200,000 nucleotide pairs. Compared with the total DNA contribution from each parent, which is about five billion nucleotide pairs, a mere 200,000 differences may seem few. In absolute value, however, they are many: they are some 1 percent of the nucleotide-pair differences that separate man from his closest zoological relatives, the chimpanzee and the gorilla.

The original source of all the differences between two individuals is the phenomenon we call mutation. When new DNA is formed by the replication of existing DNA, errors can occur. Usually such errors involve the substitution of one nucleotide pair for another, but sometimes more drastic changes, involving a cluster of nucleotide pairs or even entire chromosomes with their millions of nucleotide pairs, take place. Mutations are rare events; this is fortunate because a mutation that changes the functioning of even a single gene in a complex organism can jeopardize the life of the organism just as a clogged carburetor or an interrupted electric circuit is enough to stop an automobile. The rate at which mutations take place is of such a low order of magnitude that any individual carries only perhaps 10 to 100 nucleotide pairs, different from those present in his parents, that can be attributed to the mutation process. How, then, have we accumulated hundreds of thousands of changes?

Let us trace the history of a human mutation that has just arisen. There are three immediate possibilities: the change will affect the individual carrying it in a negative way, in a positive way or not at all. If the influence is negative, the carri-

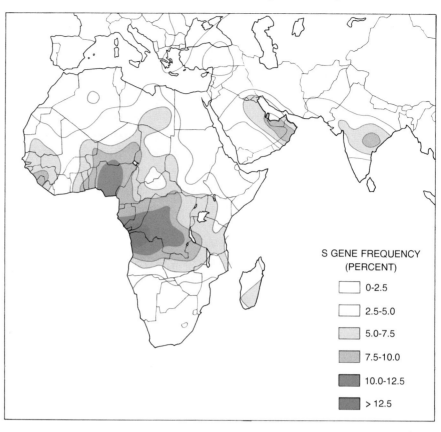

S GENE FREQUENCY (PERCENT)

☐ 0-2.5
☐ 2.5-5.0
▨ 5.0-7.5
▨ 7.5-10.0
▨ 10.0-12.5
▨ > 12.5

SICKLE-CELL GENE is commonest in populations of tropical Africa; in Zaire, for example, the S gene frequency is about 18 percent, which means that some 30 percent of the population carry the AS trait. The sickle-cell gene is also found in the Mediterranean, particularly in Greece and Turkey, in northwestern Africa, southern Arabia, Pakistan, India and Bangladesh. Individuals who carry the AS trait are more resistant to malaria than others.

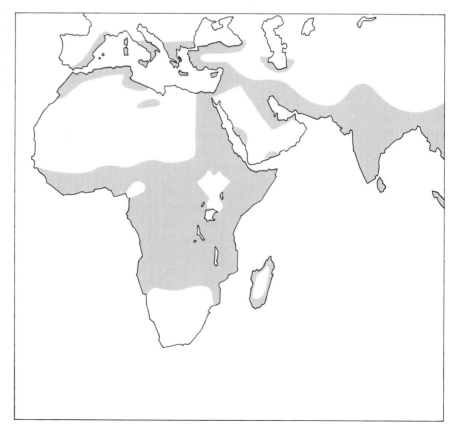

MALIGNANT MALARIAS caused by the parasite *Plasmodium falciparum* were common in the 1920's in the parts of Old World indicated on this map; data are from M. F. Boyd. Overlap with sickle-cell gene distribution is extensive, as seen in illustration at top of page.

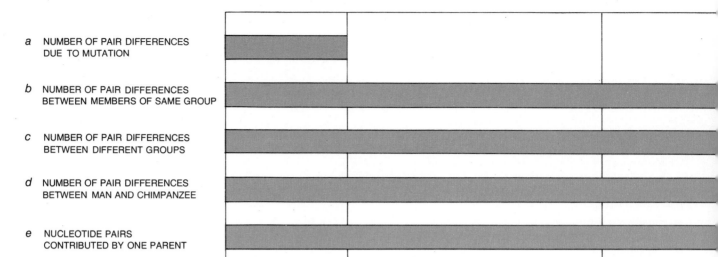

a NUMBER OF PAIR DIFFERENCES
DUE TO MUTATION

b NUMBER OF PAIR DIFFERENCES
BETWEEN MEMBERS OF SAME GROUP

c NUMBER OF PAIR DIFFERENCES
BETWEEN DIFFERENT GROUPS

d NUMBER OF PAIR DIFFERENCES
BETWEEN MAN AND CHIMPANZEE

e NUCLEOTIDE PAIRS
CONTRIBUTED BY ONE PARENT

10   1,000

ESTIMATED NUMBER O

NUMBERS OF GENETIC DIFFERENCES that are estimated to exist between individuals who are more and more distantly related are plotted on a logarithmic scale in this graph. The data used are the number of differences in the nucleotide pairs of the DNA that encodes proteins; these differences are observable as amino acid substitutions in the proteins. The observed number is then extrapolated to estimate the total number of nucleotide-pair differences. For comparison purposes the size of the haploid genome, that is, the number of nucleotide pairs contributed to an offspring by one parent only, is shown at the bottom of the graph.

er of the mutation may even die before having a chance to reproduce; then the mutation is lost. It will not be found in later generations unless it reoccurs spontaneously. If the mutation has no discernible effect on the carrier, then its reappearance in future generations is entirely a matter of chance. That is because the carrier may die before reproducing or may have no children or, even if he or she has children, may not pass the mutation to any of them. The probability that the mutation will be passed to any one child is only 50:50, so that it is possible, even if there are several children, that none of them will carry the mutated gene.

The outcome in both cases is the loss of the new mutation; that is what happens in about a third of all mutations. For another third or so there will be one descendant of the original carrier who will carry the new gene, which can then be passed on to further progeny. For the remaining third there will be more than one carrier among the progeny: two, three, four or more. Then the gene, entirely by chance, will have increased in relative frequency. Although the mutation started as a single copy, there are now several copies of it in the population.

This increase by chance can repeat itself until, after a large number of generations, the original mutant gene will be found in a great many individuals of a population. It can even happen, again always by chance, that all the individuals in a population will eventually carry the mutant gene that arose many genera-

tions earlier in a single individual. The chances of this happening are small, but they are greater than zero. Since mutations occur continuously in every new individual, this chance mechanism, known technically as random genetic drift, can contribute to the differences that we observe among individuals of a population or between populations [*see bottom illustration on page 46*].

What about the remaining possibility, a mutation that is advantageous to the carrier? This is the most interesting of the three possibilities because it allows an advance in what may be called a genetic adaptation to the environment. When a mutation confers some advantage on its carrier, the carrier may have a better chance than others to have progeny and thereby to pass on the advantageous mutation. This, of course, is the well-known phenomenon of natural selection. Chance will still play a role: even an advantageous mutation may disappear from a population as a result of random processes. On the average, however, an advantageous mutated gene will become more prevalent in a population and will eventually supplant the original gene.

Perhaps the most intensively studied example of this process is the mutation that gives rise to the sickle-cell trait. The mutation responsible for the sickle-cell trait results in three different genetic types of individuals. They are labeled *AA*, *AS* and *SS*. The *AA* type is normal. The *AS* type has the sickle-cell trait, which can be distinguished by laboratory tests, but enjoys essentially normal

health. The *SS* type has the hereditary disease called sickle-cell anemia.

It happens that in an environment where malaria is prevalent the genetic type *AS* has a distinct advantage over the type *AA*, because *AS* individuals have a 10 to 15 percent better chance of surviving invasion by the most dangerous of the malarial parasites: *Plasmodium falciparum*. The total number of *AS* types will therefore tend to increase in proportion to the other genetic types in the population by the process of natural selection. We can follow the entire process mathematically starting from one *AS* individual who arose by mutation in a population consisting only of type *AA*. At the start, and for many generations thereafter, only *AS* and *AA* individuals will be found in the population. The *AS* individuals will increase with respect to the *AA* ones because of their greater resistance to malaria. Later on, however, *SS* individuals will also appear. Unlike *AS* and *AA* individuals they are subject to sickle-cell anemia whether malaria is present or not. The *SS* individuals have only a poor chance (between 20 and 40 percent) of surviving long enough to have children.

With respect to the gene that gives rise to the sickle-cell trait, then, natural selection cannot accomplish what would seem to be (and usually is) the natural outcome of the process: the replacement of gene *A* by gene *S*. The reason is the poor viability of *SS* individuals. Their high mortality acts as a brake, and the more *AS* individuals there are, the

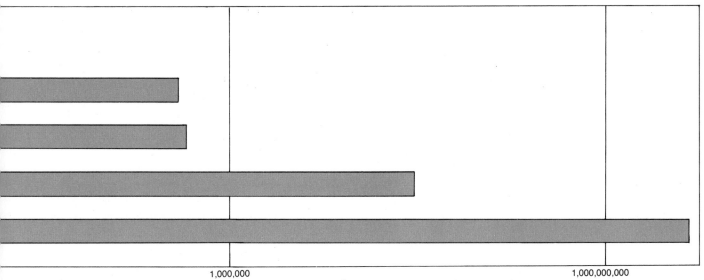

DNA NUCLEOTIDE-PAIR DIFFERENCES

It is about five billion (*e*). The smallest number of differences, perhaps as few as 10 (*a*), is the number that arises in the haploid genome because of random mutation in one generation. A much larger number of differences, half a million or more (*b*), exists between the haploid genomes of two randomly chosen members of a single ethnic group. The number is not greatly increased when the randomly chosen individuals belong to different major divisions of the human population, such as Caucasian and Oriental (*c*). Differences between man and his near relative the chimpanzee number in the millions (*d*). The figures are approximations only.

more SS individuals will be born and the more effective the brake is. Eventually an equilibrium is reached that is affected by the environmental incidence of malaria. When malaria is prevalent, as many as 30 percent of all individuals in the population can be of the AS type; at this level the frequency of SS individuals is just above 2 percent. The process comes close to equilibrium within 2,000 years or so. In biological terms that is a rapid process; the human species rarely experiences natural selection at this level of intensity.

Other kinds of genetic adaptation to malaria, involving other genes, have also occurred. Thalassemia and the disease resulting from a defect in the enzyme glucose-6 phosphate dehydrogenase are well-known examples that involve similar selection intensities. Still other genetic adaptations, although they are less well known, are believed to involve lower selection intensities. Many of them, however, are not barred from proceeding to completion by the mischance, encountered with sickle-cell anemia, that makes the SS individual the victim of a generally fatal disease. If this were not so, the population that harbors the S gene would in the end consist entirely of SS individuals.

The sickle-cell trait thus provides an example of how swiftly genetic changes can occur in a population. In almost all other cases the process is much slower. The differences we find between individuals is evidence that the process whereby one gene is substituted for another is an ongoing one. Many of these processes are clearly under way simultaneously; that is why we are able to count so many differences between two individuals. Some of the processes—an unknown number—may have reached the level of equilibrium we have noted with respect to sickle-cell anemia in the presence of malaria, namely that both gene A and gene S coexist in the population in a ratio that does not change any further, once equilibrium is reached, unless the environment also changes. This change in the environment has in fact begun to materialize. The incidence of sickle-cell anemia among blacks who have now lived for 200 or 300 years in the relatively malaria-free environments of the U.S. is only 25 percent of the incidence among equivalent populations in malarial Africa.

Many other mutant genes are similarly not at equilibrium, and their prevalence will change substantially with time. If we could visit the earth 10,000 years from now, we might find substantial changes in the comparative frequencies of all gene types. Some of these gene frequencies may change with the passage of time because one form of a gene has an advantage over another, and its frequency will tend to increase. With other genes the changes can proceed randomly. As mutations keep pouring in at every generation there is a constant state of flux.

How do such processes bear on the genetics of race? When we look at the main divisions of mankind, we find many differences that are visible to the unaided eye. It is not hard to assess the origin of an individual with respect to the major racial subdivisions: the straight-haired, tan Orientals, the wiry-haired, dark Africans and the lank-haired, pale Caucasians. If we analyze our impressions in detail, we find that they come down to a few highly visible characteristics: the color of the skin, the color and form of the hair and the gross morphology of the face, the eye folds, the nose and the lips. It is highly likely that all these differences are determined genetically, but they are not determined in any simple way. For example, where skin color is concerned there are at least four gene differences that contribute to variations in pigmentation.

If we return to the mechanisms by which differences in genes give rise to differences in proteins, we find that differences in proteins parallel the superficial differences of race only to a limited extent. The differences between individuals that have been assessed by the random sampling of enzymes total some 200,000 for any two Caucasians. Protein differences of the same order of magnitude also exist between two Orientals and between two African blacks. If, in choosing individuals for comparison, we take two Caucasians from the same village, the nucleotide-pair differences will be slightly less; if we take two Caucasians from the geographical extremes of Europe, they will be slightly more. If we compare a Caucasian with a black African, the differences increase somewhat, but not by a great deal. Much the same is true if we compare a Caucasian with an Oriental. (A black African and an Ori-

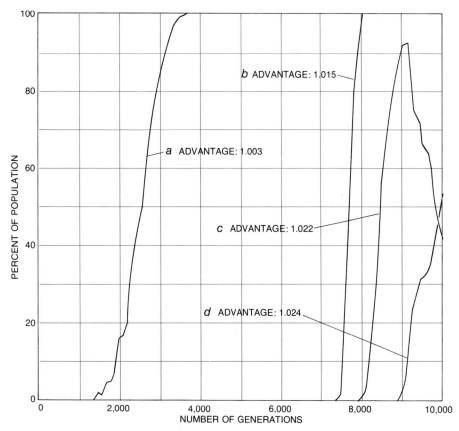

FOUR ADVANTAGEOUS MUTATIONS are traced over 10,000 generations in a computer simulation. The first to appear (*a*), with a fitness advantage only .003 greater than unity (1.0), was present in all the population some 2,300 generations later. The most advantageous mutation (*d*) swamped the next most advantageous one in only 1,000 generations.

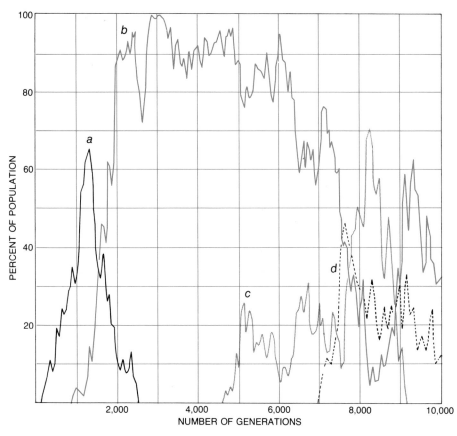

NEUTRAL MUTATIONS are traced over the same 10,000 generations in a second computer simulation. Although the gene-frequency fluctuations are random, the second mutation (*color*) succeeds in supplanting the first and even regains a majority position after a temporary swamping. Fluctuations of this kind are classified as random genetic drift.

ental may show slightly greater differences.) Race as a factor thus adds remarkably little to the differences we can detect between any two individuals. Why, then, are there such differences in some traits, differences profound enough to enable us to diagnose the origin of a Caucasian, an Oriental or an African at a glance? Which is a better measure of difference, the genes that give rise to proteins or what we perceive when we simply look at a person?

As we have seen, the genes for enzymes are similar in different populations. The same seems to be true of all the other genes we can analyze, for example the substances that account for the various blood groups: *A*, *B*, *AB*, *O* and so on. In contrast to this relative uniformity it seems likely that the genes that determine the color of the skin, the color and form of the hair and the morphology of facial characteristics are atypical in being much more diversified. How did such differences arise? Our best answer to the question is embarrassingly vague. For example, we are prepared on a commonsense basis to accept the notion that a darker skin is advantageous in the Tropics: it is less subject to sunburn. Why, however, do Caucasians have a light-colored skin? An answer has been suggested by W. F. Loomis of Brandeis University, and it is somewhat unexpected. His hypothesis is that at latitudes where solar radiation is not particularly intense the skin must be light in color if ultraviolet radiation is to penetrate it and produce enough vitamin D. An adequate supply of vitamin D is critical for growth; if it is not obtained directly through the diet (and it rarely is), it must be formed from precursors in the diet. Ultraviolet radiation is necessary to effect the transformation.

Several details of the Loomis hypothesis are open to criticism, but its general conclusion has not been refuted. Archaeology may provide substantiation; if there was a shortage of vitamin D among early Europeans, one should be able to see the effects in the form of rickets in skeletons. I have calculated that several hundred skeletons from suitable populations would need to be observed in order to test the Loomis hypothesis; so far only a small number of skeletons have been examined. The diet of the Neolithic Europeans who may have been the direct ancestors of today's Caucasians fits well, however, with the vitamin D hypothesis of skin-color selection pressure. These people were cereal-eaters and, unlike the earlier inhabitants of Europe, did not consume much animal protein. Cereals contain the precursors of vitamin D but not the vitamin itself, so that a need for ultraviolet radiation would have existed. At the time of the Industrial Revolution in England, when farming folk moved to the cities and lived in dark slums, rickets became a very common disease. Even the English were not sufficiently light-skinned when the usual quota of ultraviolet radiation was reduced. Hygienists of the period soon learned that exposure to the sun was all that was needed to prevent rickets.

Whatever role the vitamin-D need may have played in Caucasian skin color, it is likely that variations in skin color generally express genetic adaptation to climate. Hair form and such ranges of facial traits as a large nose as opposed to a small one or a narrow eye opening as opposed to a wide one may also represent adaptations to different climatic conditions. Body size too seems to be related to climate. It is always possible, of course, that sexual selection—the "tastes" of our ancestors—also played a part in shaping us one way or another. Climatic adaptation nonetheless makes sense, even if its role in selection pressure is far from being rigorously proved.

If this assumption is correct, we have a good explanation of why some differences among races are so large and others are so small. The differences we see when we look at people are genuinely superficial; the interface between the body and the environment, particularly the climatic dimension of the environment, is the body surface. It is therefore no wonder that the interface has been changed by natural selection to fit the environment to a far greater extent than the rest of our genes have.

The key prerequisite for the differentiation of any animal population into races is some kind of separation of groups that prevents interbreeding. In man's development separation must have been achieved mainly by geography. Today geographic separation has largely broken down, but even in prehistoric times there was considerable movement. An outstanding example is the migration from Asia to the Western Hemisphere across the Bering Strait land bridge roughly between 50,000 and 12,000 years ago.

Geographic distance favors local differentiation even where there are no major barriers to movement. Unless there are strict barriers of some kind, however, the differences are not sharp but gradual, continuous rather than discontinuous. This kind of gradation is characteristic of most human racial differentiation. When on occasion geological

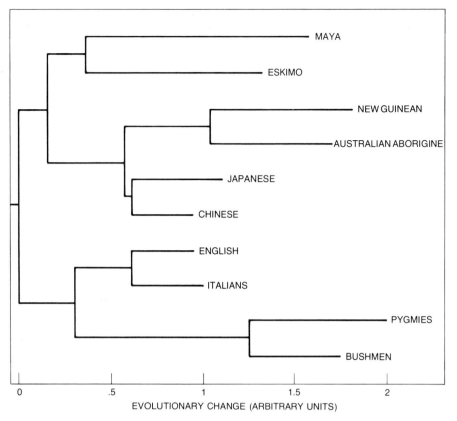

EVOLUTIONARY TREE groups 10 populations, measuring their separation from a common beginning on a scale proportional to the number of substitutions evident in 58 genes. Three main groups emerge: Africans, Europeans and one including Orientals, Oceanians and native Americans. Europeans trail in evolutionary change, possibly owing to intermixture.

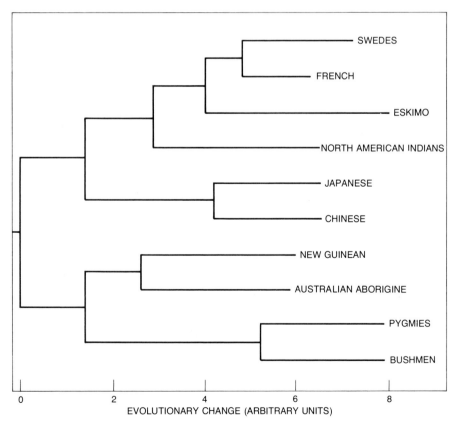

ANTHROPOMETRIC TREE, based on 26 external measurements and observations, shows 10 comparable populations; the array differs from the evolutionary tree's. Europeans now join Orientals and native Americans, whereas Oceanians are with Africans. This suggests that anthropometric characteristics are more affected by climate than genes are, so that the relations shown here are due more to similar environments than to similar descents.

events created insuperable barriers, human genetic differentiation was intensified. This is what happened, for example, when communication between southeastern Asia and Australia and between northeastern Asia and the New World was reduced or totally inhibited by an increase in sea level some 12,000 years ago.

It is possible to reconstruct in the form of a tree some of the history of the genetic differences generated in this way. The reconstruction assumes a fairly sharp separation between an original group and a group that moved away, a separation distinct enough to prevent any (or almost any) contact between the descendants of the two groups. The fact that the migrations may have taken place over long periods presents no major difficulty. Later migrations and exchanges may blur the picture, but they do not necessarily erase it.

Can one use the genetic data obtained from present human racial groups to reconstruct the history of these past separations? More than 10 years ago I undertook such an effort in collaboration with Anthony Edwards. We made use of the available genetic data on a sample of populations representing the aboriginal inhabitants of five continents. The data covered 15 different genes. With the accumulation of information on more genes, it became possible to repeat the reconstruction with a larger data base. Recently, in collaboration with A. Piazza, L. Sgaramella-Zonta and P. Gluckman, I have analyzed the data for 58 genes. The result is in remarkable agreement with the earlier one [see top illustration on preceding page].

The analysis has also made it possible to better understand the origins of many populations, such as the Lapps and the Ainu of Japan. The position of both groups has been a matter of controversy. We find, however, that the Ainu cannot be genetically distinguished from other Orientals and that the Lapps are essentially main-stem Caucasians.

It would be desirable to add time estimates to the tree to indicate the approximate dates when the separations took place. In some instances, for example the occupation of Australia or of the Americas, approximate dates are

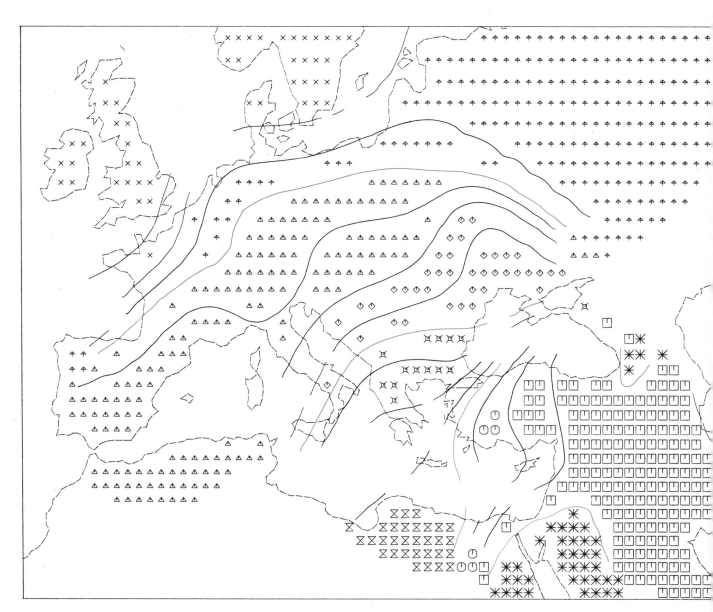

SPREAD OF FARMING across Europe from nuclear areas where agriculture was known more than 9,000 years ago is traced on this computer-generated map. Data are carbon-14 age determinations from some 90 early Neolithic sites, collated by the author and Albert J. Ammerman. The map was produced at the IBM Research Laboratory in San Jose, Calif., with Donald E. Schreiber's program for analysis and display of such data. The rate of spread proves to be about one kilometer per year. If, as is probable, not only

known. In other instances the estimates depend on the constancy of evolutionary rates, and as the tree shows such constancy has not been the case. Caucasians and some Orientals apparently have evolved rather slowly; both groups exhibit shorter branches than Africans. Even though about the same amount of time has elapsed since these groups separated, the amounts of genetic change in them are vastly different. One possible reason for these differences will be examined below.

Perhaps the most interesting estimate to be obtained in this way is the one referring to the time of the original split, the oldest separation in the tree. Allowing for the sources of uncertainty I have mentioned, the time can be given, with

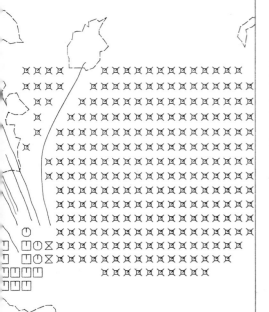

```
☀  BEFØRE  9000 B.P.
⊡  8500  TØ 9000   B.P.
◔  8000  TØ 8500   B.P.
⊠  7500  TØ 8000   B.P.
⋈  7000  TØ 7500   B.P.
◇  6500  TØ 7000   B.P.
△  6000  TØ 6500   B.P.
⚐  5500  TØ 6000   B.P.
╳  5000  TØ 5500   B.P.
```

Near Eastern farming but also Near Eastern farmers entered Europe, it could explain why modern Europeans are genetically intermediate between Africans and Orientals.

reservations, as being approximately 35,000 to 40,000 years ago. It is encouraging to note that the oldest-known fossil remains that are classified as *Homo sapiens sapiens*, that is, modern man in the strict sense, are between 40,000 and 60,000 years old. Thus two independent estimates are compatible and indicate that the differentiation among races began not long after the appearance of modern man.

The simplest interpretation of these conclusions today would envision a relatively small group starting to spread not long after modern man appeared. With the spreading, groups became separated and isolated. Racial differentiation followed. Fifty thousand years or so is a short time in evolutionary terms, and this may help to explain why, genetically speaking, human races show relatively small differences. Future discoveries may of course alter these conclusions. It should also be noted that there are fossils of manlike primates that are a great deal more than 60,000 years old. Indeed, some of these fossils may be three million years old. All of them, however, are quite distinct from the fossils of modern man.

It is interesting to pursue the genetic details of one of these differentiations, even though it is a comparatively recent one. One of modern man's most important technological innovations, the domestication of plants and animals, was achieved in various relatively restricted areas of the earth; the domestications were probably independent of one another. Of no less than three such nuclear areas, the best-known is the Near East, where the domestication of wheat, barley and other cereals and of cattle, sheep, goats and pigs began some 10,000 years ago.

With my colleague Albert J. Ammerman, an archaeologist now working at Stanford University, I have plotted the carbon-14 dates for the oldest remains of domesticated plants in Europe; this is an area where carbon-14 determinations are not only abundant but also reliable. The spread is rather regular and relatively slow [*see illustration at left*]. The average rate of spread is about one kilometer per year. We have asked the question: Did the new technology spread, or was it the people of the nuclear areas who spread, bringing their technology with them? One consequence of the introduction of agriculture, of course, is an increase in the number of people who can live in a given area. Such an increase in population is often

accompanied by a wave of expansion.

Early farming was in itself a shifting type of agriculture that required frequent movement from old fields to new ones. Furthermore, the transition from a hunting and gathering economy to an agricultural economy is a radical one. Little is known about how many people inhabited Europe just before the arrival of farming, but what data there are suggest a low population density. Therefore it is not very likely that the new technology alone spread across Europe.

There is no clear evidence, either archaeological or genetic, opposing the hypothesis that it was the farmers of the nuclear area themselves who spread to Europe, not to mention in other directions. Further analysis is needed, but the hypothesis seems a useful one. On this basis the Caucasians could be mostly the descendants of farmers from the Near East, although it is clear that they would also have mixed with the indigenous inhabitants of Europe. This could account for the fact that Caucasians are genetically somewhat intermediate between Africans and Orientals; if the Near East was their center of origin, they began as a group geographically intermediate between Africans and Asians. Their admixture with local elements during their subsequent spread (together with other factors, some of them linked to the increase in numbers following the adoption of agriculture) can also help to explain the apparent lower rate of genetic change among Caucasians.

It is worth noting that the study of single genes is probably more useful for reconstructing a common ancestry than the study of superficial traits or of bone shape and size, which are probably the effects of many genes and are subject to short-term environmental effects. This limitation is not widely realized and has been the source of some misunderstanding. Moreover, even some single genes are less useful than others for reconstructing the history of the human population. For example, genes that are rapidly selected under specific environmental conditions, such as the sickle-cell gene, may be providing us with misleading information. The fact is that we do not know enough about how natural selection affects most of the genes we study. If we knew more, we would choose those genes that show fewer (or less systematic) effects from natural selection and have differentiated in a more random fashion. Strange as it may seem, chance-determined effects are the ones most useful for reconstructing the genetic history of the human population.

5

The Migrations of
Human Populations

The Migrations of Human Populations

KINGSLEY DAVIS

Ancient migrations carried man to almost every corner of the earth; modern ones are an ebb and flow that results from technological and economic inequality. The migrations of today are the largest of all

Human beings have always been migratory. Sometime between 100,000 and 400,000 years ago man's predecessor *Homo erectus* had spread from China and Java to Britain and southern Africa. Later, Neanderthal types spanned Europe, North Africa and the Near East; modern *Homo sapiens,* originating probably in Africa, reached Sarawak at least 40,000 years ago, Australia some 30,000 years ago and North and South America more than 20,000 years ago. Excluding Antarctica, Paleolithic man made his way to every major part of the globe. Except for species dependent on him, he achieved a wider distribution than any other terrestrial animal.

Since this propensity to migrate has persisted in every epoch, its explanation requires a theory independent of any particular epoch. My own view is that the abiding cause is the same trait that explains man's uniqueness in many other ways: his sociocultural mode of adaptation. As culture advanced and diversified, a profound and distinctly human stimulus to migration developed, namely technological inequality between one territorial group and another. At the same time the possibility of migration was increased by man's capacity to adjust culturally to new environments without the slow process of organic evolution.

Although the particular conditions of each epoch shaped migration, the underlying cause remained the same. Paleolithic man, for example, was a hunter and gatherer who naturally followed his prey and forage. Urging him on was the contrast between exploited territory and virgin territory. This tendency, inherent in any predatory animal, was augmented by the unique advantages his technology gave him in hunting itself and in adapting to environments into which his prey took him. With weapons and cooperation he could quickly skim the big game from an area and move on, and with fire, skins, shelters and tools he could adjust readily to the new climatic and dietary conditions he encountered. Soon, however, most areas (and eventually all of them) would be skimmed and occupied by humans. The thrill and above all the advantage of moving into an empty land would be gone; instead migration would involve confrontation between newcomers and earlier inhabitants. At that point the difference in technology between one group and another would replace the difference between exploited territory and virgin territory as the stimulus to migration. Men with superior techniques could invade and use more fully an area occupied by others.

Whatever the specific factors, the worldwide dispersion of Paleolithic man had significant consequences. By enlarging the resource base it enabled the human population to expand to a size otherwise impossible. Men remained sparse, to be sure, but they roamed everywhere. Migration also stimulated sociocultural evolution both by making environmental adjustments necessary and by diffusing innovations. Finally, since migration also involved interbreeding, it caused man, in spite of his worldwide dispersion and his adaptation to diverse environments, to remain a single species.

Offhand one might think that the coming of agriculture and animal husbandry some 10,000 to 12,000 years ago would have reduced migration by making people "sedentary." The evidence is to the contrary. Not only did some Neolithic practices, such as slash-and-burn agri-

LONE DOG'S "WINTER COUNT," a pictographic historical chart painted a century ago on the inside of a buffalo robe (*opposite page*), chronicles 71 turbulent years in the migratory life of the Yankton tribe of the Dakota, or Sioux, Indians. The chart, in which each successive year (or winter, as the Plains Indians counted) is represented by a symbol recalling some memorable event of that interval, is dominated by encounters between the Dakotas, themselves comparative newcomers to the northern Great Plains, and other westward-migrating people, both Indian and white. This particular specimen, part of the Heye Foundation collection at the Museum of the American Indian in New York, is a copy made by the Indians for their own use from the original chart by Lone Dog, the Yankton whose task it was to record the years from the winter of 1800–1801 to that of 1870–1871 (or, according to the Dakota system, from the "Crow killed 30 Sioux" winter to the "Crow war-party surrounded and killed" winter). The record begins near the center of the robe and spirals outward in a counterclockwise fashion. The first symbol, for the winter of 1800–1801, consists of 30 black lines (representing the Sioux dead) arrayed in three rows of 10 lines each, the outside lines being joined. The last symbol, for the winter of 1870–1871, consists of a large circle (a fort) that encloses a number of smaller arcs (the Crow dead) and is in turn surrounded by figures representing the attacking Sioux; the short streaks radiating to and from the enclosure denote bullets and mark the first time on the Dakota charts that Indians are shown using firearms in battle. Other noteworthy events depicted include the outbreak of various diseases among the Indians (smallpox in 1801–1802, whooping cough in 1813–1814, cholera or measles in 1818–1819); the first appearance in their region of horses wearing shoes (1802–1803), of trading posts (1817–1818, 1819–1820, 1822–1823), of Spanish blankets (1853–1854) and of beef cattle from Texas (1868–1869). Celestial events recorded include a single bright meteor (1821–1822), a meteor shower (1833–1834) and an eclipse of the sun (1869–1870). The symbolism of the entire chart was interpreted by Col. Garrick Mallery in the Fourth Annual Report of the Bureau of American Ethnology (1882–1883).

culture and nomadic pastoralism, necessitate movement through a sizable territory but also the Neolithic transition as a whole created a gulf between peoples who had made the transition and those who had not. Furthermore, the Neolithic complex did not arise fully developed anywhere, nor did it ever cease developing; rather, technological improvements in production, weaponry and transport kept appearing, and that created inequality and hence migratory potential between one territory and another. Pastoralists or shifting cultivators could evict hunters and gatherers, because hunters and gatherers required more land per man and therefore could mobilize less manpower at any one spot. For the same reason permanent cultivators could evict migratory cultivators and herders, but they might be evicted in turn by pastoralists with superior weapons and greater mobility.

Stuart Piggott of the University of Edinburgh describes the process of domestication (sheep and goats) and agriculture (barley and wheat) starting in the Near East about 11,000 years ago and gradually spreading across Europe as the climate modified. "By 2500 B.C.," he writes, "stone-using peasant economies had been established over the whole of Europe, side by side with

[hunters and fishermen]." This wave of change was still in progress in Europe long after a new one had begun, starting with the smelting of copper in the Near East about 3000 B.C. The use of rare metals set afoot a perennial search for natural deposits and created routes between mines and trading centers. In Spain metalworking enclaves, apparently manned by foreigners, were established as early as 2500 B.C. The Near Eastern centers where the metals accumulated, however, became the foci of invasions by "barbarians." About 2200 B.C., according to Piggott, hundreds of sites in Palestine, Anatolia and Greece were sacked and pillaged. Among the invaders were Indo-European speakers originating somewhere northeast of the Black Sea. As Hittites they reached Anatolia by 2000 B.C., and as Aryans they reached India by 1500 B.C. They pushed into the Balkans and even into northern and central Europe.

Other migration streams moved in a west-east direction. There is the famous case of the bell-beaker potters, who, starting before 2000 B.C. from coastal settlements in Portugal, journeyed north and east, carrying not only their metallurgy in copper and gold but also their highly standardized pottery—so standardized that, as Piggott notes, "bell-

beakers made in Britain or Bohemia might almost be mistaken for those of Spanish manufacture." Bell-beaker settlements were established in many parts of Europe, as far away as the River Vistula [*see illustration on this page*]. In contrast to other Europeans at the time, the bell-beaker people were round-headed and strongly built.

Somewhat later than in Europe people of Neolithic culture (Melanesians and Polynesians) settled the tiny islands of the vast Pacific. By the fourth century even Easter Island, the world's most isolated piece of land, some 1,200 miles from the nearest inhabitable spot, was reached. The lateness of settlement in the Pacific islands suggests that great stretches of water were the main barrier to migration. Long before those islands were settled man had reached and had traveled throughout the Americas, where he evolved new Neolithic cultures.

With the rise of town-based and quasi-literate civilizations new kinds of inequality between one territory and another arose, generating migration. The civilized centers operated as magnets, drawing both peasants and artisans from the immediate hinterland and barbarians from beyond. The barbarians frequently came not as peaceful newcomers but as marauders or invaders. In eastern Europe and central Asia the vast steppes evidently allowed pastoralism and an increase in population but not much agriculture. From this region nomads (the word is Greek for pasturing) began their invasions, each tribe pushing the one before it. When the tribesmen learned to ride horses, by at least 1500 B.C., their rapid movement made possible the creation of empires stretching for thousands of miles. Each wave tended eventually to become sedentary itself, a target for a fresh wave of nomadic invaders.

The list of invaders from central Asia is bewildering. Among the best-remembered are the Hittites, who reached the Anatolian plateau by 2000 B.C., were masters of iron metallurgy by 1500 B.C. and succumbed to the Phrygians and others about 1200 B.C.; the Scythians, who drove and followed the Cimmerians into central Europe and raided Egypt in 611 B.C.; the Huns, who emerged in Mongolia and from the second century B.C. were the scourge of China and moved steadily westward, reaching the Volga around A.D. 250, Gaul and Italy the following century, and stopping in 453 with the death of Attila. The Roman Empire was finally subjugated by two sets of nomadic invaders: those from eastern Europe and central Asia (Goths,

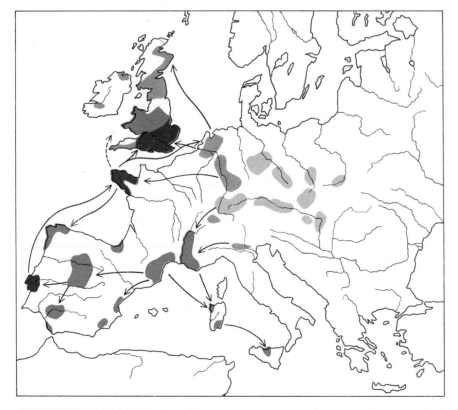

EXTENSIVE CHARACTER of prehistoric migrations is evident from this map, which shows the generalized distribution and movements of the bell-beaker potters, who, starting from coastal enclaves in Portugal, established settlements in many parts of Europe about 2000 B.C. Colored and gray areas on the map represent four different subgroups of bell-beaker culture. The map is based on the work of Stuart Piggott of the University of Edinburgh.

Vandals, Alani, Franks and Burgundi-
ans) and those from the Arabian penin-
sula. The latter expanded rapidly after
A.D. 630, until by 750 the Islamic world
extended from Spain to the Punjab.
Much of the expansion was accomplished not by Arabs, however, but by
nomads from central Asia. The Seljuk
Turks, forced out by the resurgent Chinese of the Sung dynasty, overran Persia,
Armenia, Anatolia and Syria in the 11th
century. Two centuries later Mongol
tribes under Genghis Khan conquered
northern China, eastern Turkestan, Af-
ghanistan, Persia, Russia, a large part of
eastern Europe, Asia Minor, Mesopo-
tamia, Syria and finally southern China.
As a result the Ottoman Turks were
pushed into Asia Minor in the 14th century and then to the Balkans, culminat-
ing with the conquest of Constantinople
in 1453. The Turks ruled India from the
11th to the 16th century, when the Mo-
guls (offshoots of Genghis Khan's people) took over and ruled until the British
arrived.

How much actual migration was involved in these conquests it is impossible
to say, but it was clearly from sparsely
settled territory to thickly settled and
from less advanced societies to more advanced. If it had been the only form of
movement into civilized centers, the centers could not have existed. A more normal type was the movement of peasants
and artisans into the city to sell their
wares or earn a wage. This, however, did
not suffice. The rulers and entrepreneurs
of the civilized world needed manpower
under direct control, and they took it by
force, mainly from the barbarian world.

"The old Sumerian ideograph for
slave," the historian William Linn Wes-
termann wrote, "means 'male of foreign
land,' indicating that the source of slavery was war and its prisoners." Although
slavery was not a major institution in
Egypt, it was indispensable in most of
the ancient world. At the time of Pericles,
Athens had between 75,000 and 150,000
slaves, representing between 25 and 35
percent of the population. They were the
non-Greeks who were captured wherever the Athenians were fighting. The
slaves practiced nearly all occupations; a
large contingent (approximately 20,000)
worked in the silver mines at Laureion,
and a significant number were used in
handicrafts that gave the city something
to trade for foodstuffs and materials from
distant lands.

In Athens the free immigrants called
metics, who were permanent residents
rather than passing traders, may have
outnumbered the slaves. Most of them
were Greeks, some being rural-urban mi-

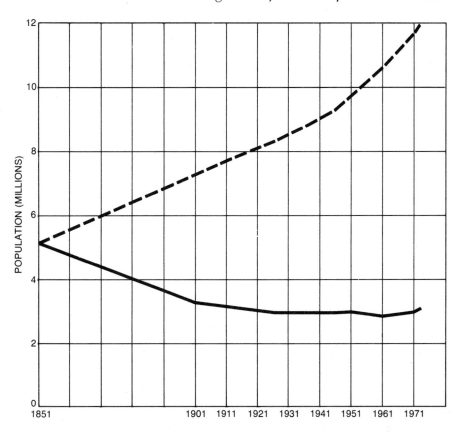

IMPACT OF EMIGRATION on the population of Ireland since 1851 is exceptional in that
Ireland was the only European country whose population declined as a result of emigration. Solid black curve shows the actual population of Ireland during this period; broken
black curve shows the projected population without emigration but with the birth and
death rates that actually prevailed. (It seems unlikely, however, that the actual rates would
have been maintained if there had been no emigration; emigration enabled the country
to keep its marital fertility higher than that of other northwestern European countries.)

grants in the sense familiar today. Count-
ing them with the slaves, at least half of
the population in the time of Pericles
consisted of migrants.

Rome was even more dependent on
slaves than Athens, but the number at
any one time hardly measures their importance, because many were freed.
Doubtless there would have been more
free migrants if there had been fewer
slaves. In Rome, where a single military
campaign might bring in 50,000 prisoners, the influx of slaves appears to have
overshadowed free migration. Tenney
Frank long ago calculated from inscriptions that at least 80 percent of the population born in Imperial Rome were of
slave extraction. Since the Romans, like
all urban populations until recently,
failed to replace themselves, the large
population of Rome (perhaps a million at
its zenith) was generated entirely by migration, much of it slave.

A milder form of migration, but still
one controlled by the civilized centers,
was colonization. Beginning before 750
B.C., the Greeks spread settlements from
Spain to the eastern shore of the Black
Sea. Whereas the Phoenicians, with the
exception of Carthage, had founded

mere trading stations, the Greeks in-
stalled full-fledged towns to serve as
trading centers and to provide opportunities for poor Greek citizens. With the
Athenian navy as the link, these towns
remained attached to Greece and were
colonies in that sense; instead of expanding territorially, however, they remained
only urban outposts. When Alexander
tried to settle Greeks in large territories,
he failed. The Romans came closer to
reaching Alexander's ideal, because they
gradually Romanized entire regions of
Europe, but they did so more by install-
ing Roman institutions than by sending
out Roman settlers. Although adminis-
trators and army veterans did go to the
provinces, the Roman population was
not large enough to supply many migrants.

Clearly, by the close of the Roman
Empire virtually all forms of migration
were known. In all of them an inequality
between areas led either to voluntary
movement or to compulsory movement
controlled by the sending or receiving
area. The modern age did not so much
invent new forms of migration as alter
drastically the means and conditions of
the old forms. The general cause was

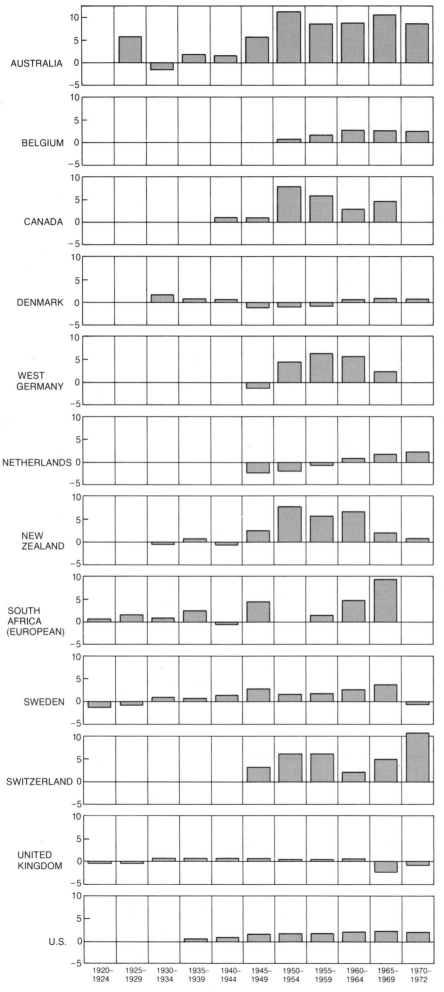

still the same: the difference between technologically advanced and less advanced. What was new was the depth of the difference, its world scope and its capacity for change.

Since Europeans initiated the technological transformation, the key to modern migration is to be found in their relation to other peoples. In the 16th and 17th centuries, for the first time, the world as a whole began to be one migratory network dominated by a single group of technologically advanced and culturally similar states. Largely as a result of the European countries' use of this network, they eventually were able to start the Industrial Revolution and thus enormously enhance their world dominance. The subsequent spread of industrialism to other parts of the world made industrialism per se, not European culture, the main basis of technological inequality.

How did the Europeans, their armies, navies and economies honed by incessant warfare among themselves, deal with the world they had discovered? Their first impulse was to skim the cream, to obtain luxuries and precious metals by confiscation, all the while preventing their European rivals from doing the same, but this could not last. Soon they followed the ancient world's example by setting up trading posts and coastal fortifications, but they needed more control over indigenous production and therefore claimed entire territories. Their handling of each territory depended on its climate, accessibility and inhabitants. In these terms four types of territory can be distinguished.

The first type, inaccessible and sparsely inhabited (such as Tibet, central Africa and the eastern Andes), was left in abeyance and need not detain us. A second type, tropical or subtropical, sparsely inhabited and accessible by sea, was immediately exploited; a third type, also accessible and lightly populated but temperate, was eventually exploited; a fourth type, accessible but thickly populated, was handled more indirectly. Let us discuss the last three types.

Warm and accessible territories were of immense potential value, because their products complemented those of Europe. When sparsely peopled by ab-

NET MIGRATION RATES per 1,000 population per year are presented in the bar charts at left for 12 developed countries in the period from 1920 to 1972. The absence of bars signifies the unavailability of data.

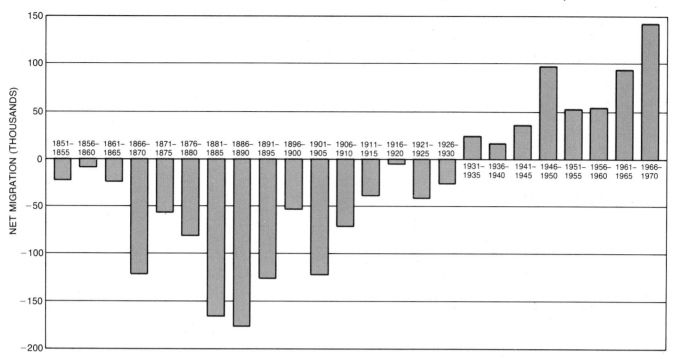

REVERSAL in the historic tide of migration in the case of a typical European industrial country is seen clearly in this bar chart, which records net migration in and out of Sweden since the middle of the 19th century. Before 1930 Sweden was a land of emigration; since then it has been a land of immigration. Other advanced European countries have exhibited a similar migratory reversal.

origines, the land required only clearing. Hence in the region closest to Europe—the Caribbean and the Gulf of Mexico and the warm coasts of North and South America—the Europeans undertook the production of indigo, rice, cotton, spices, sugar, tobacco, coffee, tea and other tropical crops. For this they needed huge inputs of cheap labor, but Europeans themselves were too expensive and too ill-adapted to such work in a hot climate, and the original inhabitants were too few and too recalcitrant. To obtain the needed labor the European managers resorted to the same device the Greeks and Romans had used: slavery. According to estimates recently evaluated and summarized by the historian Philip D. Curtin, 9.6 million slaves were imported into slave-using areas between 1451 and 1870. Since mortality during the voyages was great—normally 10 to 25 percent for slaves—the total number enslaved probably exceeded 11 million, virtually all from Africa. In distance and number this movement transcended any other slave migration in history.

When slavery was abolished in the British Empire in 1833, the British, who controlled a large share of the world's tropical lands, substituted indentured labor, and the Dutch did the same. Instead of coming from Africa, however, indentured plantation labor came overwhelmingly from densely settled areas such as southern China, Java and India, which not only were closer to new zones of

plantation agriculture in Malaya, Sumatra, Burma, Ceylon and Fiji but also were societies in which thousands of illiterate and landless workers could be induced to risk their fate in unknown places. Usually the indentured contract guaranteed the return fare after three to five years of service, but plantation managers often escaped this clause by paying a bonus for reenlistment. Migrants coming under a short-term *kangani* agreement (group recruitment under a leader, a form used for areas near the place of origin) were normally free to leave employment after a month if they paid back the cost of their journey. In some cases labor recruitment, ostensibly by contract, was achieved by force. In the latter half of the 19th century the practice of kidnapping Melanesians to work in Queensland and Fiji was notorious under the name of "blackbirding," and the impressment of Chinese coolies for naval duty gave rise to the verb "shanghai." Abusive or not, the contract system fueled plantation agriculture in tropical areas around the world. I have estimated that 16.8 million Indians left India, of whom 4.4 million stayed away permanently. It seems probable that several million Chinese left China and hundreds of thousands left Java. Although the coolie migration was historically brief, its total volume probably exceeded that of slave migration.

The third type of region, usually tropical but in any case densely settled and civilized (such as China, India, Java and

Japan), fell either under the direct control of Europeans or under their indirect influence. When the Europeans did gain control, they tended to set up estate agriculture in less populated areas, causing currents of internal migration similar to the international movement of contract labor. Europeans themselves did not migrate to these countries in any number, because they could not compete with the natives except as managers and officials, and not many of these were needed. The maximum number of Europeans ever in India was about 200,000 in 1911, representing one European for every 1,515 Indians. The centers of population in Asia were major exporters of people, not importers.

It was the fourth type of area, Temperate Zone lands with sparse and backward native populations, that attracted European migrants. These regions, comprising about a fourth of the earth's inhabitable area, were suited to European technology and temperament and offered an unparalleled opportunity for settlement. At first, however, Europeans showed amazingly little interest. Spain and Portugal, the earliest colonial powers, deliberately discouraged permanent migration. The Dutch and the French sent out few settlers. The trouble was that Europe's population was growing slowly and few people were so poor or so persecuted that they wanted to transfer to a wild area to live under subsistence conditions and battle savages. Such places were good for soldiers, criminals, adventurers and derelicts but not for ordinary citizens. For three centuries only a trickle of Europeans settled in these territories, and once there they clung to the coasts where contact with Europe could be maintained. Since the original inhabitants were decimated by even slight contact, the total population of the

Temperate Zone colonies grew slowly, more by the natural increase of the Europeans already there than by further immigration. By 1800, almost 200 years after the founding of the first permanent colony at Jamestown, the white population of the U.S. was only 4.3 million. As late as 1840, 52 years after the start of

the first penal colony in Sydney, there were only 190,000 Europeans in Australia and 2,000 in New Zealand. Similarly, Canada, Argentina, Chile and South Africa all had few white people in the early 19th century.

Only with the introduction of a new and greater technological gap produced by the Industrial Revolution did European emigration take off. Although the continent was already crowded, the death rate began to drop and the population began to expand rapidly. Simultaneously urbanization, new occupations, financial panics and unrestrained competition gave rise to status instability on a scale never known before. Many a bruised or disappointed European was ready to seek his fortune abroad, particularly since the new lands, tamed by the pioneers, no longer seemed wild and remote but rather like paradises where one could own land and start a new life. The invention of the steamship (the first one crossed the Atlantic in 1827) made the decision less irrevocable.

Little wonder that the great period of voluntary overseas European migration was from 1840 to 1930, and that the mania moved across Europe along with industrialism. At least 52 million people emigrated during that period. This equaled a fifth of the population of Europe at the start and exceeded the number of Europeans already abroad after more than three centuries of settlement.

The prime destination was the nearest Temperate Zone land, North America, but the wave spilled over to Australia, southern South America, southern Africa and central Asia. The movement fed on itself, not only because the migrants wrote back to friends and relatives but also because the new lands underwent rapid development. They turned out crops and products that competed with those of Europe, worsening the plight of many Europeans and improving the prospects for migrants. By World War I, 65 years after the big wave had started, the New World countries already rivaled northwestern Europe economically.

The new lands were so vast that not all parts could be settled simultaneously. In Russia settlement began beyond the Urals, but elsewhere it hit the seacoasts first and worked its way inland. The moving frontier became a part of life and folklore.

What were the consequences of the migrations of slaves, indentured laborers and free migrants in the four centuries preceding the Great Depression? One was a steep rise in world population

CHANGING COMPOSITION OF IMMIGRANTS to the U.S. is evident in these bars, which break down the immigration totals for each decade from the 1830's through the 1960's according to whether the area of origin was northwestern Europe (*dark color*), the rest of Europe (*gray*) or the rest of the world except Canada (*light color*). The bars reflect how eastern and southern Europe gradually replaced northwestern Europe as the main source of immigration to the U.S. and how these regions were in turn displaced by Latin America and Asia. (Immigrants from Canada are omitted from the chart because a substantial number of them were not originally Canadians but recent migrants to that country.)

growth after 1750, because in the regions of origin (except in Ireland) the migrations did little to damp population increase, whereas in the regions of destination, after initial setbacks, they greatly stimulated it. The sending areas, by the standards of the time, were densely settled. Emigration therefore enabled them to postpone an inevitable change in birth or death rates. Comparative data show that in Europe the countries with the highest rates of emigration postponed longest the reduction in their birth rate. France, with little emigration, had the lowest birth rate; Ireland and Italy, with much emigration, had high birth rates. Ireland was the only country whose population declined; if it had had no migration but had exhibited the birth and death rates that actually existed, its population today would be nearly 12 million instead of about three million [*see illustration on page 55*]. In Europe as a whole emigration did little to hold down population growth; the population rose from 194 million in 1840 to 463 million in 1930—about double the rate for the world as a whole. Emigration had even less effect in Asia and Africa.

In contrast, in the areas of destination the effect was electric. Even the primitive peoples after initial decimation generally made a strong comeback, and the descendants of African, Asian and European immigrants multiplied so fast that they were widely cited as being an illustration of the biological maximum of human increase. The reason for the growth was that entire new continents were being transformed overnight from stone-age technology to modern technology. This was a much greater transition than what was happening in Europe itself; in fact, it was the most fantastic jump in cultural evolution ever known, and it took the lid off population growth. Between 1750 and 1930 the population of the main areas of destination increased 14 times, while the rest of the world increased only 2.5 times.

Another consequence of the migrations was a geographic redistribution of the world's population. In 1750 the new regions, which accounted for half of the world's land area, held fewer than 3 percent of its people; by 1930 they held 16 percent.

At the same time the world's racial balance was altered. Certain groups became extinct, others disappeared by hybridization and still others made great gains. Caucasians increased 5.4 times between 1750 and 1930, Asians 2.3 times and blacks less than two times.

Even more dramatic was the geographic displacement of races. By 1930

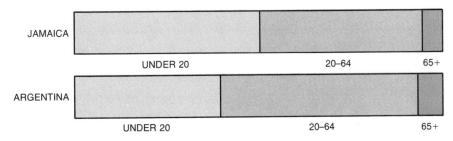

AGE STRUCTURE of a typical country of emigration (Jamaica) is contrasted with that of a typical country of immigration (Argentina). Migrants tend to be in the middle age range.

approximately a third of all Caucasians (and by 1970 more than half) did not live in Europe and more than a fifth of all blacks did not live in Africa. If all Europeans had stayed in Europe and had had the same natural increase that Europeans exhibited everywhere, there would have been 1.08 billion people in Europe in 1970 instead of 650 million. The earliest immigrants exercised a disproportionate influence on subsequent racial distribution because their natural increase lasted longer than that of later immigrants. Although the immigration of blacks into the U.S. was minuscule after 1850 compared with European immigration, they almost held their own by sheer excess of births over deaths. Blacks represented 15.7 percent of the American population in 1850 and 11.1 percent by 1970.

Although most of the migrations involved no drastic shift in climate, some of them did. In the U.S. there are now 11 million blacks outside the South and 50

million whites (mostly northwestern Europeans) in the South. In Queensland in Australia there are about 1.7 million whites and in sultry Panama about half a million.

As a result of the displacement and mixing of races there are more racial problems in the world today than at any time in the past. In nearly all immigrant countries, in the Americas, Southeast Asia and southern Africa, race is one of the most important bases of political division. In some countries particular hybrids have become separate groups, for example the "Coloureds" who comprise 9.4 percent of the population of South Africa and the "Creoles" who make up 35 percent of the population of Surinam. Among immigrant countries Australia has been most effective in excluding racial minorities. Australia's freedom from racial strife compares with that of Sweden or Denmark.

It is often thought that with two world wars, a Great Depression and restrictive

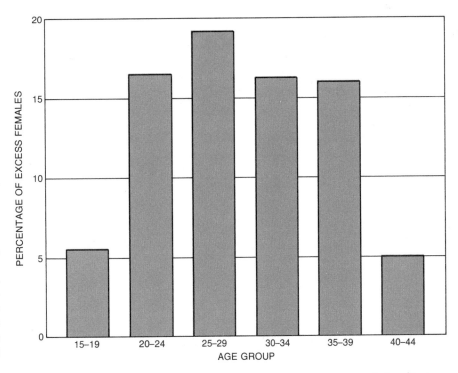

SEX RATIO in a country of emigration such as Jamaica also tends to be unbalanced, since men (particularly young men) participate in international migration more than women.

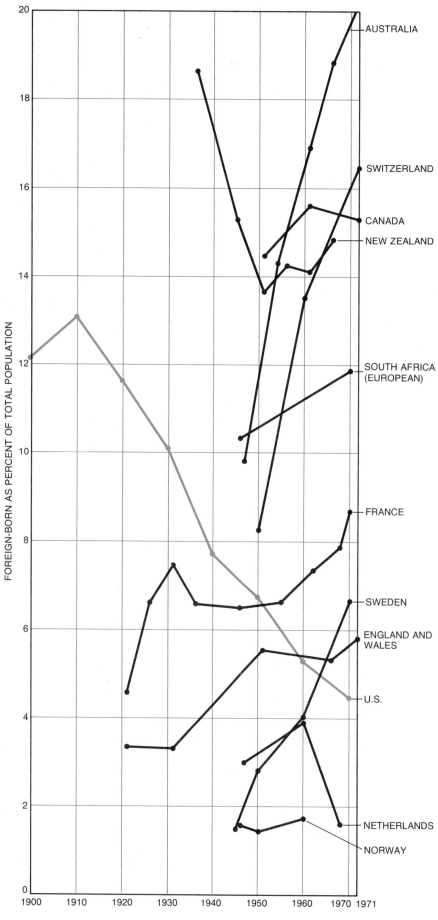

FOREIGN-BORN AS PERCENT OF TOTAL POPULATION

AUSTRALIA

SWITZERLAND

CANADA

NEW ZEALAND

SOUTH AFRICA
(EUROPEAN)

FRANCE

SWEDEN

ENGLAND AND
WALES

U.S.

NETHERLANDS

NORWAY

1900 1910 1920 1930 1940 1950 1960 1970 1971

FOREIGN-BORN POPULATIONS of a selection of countries are plotted as a percentage of each country's total population. In most developed countries proportion has been rising, and in some of older industrial countries of Europe it now exceeds proportion in U.S.

legislation the volume of international migration has declined. This illusion appears to be born of the preoccupation with free migration from Europe to the New World. In 1942 an Australian, W. D. Forsyth, pointed out in *The Myth of Open Spaces* that desirable lands sparsely occupied by primitives no longer existed, that Europe's population had virtually ceased to grow and that therefore the traditional flow of migration from the Old World to the New World was over. He was right, but he did not foresee the magnitude of two developments then already under way: the rebirth of forced migration in the world and a massive reversal of migration between the developed countries and the underdeveloped ones.

To understand these two developments one must recall the principle that migration is generated by significant differences between one area and another. In the 20th century some of these differences have been political and ethnic. Two world wars ignited by a nation obsessed with the separateness and solidarity of its own folk were ironically ended by a legitimation of that obsession for nations in general. Under the Wilsonian banner of "national self-determination" it was all peoples, not only the Germans, who could claim folk sovereignty. Carried to its extreme, this ideal, which justified the dismemberment of the defeated German, Turkish and Austro-Hungarian empires, encouraged every minority to seek a territory of its own and every colony to seek "independence." In a world where most states had minorities and many had colonies the result was to frighten them into seeking ethnic purity and to release former colonial areas. Between 1900 and 1970 independent nations multiplied 2.5 times, from 56 to 142. The combination of political independence and economic weakness made the greatly expanded phalanx of underdeveloped states receptive to systems of government that promised shortcuts to Utopia in exchange for political freedom. The wars, revolutions and ideological struggles that accompanied these changes not only uprooted people against their will but also made migration a political instrument. Unlike slavery or kidnapping, the force was usually applied by the sending region rather than the receiving one, and in the name of ethnic purity or ideological correctness rather than personal gain.

Ethnic purity was easiest to attain when two countries had minorities that "belonged" to each other and could therefore be "exchanged." Thus the

Treaty of Neuilly (1919) sanctioned an exchange of some 46,000 Greeks for about 120,000 Bulgarians; the Treaty of Lausanne (1923) provided for the transfer of 190,000 Greeks from Turkey to Greece and 388,000 Muslims from Greece to Turkey. In 1945 and 1946 population-exchange agreements were made between Czechoslovakia and the U.S.S.R. and between Hungary and Yugoslavia. Some of the exchanges were more like panics and less like trades than the treaties imply. In the Czechoslovak-Russian exchanges migration was virtually all one way—out of the U.S.S.R.

Cases of exchangeable minorities are rare, however, because many minorities have no state to which they belong, and when they do, they are seldom paired there with a reciprocal minority. Minorities were more often expelled than exchanged. After World War II some 2.7 million Sudeten Germans were transferred to Germany and 415,000 Karelian Finns were moved to Finland. Even if a group had nowhere to go, it might still be expelled or forced to flee, as were 250,000 Armenians who survived Turkish massacres, a million White Russians, 2.5 million Chinese and 200,000 Hungarians.

In the effort to provide a separate territory for each ethnic or ideological camp, nations have been carved up, as in the partition of India, Korea, Vietnam and Palestine, often creating two minority problems where one existed before, but in any case setting in motion a forced migration. Following the partition of India some 15 million people survived the flight to or from Pakistan, yet there are still Muslims in India and Hindus in Pakistan. A difficult minority problem was created in Palestine by legal and illegal immigration of Jews from other countries where, in nearly all cases, a Jewish minority remained. In 1946 there were approximately 650,000 Jews and 1,044,000 Arabs in Palestine. In the war following the proclamation of the state of Israel in 1948, more than 500,000 Arabs fled, leaving an Arab minority of almost 200,000 in the four-fifths of Palestine that became Israel. After the "six-day war" in 1967 the entire territory controlled by Israel contained about 2.4 million Jews and more than a million Arabs. The original Palestinian refugees and their descendants, now approaching a million, were scattered as minorities in several surrounding countries.

The noted authority on European migration Eugene Kulischer compiled a table of population displacements in Europe from World War II to 1948. Omit-

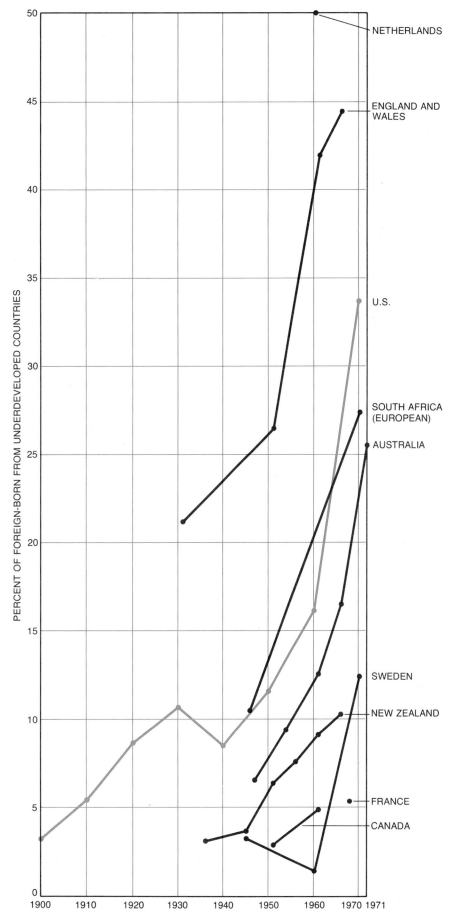

FOREIGN-BORN FROM UNDERDEVELOPED COUNTRIES make up an increasing proportion of the total foreign-born populations of most developed countries, as this graph demonstrates. The U.S. totals for 1940 and 1950 count white foreign-born population only.

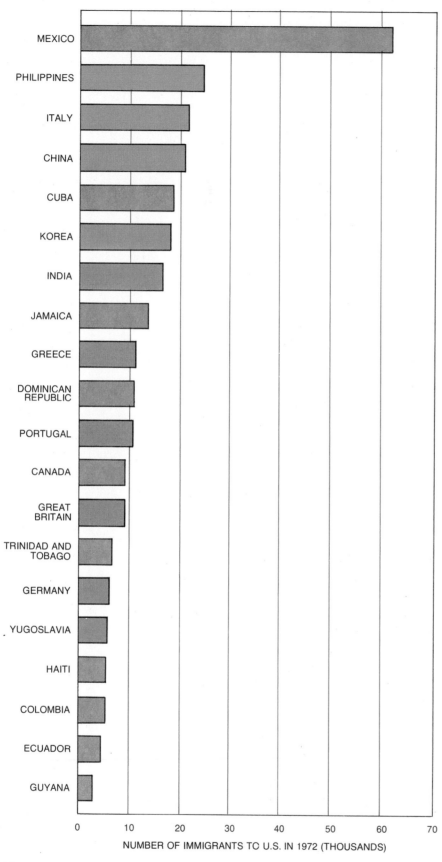

NUMBER OF IMMIGRANTS TO U.S. IN 1972 (THOUSANDS)

SOURCES OF CURRENT IMMIGRATION TO U.S. are ranked here in descending order, with the top 10 countries of origin in the Western Hemisphere in black and the top 10 in the Eastern Hemisphere in color. The figures for each country in the Western Hemisphere (except for Cuba) represent the number of visas issued in fiscal year 1972; the figure for Cuba includes 16,380 "adjustments of status" granted by the Immigration and Naturalization Service to aliens subject to numerical limitations. The figures for the Eastern Hemisphere represent the number of visas issued in fiscal year 1972 (excluding recaptured visas) together with the number of adjustments of status and conditional entries granted to aliens subject to numerical limitation. Chart is based on 1973 data from U.S. Department of State.

ting internal displacements, some of which were enormous, the total comes to 18.3 million. For the periods from 1913 to World War II and from 1948 to 1968 I have tallied exchanges and refugee movements totaling 28.7 million. If we add similar displacements in Asia, Africa and the Western Hemisphere, the grand total for the world during the period from 1913 to 1968 comes to 71.1 million. This number of migrants is considerably higher than the estimated 52 million who left Europe of their own free will in the heyday of the transatlantic movement from 1840 to 1930, in spite of the fact that the period is shorter (55 years compared with 90).

Clearly the amount of forced migration since 1913 belies predictions that world migration would diminish. But what about free migration? The answer is that it has not diminished either, but it has changed direction. Instead of flowing from the crowded industrial countries of Europe to open spaces in the New World, it has gradually shifted until it is now flowing toward developed countries everywhere. The nations of northwestern and central Europe, exporters of people for so long, are now net importers. The New World industrial countries, still relatively uncrowded, receive professional and highly qualified immigrants from industrial Europe, but increasingly their migration is from less developed countries in southern and eastern Europe, Asia, Latin America and Africa.

Evidence of the surge into developed nations is abundant. Four New World countries—Australia, Canada, New Zealand and the U.S.—received a net total of 13.9 million migrants between World War II and 1972. The U.S. alone, still admitting more foreigners than any other nation in the world, received 9.2 million during that period. More surprising is the tide of migrants into industrial Europe; for example, Sweden, for centuries a country of emigration, became a country of immigration after 1930 [*see illustration on page* 57]. Other advanced countries in Europe have shown a similar reversal, some more sharply than Sweden. Data on seven such countries, including Sweden, reveal a net migration of 6.3 million between 1950 and 1972. Adding this figure to the one for the four New World countries gives a total of 20.2 million net migrants to 11 industrial countries during the period.

What explains the reversed migration into industrial Europe and the continued migration into New World industrial nations? In my view the driving force is the widening technological and demographic gap between the developed nations and the underdeveloped three-fourths of the world. The gap differs in several important respects from the former differences between Europe and the rest of the world. First, the developed nations are now scattered over the entire world instead of being concentrated in Europe. Second, the underdeveloped countries are no longer overwhelmingly colonies but rather are independent nations. Third, the technological gap has widened in absolute terms while commercial and intellectual communication has drawn the two classes of nations closer together. Fourth, the demographic contrast between the two groups has been reversed. Formerly the technologically advanced nations had the most rapid population growth; now it is the technologically backward nations, and their rates of growth are without precedent. The population of the 176 countries I classify as underdeveloped in 1950 increased by 1.04 billion from 1950 to 1972, while the population of the 47 developed countries increased by only 200 million. Originally more sparsely populated, the underdeveloped countries as a whole were already more densely settled than the developed ones in 1950. Their comparative density was still greater by 1970: 36.3 persons per square kilometer compared with 17.2 in the developed countries.

As a consequence of the gap as it is now constituted the advanced countries have on the average more resources per person, more workers in relation to dependents, more capital generated from savings and more investment and trade. They therefore have more jobs and offer higher wages. Their native populations have become so educated, comfortable and upwardly mobile that in times of labor shortage they refuse to fill low-paying, low-status or disagreeable jobs. Millions of workers in the bulging underdeveloped countries are eager to take those jobs, and employers are anxious to hire them. Hence legally or illegally the migrants come, their transit facilitated by modern means of travel and communication and even by government and international assistance.

The dichotomy between developed and underdeveloped is, of course, arbitrary. Special geographic and political circumstances aside, the general principle is that a nation tends to gain migrants from countries less developed than itself and to send migrants to countries more developed. When an underdeveloped nation is close to a developed one (as Mexico is to the U.S. or Greece is to Germany) or has special ties with a de-

veloped one (as Britain's ex-colonies have with her), the migratory pressure is very strong. In the U.S. the 1970 census counted 4.53 million people of Mexican origin, more than the number from the rest of Latin America combined but equivalent to only two years of current population increase in Mexico. In Germany the number of foreign workers, 167,000 in 1959, rose to 2,345,000 in 1973, 82 percent of whom came from six countries (Greece, Italy, Portugal, Spain, Turkey and Yugoslavia).

That the immigrant stream is being increasingly drawn from underdeveloped countries is easy to see. In the U.S. the current shifted from northwestern and central Europe to southeastern Europe, and then to Asia and Latin America. In European countries Africa and Asia are playing an increasing role in immigration.

What are the effects of this new free migration? Let us look first at the receiving nations. A few of these are "churners," nations in which immigration and emigration are nearly balanced, leaving only a small net migration. In their case the main effect is not on the population's growth but rather on its composition. Since the immigrants increasingly come from the underdeveloped countries and the natives go to the developed ones, the churners are on the whole taking in untrained people at the bottom of the social hierarchy and sending out trained people at the top. Britain provides an example. Since 1930 she has had a small net intake but large movements in and out. The inward migration has given the country a large foreign-born population (2.5 million in England and Wales by 1966, representing 5.4 percent of the total population). The outward movement has in turn caused a comparable loss of natives: about 3.1 million people born in Britain now live elsewhere. More than a million of the foreign-born are from Africa, Asia and the Caribbean. Although some of them are well educated, the majority are not. On the other hand, 97 percent of Britain's exiles live in five advanced countries: Australia, Canada, New Zealand, South Africa and the U.S. They are mainly well qualified. Evidently Britain is importing relatively unskilled foreigners from the underdeveloped world and sending out her own professional and skilled citizens to more prosperous nations. To a lesser extent the Netherlands is doing the same.

The most prosperous countries are the ones that have the largest net immigration. The influx not only gives them a

large foreign population but also adds to their population growth. The growth comes in two ways: directly as a result of the net migration itself and indirectly as a result of the immigrants' natural increase after they arrive. The indirect effect is greater the longer the period of time under consideration is. (The entire population of the U.S. is the result of immigration at some time in the past.) For a period less than a generation the indirect effect is a function of the migrants' fertility and age-sex structure. Normally, since young adults are more numerous among immigrants than among natives, their crude birth rate is higher. On the other hand, international migration ordinarily includes more males than females, thus depressing the crude birth rate. In recent years this rule has not held for the U.S., but in the receiving countries of Europe contemporary free migration, often called "labor migration," is largely composed of young males. In West Germany in 1970–1972, for example, foreign workers were 71 percent male. Finally, the indirect effect of immigration on population growth depends on the fertility of the immigrant women. Insofar as they come from underdeveloped countries, their fertility is high compared with that of native women. In the U.S. in 1970 the number of children ever born to women aged 40 to 44 was 4.4 per woman for those of Mexican origin and 2.9 for all women. In Sweden the fertility of foreign women in 1970 was 28.3 percent higher, age for age, than that of native women. An approximate calculation indicates that about 42 percent of Sweden's increase in population (1.04 million) between 1950 and 1970 was contributed by net immigration: 33 percent by the entry of immigrants themselves and 9 percent by their natural increase during the period. Hence direct immigration accounts for a large share of the growth of the major industrial nations.

Where the economy is concerned net immigration should have a stimulating effect because it adds more workers than dependents, but this benefit is more or less canceled by several factors, including the lower average skills of immigrant workers compared with those of native workers. Since it is the sheer availability of jobs (jobs unacceptable to native workers) rather than wages or conditions that attracts workers from underdeveloped countries, the question is: What would happen if immigrants did not come? One possibility is that certain jobs would be eliminated, jobs too unproductive to justify making them attractive to native labor. More immigrant workers come to the U.S. as live-in maids than as anything else; it would be no great loss to the economy if this category of employment were reduced. Other jobs characteristic of immigrants would be improved with respect to wages and conditions to make them attractive to natives. In other words, immigration enables employers to fill unproductive jobs or to forgo capital improvements, thus slowing the rate of technological progress. These effects are minimized but not eliminated by countries that select their immigrants carefully, such as Australia. For example, a large immigration of physicians and other professionals from underdeveloped countries not only deprives natives of opportunities for upward mobility but also allows inade-

quacies in the system of professional training to persist.

The assertion that natives will not take the jobs that immigrants fill is curious in view of the considerable unemployment in the industrial countries. Comparisons are misleading because of unstandardized definitions, but unemployment appears to have been rising. It is particularly high in precisely those groups—the least skilled, youths just entering the labor market and poorly educated minorities—that most directly compete with immigrants. In addition, if the industrial countries actually have a labor shortage, there is a reserve labor force that could be tapped to a much greater extent, namely women. In view of the low birth rates prevailing since the

late 1950's, there would seem little hindrance to using this reserve and obtaining workers more competent than those from the underdeveloped countries.

Even if the labor shortage is real, immigration is a clumsy way of meeting it. Labor shortages come and go, but whether the migrant workers intend to stay or not, their move is often permanent. Moreover, immigrants do not stay in their first occupation. It is estimated that 57 percent of immigrants certified for a job on entering the U.S. change occupations within two years. Thus extremely short-run problems in labor supply are met by means that incur long-run population growth, the effect of which is to reduce the ratio of resources to people and to make the industrial level of living

EXTREME URBANIZATION of the eastern half of the U.S. is evident in this night infrared photograph made recently by an Air Force weather satellite. The patterns of heat concentration recorded by the infrared film reflect the distribution of population.

still more dependent on draining the rest of the world. There is also the difficulty of assimilation. Immigrants give rise to school problems, health risks, welfare burdens, race prejudice, religious conflicts and linguistic differences.

So dubious are the advantages of immigration that one wonders why the governments of industrial nations favor it. Why do they use such devices as advance job placement, housing aid, bilateral agreements on visas and work permits, and (in countries of origin) official propaganda, recruiting offices and preparatory training programs? Strictly speaking, except where former colonies are involved, their efforts are not directed to the most backward countries but to quasi-developed ones. Still, why invite immigrants at all?

One will find few clarifications, but official statements hint that the goals are to fill essential jobs and to stimulate population growth. One suspects that the actual causes are government inertia and pressure by employers to obtain cheap labor. Given strong employer demand and a limitless supply of job-hungry people in the underdeveloped countries, migration will occur whether it is encouraged or not. To stop it requires a great effort; to permit it requires none. Estimates of all illegal aliens in the U.S. run as high as two million. The tendency to reward illegal entry is illustrated by the announcement in San Francisco on June 4 of this year that the immigration service had resumed its "confession" program. According to the *San Francisco Chronicle*, "aliens who gained entry illegally may confess and have their status adjusted to permanent residency." "Have no fear," the immigration official reportedly said, "we are not out to deport anyone."

Special interests favoring immigration seem better able to influence the government than those opposing it. In a 1951 poll in France 93 percent of the respondents said there were enough foreigners in France. Nevertheless, the French government thereafter pursued one of the most active proimmigration policies in Europe, increasing the proportion of foreign-born from 6.5 percent to 8.7 percent by 1970. Polls in 1965 and 1971 still found the public more than 90 percent opposed to immigration, but French officials were evidently not listening. The respondents in 1971 felt that immigrants from countries closest to France adjust best to French life, yet in 1970–1971, as nearly as can be determined from French data, the government admitted at least 200,000 people

from groups considered as being the least assimilable. In Germany 51 percent of those polled in 1965 opposed bringing foreign workers into the country and only 27 percent favored it. Most of those opposed (30 percent) mentioned difficulty of employment as the reason. In Switzerland in 1965, 47 percent of native Swiss employees said they would be willing to work overtime in order to decrease the number of foreign workers in Switzerland. Shortly after some 200,000 Cuban refugees were admitted to the U.S. a poll in Minnesota found 51 percent opposed to admitting them and only 36 percent favorable. In Britain, after a Labor government earlier than the current one had come to power, a poll asked what matters the respondents would like to see the government concentrate on. The third most frequently mentioned item on a list of 13 was "Keep strict controls on immigration." Governments in Europe's industrial countries are now having second thoughts about immigration; although free movement is a basic principle of economic union, it seems likely that the recent volume will be reduced.

Contemporary migration has drawbacks for the sending countries as well as the receiving ones. They derive chiefly from the fact that migration is inevitably selective. Although the quality of migrants may be lower on the average than that of natives in the developed countries, it is higher than that of natives in the underdeveloped nations. Since the developed countries cannot admit all who wish to come, they can pick and choose as the interests of their employers dictate. This means that the underdeveloped country does not simply lose untrained manpower but often loses trained manpower that is scarce and costly to produce. In the U.S. in 1972, of the immigrants admitted who had an occupation 31.1 percent were classified as "professional, technical and kindred workers," compared with only 14 percent in this category in the U.S. labor force. In 1971 there were 8,919 medical degrees conferred in the U.S.; in the same year 5,748 immigrant physicians were admitted and in the next year 7,143 were admitted. At the same time many thousands of American youths failed to gain admission to medical school. Even when, by the standards of the receiving country, the foreign workers are relatively unskilled, they are often on the average better trained than the ones who do not move. In any case emigration removes people of productive age and leaves children and old people,

thereby raising the underdeveloped country's already high dependency ratio. The value of remittances sent back home may partly compensate for those losses, but the remittances are uncertain and subject to stoppage or control in times of crisis. Indeed, migration itself may be cut off and migrants may be returned precisely when the sending country is in its worst condition. How ominous that prospect can be is suggested by the fact that in Germany alone the number of Greek workers is equivalent to 8.4 percent of Greece's entire labor force and the number of Portuguese workers is equivalent to 4.7 percent of Portugal's labor force.

For the underdeveloped country emigration appears to be a stopgap allowing postponement of internal economic and demographic changes that would make emigration unnecessary. It is like borrowing money at high interest to pay off debts that one's income could not support in the first place. As the underdeveloped countries become still more crowded, there will be increasing pressure for greater admission to developed countries, on humanitarian grounds if for no other reason. By and large, however, the problems of underdeveloped countries are beyond solution by emigration. If developed nations tried to accept as migrants the excess population growth of the underdeveloped ones, they would currently have to receive about 53 million immigrants per year. This would give them a population growth of 5.2 percent per year, which added to their own natural increase of 1.1 percent per year would double their population every 11 years.

In the future the failure of international migration to solve problems will not necessarily prevent its happening. The present wave of voluntary movement from underdeveloped nations to developed ones may reach a maximum and be reduced, but if so, it will be replaced by other waves. Although particular migratory streams are temporary, migratory pressure is perpetual because it is inherent in technological inequality. In the past migration has helped to fill the world with people. That the world is now full is a new condition that complicates prediction. Another new condition is the degree to which nations can, if they wish, control their borders. Nations strong enough to prevent voluntary migration, however, are also strong enough to engender forced migration. Whether migration is controlled by those who send, by those who go or by those who receive, it mirrors the world as it is at the time.

6

The Populations of the Developed Countries

The Populations of the Developed Countries

CHARLES F. WESTOFF

These populations, a little more than a fourth of the human species, may be well on the way to long-term numerical stability. This state of affairs appears to have been achieved largely by personal choice

One result of man's social evolution has been the rise of a group of populations living in countries commonly described as developed. The populations of these countries enjoy better health, longer life, better education, wider occupational opportunities and a greater variety of amenities than the populations of less fortunate lands. If it is true that a third or a fourth of the human race still go to bed hungry every night, it is also true that a large fraction of a billion people now have access to a kind of life that two centuries ago was known to only a privileged few.

Understandably the inhabitants of underdeveloped lands look to the day when their own country will cross the imaginary and elusive line that separates the haves from the have-nots. In 1974, measured in terms of the steadily depreciating U.S. dollar, that line might be represented by an annual per capita income of something like $750. Comparable figures for an inhabitant of the U.S. or Sweden are between $4,000 and $5,000.

If the line separating the haves and the have-nots is elusive, it is sharply drawn in demographic terms. In developed countries the average life expectancy at birth has climbed to more than 70 years compared with about 50 years in the underdeveloped countries. Much of the difference is attributable to high infant mortality: anywhere from 50 to more-than 250 deaths per 1,000 births in underdeveloped regions as against fewer than 25 deaths per 1,000 in most developed countries.

The demographic index that probably has the greatest significance for mankind in the long run is the rate of population growth. It too shows a sharp line of demarcation between the underdeveloped and the developed regions of the world. The former have high population growth rates (averaging 2.5 percent per year) whereas the latter have rates that not only are low (less than 1 percent) but also are still falling. In fact, among 30-odd countries that can reasonably be described as developed, the fertility rate is at, near or below the replacement level in the 20 that have 80 percent of the world's total developed population. If these low fertility rates continue for two generations, population growth will cease and the developed world will reach zero population growth, the culmination of a historical process in which birth rates slowly fall to the low magnitudes of the death rates achieved some generations earlier. The balancing of these vital rates at very low levels can be viewed as the end of a major demographic transition, a process involving the entire economic development and accompanying transformation of social institutions that can be called for want of a better term modernization.

Before one predicts too confidently that the end of the demographic transition is in sight, however, one must recall that the same was predicted once before, back in the 1930's when the rates of population growth in the industrialized countries of the world had reached all-time lows. That the next generation of parents did not exactly follow the script of the demographers is now all too clear and has proved a continuing source of embarrassment to the experts.

From one point of view the fact that the demographic transition appears to be entering its terminal stages a generation later than was predicted could be regarded as no more than a slight interruption in a long historical process. On the other hand, the "baby boom" that occurred in many of the developed countries during the late 1940's and subsequent years has already added more than 10 percent to the populations of those countries: nearly 100 million more people who are now themselves reaching the age of parenthood and who constitute an enormous potential for a second baby boom. At the beginning of World War II the combined population of the then developed world—the U.S., Europe (including all the U.S.S.R.), Canada, Australia and New Zealand—stood at about 720 million. If the expectations of demographers had materialized, the population of these countries today would be around 845 million instead of the currently estimated 940 million.

One can disagree about the list of countries that can be described as developed. For the purposes of this article

I have selected 31 nations, representing most of the conventionally defined developed countries of the world, including all the nations of Eastern Europe, plus Portugal, Spain, Greece, Japan and Israel. I have omitted Venezuela and Argentina, which have per capita gross national products substantially higher than the poorest of the European countries (Portugal and Yugoslavia), because their vital statistics are incomplete. The oil-rich countries of the Middle East are also excluded because they still lack most of the characteristics of industrialized nations in spite of their high per capita gross national products. Hong Kong, which has a population of about 4.5 million, could probably also qualify today as a developed country but its records too are inadequate.

It is appropriate to concentrate on fertility and ignore mortality because death rates are uniformly low in the developed countries; thus population growth in the aggregate depends mainly on the future course of fertility. I have selected the "total fertility rate" from among various alternative measures because it summarizes several demographic dimensions simultaneously in a single number that has familiar properties: the average number of births per woman. More precisely, the total fertility rate can be regarded as the average number of births women would have as they pass through to the end of their childbearing years provided that they continue to reproduce at the observed rates for women at different ages as determined for any given year. If the total fertility rate persisted at approximately 2.1 births per woman, what demographers refer to as replacement fertility, then each generation would merely replace the next and eventually (after the effects of the disproportionately larger numbers of young people due to past growth diminished) birth rates would equal death rates and the population would stop growing (apart from immigration). The time required to reach a zero rate of natural increase varies, depending on the history of past growth. Some countries, most recently West Germany, have already dropped below zero natural increase; others, such as Australia and New Zealand, have a long way to go both because of their more youthful age structures and because their fertility rates, although declining, are still well above replacement.

As a demographic index the total fertility rate shares the inherent problem of any period rate used as an indicator of future trends. The "if" in one of the demographer's most frequent statements, "If current trends continue...," is patently treacherous, as one can readily see by glancing at the variations over a period of time in the different countries.

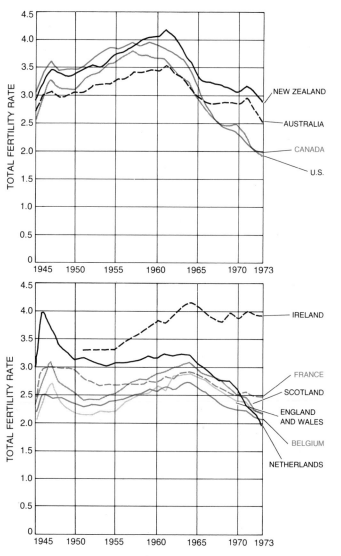

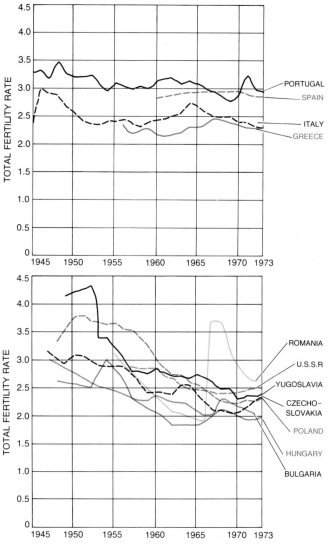

POSTWAR "BABY BOOM" was most pronounced among overseas English-speaking populations (*top*). Sharp declines began in the 1960's. The postwar surge in fertility in Western Europe (*bottom*) was brief. Fertility fell sharply, climbed again slowly and has been declining for 10 years. Fertility in Ireland is quite different.

SLOW DECLINE IN FERTILITY seems to be taking place in Portugal and Italy (*top*). There is no clear trend in Spain and Greece, but data are limited. In Communist countries of Eastern Europe (*bottom*) fertility has generally been falling, except for a brief sharp rise in Romania when abortion law was tightened in 1967.

Not only is the reproductive behavior of people difficult to predict, except very roughly, but also a measure of fertility for a given period of time can be misleading because the magnitude of fertility can be confused with the timing of births. The currently low fertility rates in some countries may imply only a postponement of childbearing that could be made up in later years, resulting in an underestimate of the completed fertility of those women. Finally, the overall rate is the simple sum of the rates for all ages within the range of reproductive years and thus can obscure countervailing trends among younger and older women.

Since World War II the trend in fertility in the developed world has followed a variety of patterns in different regions. To summarize these patterns the 31 selected countries of the developed world are divided here into eight different regional or cultural groupings [see illustrations on these two pages].

The U.S., Canada, Australia and New Zealand (current total population 250 million) experienced sustained baby booms from the end of the war, rising through the next decade and reaching highs ranging from 3.5 to 4.2 births per woman in the four countries. These baby booms added about a third more people to the 1970 population of these countries than hypothetically would have been added if the prewar fertility rates had continued. This historically unprecedented increase has been followed in the past decade or so by a dramatic and continuing decline, which has set record lows in the past two years. In the U.S. and in Canada the fertility rates declined by nearly 50 percent in 15 years, down to fewer than two births per woman by 1973. If this below-replacement level in the U.S. were to continue unchanged, the population would stop growing in less than two generations and would begin to decline, unless it was bolstered by immigration. Even if immigration were to continue at its current level (a net of some 400,000 per year), any further drop below the 1973 fertility rate would still lead ultimately to a population decline.

The pattern in Western Europe has been different. Britain, France, Belgium and the Netherlands (current total population 130 million) experienced only a temporary rise in fertility immediately after the war, followed by a resumption of the downward movement for five years or so and then a gradual increase in fertility (a fairly marked increase in England and Wales from 2.2 births per woman in 1951 to 2.9 in 1964), followed by another decline continuing to the present. Italy, grouped in the charts with Spain, Portugal and Greece (current total

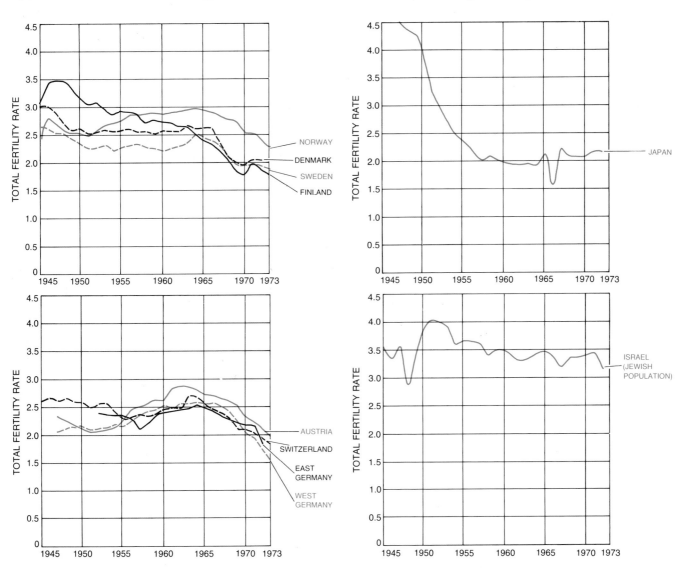

SCANDINAVIAN COUNTRIES (*top*), except for Sweden, showed a brief postwar surge in fertility. The decline since then has been sharpest in Finland. Countries of Central Europe (*bottom*) have followed a fertility pattern similar to that of Western Europe. West German fertility is now the lowest among all developed countries.

TWO NEWLY DEVELOPED COUNTRIES, Japan (*top*) and Israel (*bottom*), show markedly different fertility patterns. Drop in Japanese fertility followed the adoption of a permissive abortion law. The curve for Israel applies only to Jewish population. Fertility of the Arabs in Israel is currently more than twice as high.

population 110 million), exhibited a fertility pattern closely resembling that of its northern neighbors. In Portugal, by way of contrast, the fertility rate is unusually stable: there are only small annual fluctuations around an average of three births per woman, with some suggestion of an overall downward trend. The records for Spain and for Greece are less extensive, but the recent experience in these two countries shows a fairly stable fertility at quite different levels: Spain hovers just below three births per woman and Greece just above two births per woman.

Ireland, although grouped with its British neighbors in the charts, has a fertility pattern that is unique among the 31 nations in the postwar period. (Ireland's population is only three million.) Superficially the trend, based on incomplete data, corresponds more closely to that of the overseas English-speaking populations of European origin (the U.S., Canada, Australia and New Zealand) than it does to that of Britain, at least through 1960, except that there is no evidence of any recent sustained decline. Irish fertility has remained just under four births per woman.

The Central European countries of Austria, Switzerland and the two Germanys (total population 93 million) have followed a pattern similar to that of the countries to their west, at least since 1955. There was a gentle rise in fertility, peaking at levels between 2.5 and 2.8 births per woman and then declining rapidly. The total fertility rate of 1.5 births per woman in West Germany is unquestionably the lowest in the world. All four of these Central European countries are now significantly below population replacement.

The Scandinavian countries, except for Sweden, which escaped the war, experienced a brief postwar baby boom, followed by patterns very similar to those of Central and Western Europe. Norway was slightly anomalous in showing an increasing rate for a decade, beginning in the early 1950's. The decline in Finland has been precipitous, from 3.5 births per woman in the immediate postwar years to an estimated 1.8 in 1973. Fertility in all the Scandinavian countries (total population 22 million) is now below the replacement level except in Norway, which at the current rates of decline will join its neighbors demographically in a few years.

According to a recent analysis by Arthur A. Campbell of the National Institute of Child Health and Human Development, most of the rise in fertility in the developed countries during the postwar period was due to increases in the fertility of women in the younger age groups, resulting in a significant decline in the average age of childbearing. Involved in this change were sharp increases in proportions of women marrying at younger ages. The baby boom was therefore to a large extent a result of changes in the age distribution of childbearing rather than of changes in completed fertility; it was clearly not a return to the large families of earlier times.

The U.S.S.R. and the other countries of Eastern Europe (total population 356 million) reveal a different pattern of a fairly uniform decline in fertility, aided by the wide availability of abortion, reaching very low levels earlier than the other developed countries. In some years the number of abortions has exceeded the number of births. In Hungary the total fertility rate had dropped to 1.8 births per woman by 1962, when the U.S. rate, for example, was still at 3.5. Romania's fertility dropped precipitously from 3.1 births per woman in 1955 to 2.0 by 1962 and to a low of 1.9 in 1966. In that year the Romanian government, alarmed at the rapid decline, reversed its permissive abortion law, with the result that the fertility rate doubled to 3.7 the following year. The liberalization of abortion laws in Eastern Europe had been intended primarily to promote maternal health and to facilitate the employment of women, but the resulting low rates of population growth have caused official anxiety. Since the tightening of the abortion law in Romania fertility has once again resumed its decline as contraception and illegal abortion have taken the place of legal abortion.

The data for the U.S.S.R. are incomplete. Postwar fertility records begin only with 1957, when the rate was 2.8 births per woman. The trend during the following decade was slowly downward, but the fertility rate seems to have stabilized at around 2.5 births per woman in the past several years, which is higher than that of any of the other Eastern European countries except Romania. According to other evidence, the European regions of the U.S.S.R. have a fertility rate quite similar to that of other European countries; it is the high fertility of the Asian regions that accounts for the higher overall national rate.

The less developed eastern countries of Poland and Yugoslavia have experienced radical declines in fertility since the war. In Poland the rate dropped from 3.7 births per woman in 1954 to 2.2 in 1969; in Yugoslavia the rate dropped from a high of 4.3 births per woman in 1952 to 2.3 in recent years.

Only the Jewish population of Israel (2.8 million of a total population of 3.2 million) is included in this review because of the enormous differences, demographic and otherwise, between the Jewish and the Arab components of the country's total population. In 1972 the total fertility rates for the Jewish and the Arab populations were respectively 3.2 births per woman and 7.3. A demographic cynic has recently calculated that if current trends continue, the Jewish population will be a minority in Israel within three generations. Although Jewish fertility is changing slowly, its trend is clearly downward, and it will probably continue to decline during the remainder of this decade. It is nevertheless consid-

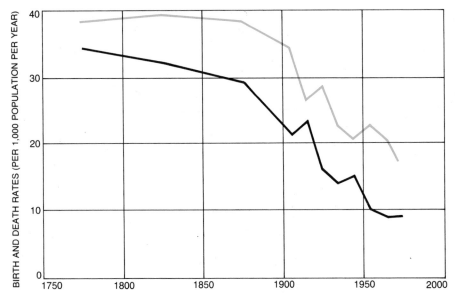

HISTORICAL DOWNTREND of birth rates (*color*) and death rates (*black*) per 1,000 population per year are compared for the currently developed regions of the world. Short-lived baby booms followed both world wars, which produced the two peaks in death rates.

erably higher than the estimated rate for the Jewish population in the U.S. For that matter, it is probably higher than that for Jewish populations in any developed nation.

The last country on the list, Japan (population 108 million), has been frequently referred to as the modern demographic miracle and an example of what the introduction of a permissive abortion law can do to the birth rate of a population that practices little contraception. Japan's total fertility rate dropped from 4.5 births per woman in 1947 to 2.0 a decade later. As the curve in the illustration at the right on page 71 shows, the rate fell to 1.6 births per woman in 1966. That was the Year of the Fiery Horse, which comes every 60 years. According to Oriental astrology, girls born that year may murder their husbands, which tends to reduce their marriageability. Japanese parents evidently decided to cut their chances of having a girl child in 1966. Japanese fertility is now still around replacement, having climbed slightly above the rates prevailing in most of the preceding decade.

The variety of patterns in these 31 countries should not obscure the central and most important fact that fertility in most of the developed world has virtually collapsed. Only New Zealand (in which fertility has been declining), Ireland, Spain, Portugal and the Jews of Israel still have relatively high rates, ranging between 2.8 births per woman and 3.9. In 20 of the 31 countries the total fertility rate is not far from, and in some cases is below, the replacement level of 2.1 births per woman; it appears to be headed in that direction or hovering around 2.3 births in most of the remaining 11 countries. The average fertility rate for all 31 countries is currently 2.3 births per woman. If the figure is weighted for population, the average drops to 2.2 for the total population of the developed world. The population growth rate in all but a few developed countries is now less than 1 percent.

What lies ahead? Will fertility stabilize at replacement levels? Or will it continue to decline, resulting in the prospect of populations of rising average age and actual declines in numbers sooner or later? Although it seems unlikely now, it is also quite possible that fertility rates could do an about-face and rise again. These are not easy questions to answer, and one should approach any portrait of the future with particular hesitancy in view of the failure of prediction in the 1930's, when fertility was at similar low levels.

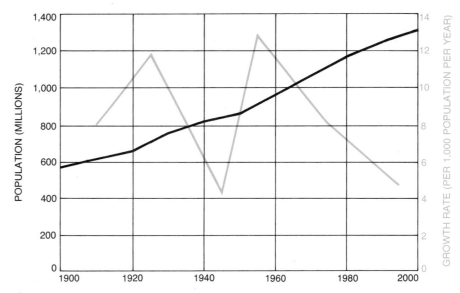

TOTAL POPULATION and growth rates per 1,000 population per year are plotted for developed regions of the world. Broken lines are unpublished United Nations projections.

We should continually remind ourselves that the evidence we have to rely on, annual total fertility rates, can be quite misleading as a guide to the long-range behavior of women passing through three decades of reproductive life. What can be postponed today can be made up tomorrow. Nevertheless, there is some independent evidence in support of the inference that the current low fertility rates indeed reflect the longer-range intentions of younger couples. Fertility surveys were conducted in 10 developed countries between 1966 and 1972; married women were asked the number of children they wanted or expected to have. When their replies are tabulated by the number of years they have been married, there is a clear decline in the anticipated number of children for women married before 1951 as opposed to those married since 1966, which is quite consistent with the picture of decline presented by the series of annual rates.

For example, the women in the Finland survey, married for 20 years or longer, expected a total of four births, whereas those married five years or less expected to bear only two children. A similar decline in the U.S. was evident by 1970, from 3.5 births for those married 20 years or more down to 2.5 among newly married women. A further decline to 2.2 was found in a 1972 survey. Comparable low values were recorded for recently married women in Belgium (2.2), Czechoslovakia (2.2), Poland (2.2), France (2.1), Yugoslavia (2.1), Hungary (1.9) and England and Wales (1.8). Even in Turkey, a country not included among the developed nations of the world, the average number of births expected had

declined from 6.6 for women married for 20 years to 3.8 for those most recently married. Of course, these expectations might well increase as the younger women grow older and experience unplanned pregnancies.

The same surveys revealed, however, that an average of more than 80 percent of the women in these countries (excluding Turkey) who were exposed to the risk of pregnancy were currently practicing birth control. Improved contraceptive methods are widely available, the practice of sterilization has become increasingly common in a few countries (in the U.S. it has become the most popular method among couples with wives aged 30 to 44) and legalized abortion has become more available for situations where contraception fails. This does not mean that unplanned and unwanted pregnancies have disappeared or even that they are about to disappear. The practice of male withdrawal was the most common method used by couples in half of the countries surveyed; the modern methods of contraception are far from universally available. It does mean, however, that the small families expected by younger couples today have a greater chance than ever before of being realized.

The pervasiveness of the decline of fertility throughout the developed world should caution us against invoking currently fashionable causal explanations such as the women's rights movement, the "pill," "zero population growth" or the recent concern for the environment, although these factors have undoubtedly played a role in some countries, such as the U.S. and Canada. One can think

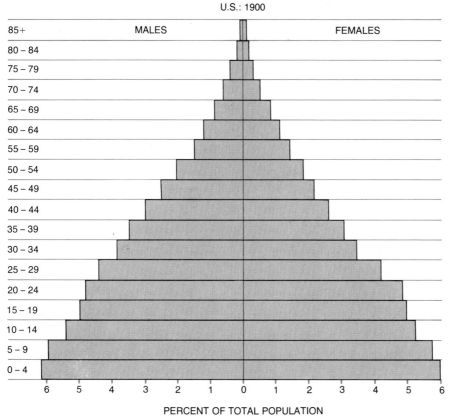

U.S.: 1900

MALES — FEMALES

PERCENT OF TOTAL POPULATION

U.S. POPULATION OF 1900 had the age composition shown in this pyramid. Its shape is characteristic of a fast-growing population with high birth and death rates where the average life expectancy is under 60. A third of Americans were under 15 years of age.

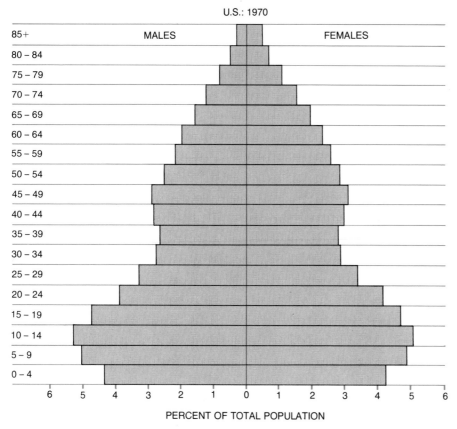

U.S.: 1970

MALES — FEMALES

PERCENT OF TOTAL POPULATION

U.S. POPULATION OF 1970 gave rise to a pyramid whose sides are pinched in because of the low birth rates that prevailed during the years of the Great Depression. The bulge centered on the 10-to-14-year-old age group is a consequence of the postwar baby boom.

of particular factors relevant to fertility that have operated in certain countries, such as abortion in Japan and a chronic housing shortage coupled with easy abortion and a demand for women in the labor force in Eastern Europe. A more persuasive case can be made, however, by taking the long-term historical view that links the demographic transition with the development of an industrial society, with secularization, with education and with the emergence of the demands of the individual over and above those of the family and the community. This transition has been proceeding in the U.S. and France since about 1800 and in the rest of Europe for about a century.

Although the pill, intrauterine devices and legalized abortion are appealing as ready explanations of the low fertility rates of recent years, one should remember that the rates were even lower in the 1930's. With only a few exceptions every Western European nation recorded total fertility rates at or considerably below the replacement level (as low as 1.5 births per woman in Czechoslovakia and Austria), and this was before abortion was readily available and before the modern methods of contraception appeared. Fertility was also at the replacement level in the U.S., Australia and New Zealand. Evidently the motivation to control reproduction was so intense in those years that delays in marriage, illegal abortion, abstinence (probably) and the more effective use of conventional contraceptive methods combined to produce the lowest fertility in history. Granting that the Great Depression may have contributed to the rapidity and depth of the decline, the fact remains that if one projected the fertility rates of the 1930's from previous trends, the curve would look much like what actually happened. From this perspective the phenomenon that still remains to be satisfactorily explained is not the decline in fertility of the past 15 years, which is part of a longer historical process, but rather the baby boom, which was particularly sustained in the English-speaking populations of European origin.

One certainty about future population trends in the developed world is that the rate of natural increase will not be exactly zero. As fertility becomes increasingly subject to voluntary control—the closer we approach the situation in which every child born is planned—the more vulnerable annual fertility rates will be to short-term variation. My guess is that we can expect swings in fertility rates of five to 10 years' duration, ranging perhaps from as low as 1.5 births per woman to as high as 2.5 as fertility responds to short-term economic changes and to various other changes in ideology and fashion. There is no reason in principle that fertility could not rise above or fall below this range in some countries, but it seems unlikely that the developed world as a whole will experience such wide swings. It is also unlikely that the swings will be anywhere near as violent as the Romanian experience, where the number of births in 1967 was double the number in 1966. This bumper crop of babies is now creating overcrowding in the Romanian school system, and beginning in 1984 there will probably be severe unemployment or an out-migration of surplus labor as the 1967 cohort begins to enter the labor force at age 18. If one wanted to draw a demographic blueprint for a meritocracy, it would feature a uniform stream of births from year to year in order to equalize opportunity. The avoidance of large swings would eliminate both the competitive advantages enjoyed by small numbers in great demand and the disadvantages experienced by those born in years when birth rates were high, who are forced to compete for limited opportunities and rewards.

Even if replacement fertility for the developed world as a whole were maintained for the foreseeable future beginning in the 1980's, the population, because of the age composition resulting from its past history of growth, would increase by more than a fourth, adding some 300 million more people. Of that total about two-thirds would have been added by the year 2000. Of course, if fertility remained below the replacement level, the end of population growth would come sooner and would result in a smaller increment. Although it is possible that this may happen, it does not appear too likely at this juncture. The demographic situation seems to be changing so rapidly, however, that what appeared likely a scant five years ago no longer appears so, and by the same logic today's picture may appear badly out of focus from the perspective of 1980.

What does seem plausible today is that the population of the developed world will average replacement fertility by the early 1980's. If that level is continued in the future, the developed population will continue to increase for a good part of the next century, stabilizing just below 1.5 billion. Apart from the effects of the sheer increase in numbers (half a billion more than today), the age structure of the population will change in several significant respects. The proportion of youths—those under 20 years

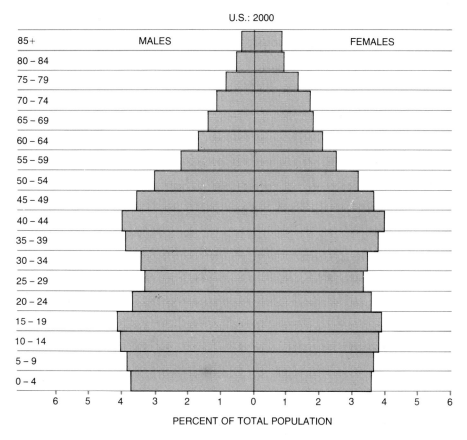

U.S.: 2000

PERCENT OF TOTAL POPULATION

U.S. POPULATION OF YEAR 2000 will form this age pyramid if fertility stabilizes at replacement levels from now until the end of the century. Five-to-19-year-olds of 1970, who will then be 30 years older, will have produced a second bulge of five-to-19-year-olds.

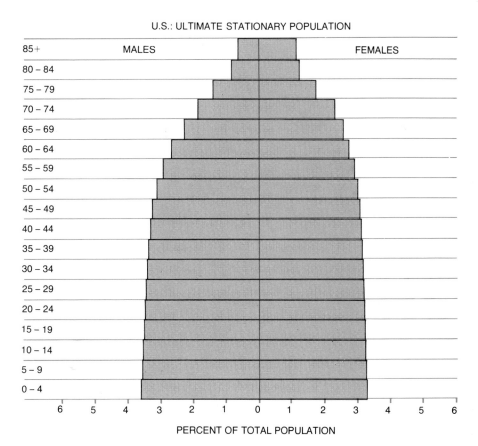

U.S.: ULTIMATE STATIONARY POPULATION

PERCENT OF TOTAL POPULATION

ULTIMATE STATIONARY POPULATION, if it is achieved in the U.S. during the next century, will have the age composition shown here. A third of the population will be under 25 years of age, a third will be between 25 and 50 and another third will be over 50.

of age—will decline from roughly a third to a fourth of the total by the time the population stops growing, but because of the increasing population base the number of young people will remain about the same as it is today. The number of aged people—those 65 and over—will increase dramatically from about 120 million to 175 million by the year 2000 and to 275 million in the stationary population; now 11 percent of the total population, this age group will ultimately constitute 19 percent. The increase of 55 million aged people that will take place by the end of the century is not a matter of conjecture; they will be the survivors of people 40 and over who are alive today. For societies that do not seem to have been doing an outstanding job in the integration of the aged, the prospect of such growth is sobering.

The age structure of the population that is in prospect for most developed countries is foreshadowed in Sweden and a few other countries that have experienced very low rates of growth for a long period of time. Some observers have maintained that older populations will discourage innovation and will be more conservative, less exciting societies in which to live. Others who have lived through recent excesses of youth feel less apprehensive about the prospect. Little is actually known about the effects of age composition per se because its change is relatively slow and is intertwined with numerous social and economic factors that become part of the total process. The components of broad social change cannot be so neatly disentangled that the social scientist can isolate age composition as a determinant of other changes. One advantage is that the prospect of an increasing number of older people is completely predictable; the governments of the developed countries therefore have time to plan their accommodation. Regrettably, governments in general are not noted for their capacity for long-range planning.

After another generation or so of continued low fertility many developed countries will have reached the point where below-replacement fertility will mean an absolute decline in numbers, such as both West Germany and East Germany are now experiencing. When that happens, and probably long before, the occasional cries of alarm we now hear about labor-force needs or national security or national virility will increase in both number and volume.

How do governments react to population change? Most of the talk about population has understandably focused on the problems of growth in the developing countries. Back in the late 1930's population was on the mind of a country such as Sweden that was facing an impending decline in numbers, resulting in one of the first modern population policies. Population was also a matter of great interest to the German and Italian governments for different reasons. France, which had long been sensitive to problems of national security, had earlier enacted pronatalist legislation designed to strengthen the family. Apart from these sporadic displays of interest, however, the subject of population has never been high on the agenda of national priorities.

A similar, although perhaps changing, situation obtains today. In general the subject of population is not a pressing one in the government offices of the developed countries. The topic seems to emerge only when the aggregate consequences of individual behavior are perceived to threaten the national welfare. Thus the U.S. and Australia formed national panels to inquire into population as environmental problems became linked with population. Britain recently established an "inquiry" and the Netherlands a royal commission to evaluate the consequences of expanding populations. Ironically a royal commission in Britain and an official committee in the U.S. had been appointed only a generation earlier because of concern about the threat of a declining population. Japan has had a population advisory panel for several years; Israel, with its political concerns both about its numbers in relation to its hostile neighbors and about the different growth rates of ethnic segments of its own population, has had a Committee for Natality Problems for more than a decade. Virtually all developed countries have or have had some official group concerned with population (frequently in connection with labor migration), but few can be said to have articulated what might be termed explicit population-growth policies and programs. The World Population Conference, held this summer in Bucharest, has stimulated the development of population policy if for no other reason than that the official delegations were expected to take positions on a draft "World Population Plan of Action."

On balance, the direction of official thinking on the subject in the developed countries is pronatalist. For the most part the official attitude is to promote family welfare for various reasons largely unrelated to fertility but with the expectation, or hope (the little evidence that exists is not reassuring), that by reducing the costs of parenthood through family and child allowances, maternity benefits and sundry other benefits couples may be less reluctant to have another child.

Fertility and population growth are not the sole reasons for official concern. The increasing concentration of population in metropolitan areas presents special problems; also in some countries the depopulation of rural areas is worrisome. From time to time the desirability of immigration has loomed large in the thinking of Australia, Britain, Canada, Israel, New Zealand and the U.S. Other countries, such as Finland, Greece, Ireland and Sweden, have long been concerned about the loss of population through emigration. Some countries, such as the Netherlands, Switzerland and West Germany, are concerned about the problem of accommodating foreign workers.

By and large, however, the pronatalist sentiments of most of the developed countries are motivated by the impending threat of a declining population. Some countries, such as Japan, are concerned about the economic implications of declining numbers of young workers. The countries of Eastern Europe are similarly worried about the economic consequences of periods of low fertility. Other countries have nationalistic anxieties—an attitude that never lies much below the surface. For example, shortly before his death President Perón of Argentina announced a pronatalist population policy because of the rapid population growth of some of Argentina's neighbors. He made oral contraceptives illegal and reminded Argentine women of their maternal responsibilities.

That harsh response, however, is exceptional. Most pronatalist "policies" do not preclude the availability of contraceptive supplies or, in some instances, abortion services. A survey of 24 developed countries made by Bernard Berelson of the Population Council shows that before Perón's action only Ireland interposed legal obstacles to distribution of contraceptives, and this now appears to be changing. About half of the countries in Berelson's review had provisions for legal induced abortion, although they varied in the degree of permissiveness. Therefore, in spite of the pronatalist orientation of most of the developed countries, the majority of governments provide fertility-control services in public health programs.

What will happen if fertility continues to decline, or if population actually begins to drop, is another matter. It seems unlikely, however, that there will be any wholesale removal of family-limitation supplies or services. These apparent conflicts in policy underscore the fact that fertility-control policies were prompted in earlier days primarily not by demographic considerations but rather by concern over women's health and, in some instances, women's freedom of choice, and by the desire to achieve economic objectives by enabling women to work. There has been talk in some governments (for example Japan's) about tightening permissive abortion laws, and in recent months Czechoslovakia and Hungary have narrowed the conditions under which abortions can be obtained. The motivation is a concern both about very low fertility and about rising rates of premature births resulting from earlier abortions. Both countries are nonetheless promoting alternative forms of birth control.

The reports of the most recent American and British population panels were released respectively in 1972 and 1973, and they were quite similar. They regarded population growth as aggravating environmental and social problems, but the tone of the reports was far from alarmist. They both subscribed fully to maximizing freedom of choice in connection with reproduction. During the preparation of the U.S. report and since its release fertility in the U.S. has declined sharply, removing much of the immediate concern about population growth. Moreover, the unenthusiastic response of the White House to the report, which was issued at the beginning of the 1972 Presidential campaign, was hardly conducive to development of an official population policy. Probably the only developed country that is still concerned about too much population growth is the Netherlands, with its past history of high fertility, its high density and its dependence on external resources.

Governments in general are not particularly enthusiastic about adopting population policies because of the moral, ethnic or political sensitivities involved. Therefore, unless rates of growth decline further, which of course they may do, there does not seem to be much prospect of further developments in policies concerning population growth in the advanced countries of the world. If any population goal at all is emerging in the developed world, with some exceptions it seems to be in the direction of population stabilization. All the talk about what governments do or do not do about population should not, of course, obscure the fact that the trend of the birth rate has been much more a response of couples to their perception of their own welfare than a result of deliberate government policy.

7

The Family in Developed Countries

The Family in Developed Countries

NORMAN B. RYDER

Such countries have the same level of fertility and the same kind of family. Although that family is more specialized than it was in the past, it remains essential to both the individual and society

The type of family that is idealized in a society is congruent with the level of economic development. Throughout the currently developed societies the conjugal family prevails as an ideal; in underdeveloped societies the norm is typically one or another variant of the consanguineal form. The essential distinction between the two types is the extent to which the individual's family of procreation (in which he or she is a parent) is independent of the individual's family of orientation (in which he or she was a child).

The characteristic features of industrialism that have special relevance for family form are specialization, education, mobility and particularly individualism. Industrialism is essentially a system for increasing productivity by the division of labor in all societal spheres. Units with specific tasks are highly differentiated and human resources are exploited on a rational basis in terms of individual merit, regardless of other considerations. A specialized and efficient labor market requires technical education and individual mobility; job decisions are made by and about individuals rather than families.

The specialization of production units by task implies the withdrawal of the family from many activities it had performed in a less differentiated context. The society largely supplants the family as the instrument of technical education, the avenue of employment, the channel of credit and social security and the source of protection and defense. Rather than emphasize the way in which a family is stripped of its functions in a developed society, however, it is more useful to consider that the family becomes a much more specialized institution.

In every society, regardless of the socioeconomic setting, the family has the primary responsibility for population replacement. The question that will be addressed in the first part of this article is the extent to which that responsibility is met by the conjugal family in an industrial society. In every society the family also has the principal responsibility for the development and maintenance of the individual self; the case is made in the second part of this article that the individual in a developed society has a greater need for emotional support and that the conjugal family is more exclusively the source of that support.

The first evidence to be presented concerning the performance of the conjugal family in a developed society is the pattern of nuptiality in the U.S. (largely because that is the population with which I am most familiar). The term nuptiality is used to signify the incidence of marriage by age and sex. From census data for the U.S. I have reconstructed the two most useful indexes of nuptiality for the years 1923 through 1960. These indexes are the proportion married (at least once) and the mean age at first marriage up to age 45 (selected to represent the upper limit of the childbearing ages). The measures are calculated from the histories of cohorts of women (those born in successive years) and dated at the time corresponding to each cohort's mean age at first marriage. From an already high level at the beginning of the period the proportion married rose to a plateau close to 97 percent, where it remained for several decades without showing any response to either war or the business cycle. Movements of the mean age at marriage are more volatile; it appears that changes in the economic and political climate cause women to marry sooner or later than they otherwise would but do not modify their likelihood of marrying eventually. We know from other sources that the age at marriage had been declining before 1923. There was a small reversal of this trend for those marrying in the late 1920's and early 1930's. Then a long and strong decline

"THE MARRIAGE OF GIOVANNI ARNOLFINI AND GIOVANNA CENAMI," painted by Jan van Eyck in 1434, is in effect a pictorial marriage certificate. (Although the woman appears to be pregnant, she is not; the effect is due to the way she is holding her dress.) The Flemish bridal chamber is filled with symbols that reflect the social and economic role of marriage in that society. The rich furnishings and cloth are symbolic of the husband's obligation to provide material goods and protection for his wife. The man and woman have removed their shoes in recognition that they are standing on "holy ground" while they exchange their marriage vows. They seem to be alone, but when the images in the small mirror behind them are examined, the reflections of two other people, witnesses to the marriage, can be seen. Above the mirror is written *Johannes de eyck fuit hic* (Jan van Eyck was here) and the date 1434. To the right of the mirror is a high-backed armchair with a carving of St. Margaret, patroness of childbirth. It is suggestive of the role of the wife in marriage. Behind the wife is the bridal bed on which the marriage is to be consummated in order to make it legally binding. With her left hand the woman is lifting up her dress to expose her blue underdress, a sign of acquiescence. The terrierlike dog in front of the couple is a symbol of fidelity. The candle in the chandelier, burning in daylight, stands for the all-seeing wisdom of God. Apples by the window are a reminder of the original sin, and the 10 passion scenes around the mirror symbolize the forgiveness of the original sin by the crucifixion of Christ. The painting is in the National Gallery in London.

began, from an age a little under 23 to one slightly over 21. This movement apparently stopped during the 1950's.

For the years since 1960 we must rely on somewhat less satisfactory information. The Current Population Survey of the Bureau of the Census provides a series of median ages at first marriage for the years 1947 through 1973 [see illustration below]. For the years 1949 through 1962 that average was approximately 20.3 years, but since then it has climbed by almost a year. The crude marriage rate (the number of marriages per 1,000 population per year) has recently increased somewhat (from 10.4 in 1968 to 10.9 in 1973). One cannot, however, infer that nuptiality is once again embarked on an upward course, because the crude marriage rate is an unsatisfactory measure. I have eliminated from the numerator remarriages (they have recently been increasing as a proportion of all marriages) and from the denominator all but the single women aged 18 through 24 (those most relevant to the process); with these refinements it appears that the probability of first marriage for a young woman has declined by more than 10 percent in the past five years. The inference is that the age at first marriage is still rising (provided that there has not been an unprecedented decline in the proportion of women eventually marrying).

The high proportion married and the early age at marriage manifest the prevailing social norms. Almost from the beginning of life one learns that marriage is a virtually obligatory state for an adult. The atmosphere in which a teenager lives is charged with encouragement for marriage, from parents, peer groups and the mediums of mass communication; society as a whole registers its tangible approval through various forms of subsidy. Yet it remains a remarkable fact that the age at marriage would continue to decline in spite of a substantial rise in the school-leaving age. According to the census, those who complete their education with high school graduation tend to marry about two years later than those who have dropped out and about two years earlier than those who go on to college. Since the average number of years of schooling has increased for women (by about two years in the past generation), one would expect a rise rather than a fall in the marriage age. On the contrary, the effect of additional schooling has been more than counterbalanced by the concurrent decline in marriage age for every level of educational attainment. Within a generation the time lag between leaving school and getting married has narrowed from about six years to about two.

A substantial contribution to the lower marriage age has been made by an improvement in the efficiency of the American marriage market. For example, it was not so long ago that each of the diverse subcultures in American society maintained a more or less closed marriage system. The gradual evolution of a homogeneous culture, the increase in social and spatial mobility and the declining relevance of parental characteristics in the choice of a partner have effectively enlarged the size of the market and thereby have improved the probability of marriage for each individual. Furthermore, increasing education has probably helped to reduce the marriage age. As long as the school-leaving age was lower than the age of sexual awareness school enrollment was essentially irrelevant to nuptiality. Now, however, a considerable majority of boys and girls

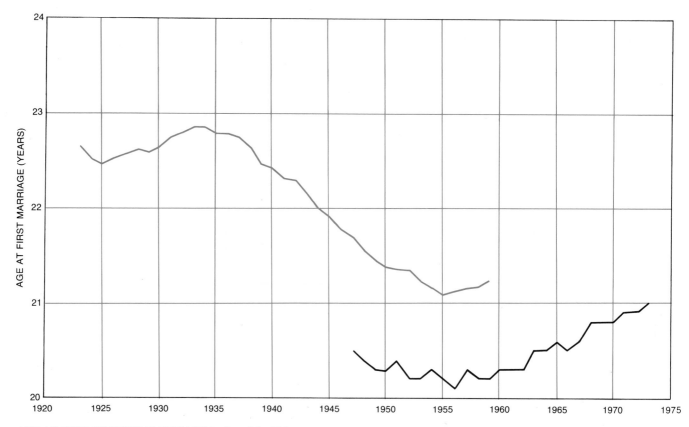

AGE AT TIME OF FIRST MARRIAGE is plotted for U.S. women. For the years 1923–1960 (colored curve) the age plotted is the arithmetic mean for birth cohorts, dated at the time corresponding to that mean. For the years 1947–1973 (black curve) the age plotted is the period median, the age that divides the married population of the U.S. under age 45 into two equal groups; the people in one group are younger than the median and the people in the other group are older. Before 1923 the mean age at marriage had been declining. The direction of change was reversed around 1930, but the decline resumed in the mid-1930's and continued until the mid-1950's. More recent data shown in black curve indicate that median age at first marriage has risen from 20.1 in 1956 to 21.0 in 1973.

remain in school until 18. The American high school has all the requisites of an institution designed to promote mating: single males and females are assembled in substantial and equal numbers, are residentially selected for social homogeneity, are organized on an age-graded basis and are exposed to one another in a variety of social contexts over extended periods. In addition, the more education one has, other things being equal, the more desirable one is in the marriage market; census data show that the time lag between leaving school and entering marriage varies inversely with the level of education.

Particular characteristics of the American economy since the end of World War II have probably played an important role in the decline of the marriage age and in its subsequent rise. Because of the marginal status of young adults in the labor force, they are peculiarly sensitive to labor-market conditions. In the immediate postwar period employment opportunities were generous for young adults because a high rate of economic growth produced a strong demand for their services at a time when the supply of those services (the number of young adults) was small. Furthermore, the Government provided not only veterans' benefits, housing loans and educational subsidies but also tax advantages for married couples. And there was less competition among siblings for parental assistance because the number of siblings with whom the young adult had to share the assistance was smaller on the average than it had been at any time in history.

Recently, however, the rate of economic growth has been lower, and the supply of young adults has been increased greatly by the "baby boom." There has probably also been an increase in the competence with which unmarried people can prevent pregnancy from propelling them into an early marriage. Finally, the school-leaving age has risen substantially, to the point where it may now be having a net effect on age at marriage. The probability of graduating from high school increased from 50 percent in 1950 to 75 percent in 1970. In the decade from 1960 to 1970 female college enrollment swelled from 1.25 million to more than three million. Under the circumstances a rise in the marriage age is not surprising.

The dominant feature of recent American fertility has been the baby boom. Even though it has long since subsided, an appreciation of current developments requires an understanding of exactly what caused it. The baby boom can be specified as a rise in the annual number of births from 2.46 million in 1936–1940 to 4.28 million in 1956–1960, that is, a 74 percent increase in births over a period during which the population as a whole increased by only 33 percent. The measure customarily used by demographers to chart movements of fertility from both the size and the age-sex distribution of the population is the period total fertility rate: the sum over all ages of the birth rates calculated for women of each individual age in the period concerned. This measure has a useful descriptive dimension: it represents the mean number of births a woman would have in her lifetime if she experienced the specified birth rate at each age. From 1936–1940 to 1956–1960 the period total fertility rate rose by 69 percent, from 2.17 to 3.67 [*see illustration on next page*].

This measure cannot, however, be accepted as a valid indication of the underlying change in fertility, because it is a cross-sectional index that may not reflect the actual lifetime experience of any of the cohorts of women who have contributed fertility to the period in question. I have made the same kind of calculation for each birth cohort, and in order to allow comparison of the two series I have dated the result as of the time when the cohort reached its mean age of fertility. The cohort fertility measure rose only 42 percent (from 2.28 to 3.24). Although this is a substantial increase, it is much less than that for the cross-sectional index. The source of the discrepancy is that whenever successive cohorts are having their children at progressively older ages, the period total fertility rate is depressed below its cohort counterpart, because the earlier (older) cohorts are having lower proportions of their fertility in the same period that the later (younger) cohorts are having lower proportions of their fertility. Over the years 1936–1940 the mean age of cohort fertility was rising (by about .1 year per year); the period total fertility rate was accordingly lower than the same measure for cohorts. The opposite phenomenon occurs when the age distribution of cohort childbearing is shifting downward. Over the years 1956–1960 the mean age of cohort fertility was falling (by about .2 year per year); the period total fertility rate was accordingly much higher than the same measure for cohorts. The approximate algebraic relation is as follows: The ratio of the period total fertility rate to the cohort total fertility rate is equal to the complement of the annual change in the cohort mean age of fertility. This relation implies that large movements upward or downward in births from period to period are not necessarily inconsistent with a constant level of cohort fertility; they may be generated by changes in the age distribution of cohort childbearing.

That circumstance is essential to an accurate interpretation of the current level of American fertility. It is not possible to calculate directly the cohort total fertility rate corresponding to any recent year because the cohorts now at their mean age of fertility have many years of childbearing still ahead of them, but one can make an inference about the cohort total fertility rate if one has evidence about both period fertility (which can be calculated) and the direction of change in the age distribution of cohort childbearing. As one could infer from a rising age at marriage, women are at present having their first and second children at higher ages than in the recent past, but this trend is being counterbalanced by a decline in the relative frequency of births of higher order (which tend to occur at later ages). In my judgment it is unlikely that there is currently much change in the mean age of cohort fertility. Accordingly the level of period fertility (which was 2.08 for the years 1971–1973) gives a fair indication of the level of cohort fertility. I conclude that the cohort total fertility rate is now lower than it has been at any time in American history.

One further statistical step is useful in characterizing the increase in cohort fertility from 1936–1940 to 1956–1960. The cohort total fertility rate is algebraically identical with the sum of (the product of the proportion of women having at least two children, and their mean number of children) and (the proportion of women having only one child). The numbers in this equation for the cohorts representing the two periods in question are as follows: $2.28 = (.573) \times (3.61) + .21$ and $3.24 = (.838) \times (3.76) + .09$. Clearly the dominant source of increase in the total has been the 46 percent rise in the proportion having at least two children.

There has always been strong social pressure for married couples to have at least two children, but not if they are unable to afford them. Between the 1930's and the 1950's there was not only a substantial rise in real per capita income but also an increase in pronatalist intervention by the Government, particularly through the tax structure and the

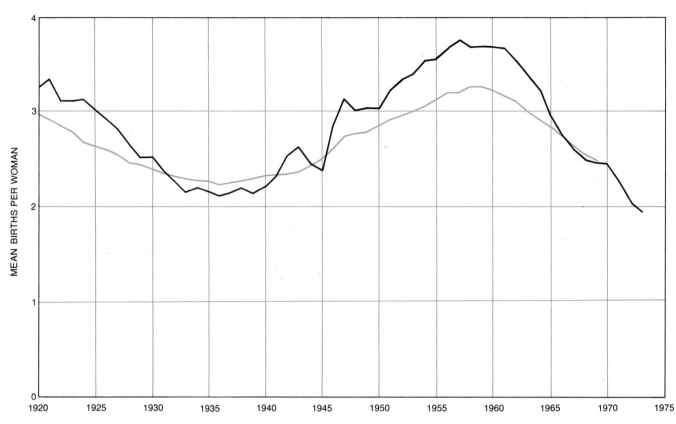

TWO FERTILITY-RATE SERIES for U.S. women are plotted for the years since 1920. The cohort rate (*colored curve*) indicates the average number of births per woman, dated at the time corresponding to the mean age of that cohort's fertility. The cohort total fertility rate fell from 2.97 in 1920 to 2.23 in 1936, rose to a peak of 3.28 in 1958–1959 and by 1969 had subsided again to 2.50. The period rate (*black curve*) gives the same kind of information, but it is based on the cross section of age-specific birth rates for each successive year. Amplitude of fluctuations in period-rate curve is substantially larger than that of fluctuations in preferred cohort curve.

subsidization of education. Demographers have been reluctant to acquiesce in the idea that fertility varies directly with income, mainly because the time series for individual countries, the comparisons between countries and the differentials within countries all tend to show the contrary. Furthermore, the major decline in American fertility preceded the Great Depression, and the decline actually came to a halt during the 1930's; moreover, the subsequent rise in fertility was much more impressive for those of higher income than for those of lower income. In my opinion these pieces of evidence against an income theory of fertility are less than compelling because the fertility differentials observed are mainly reflections of differences in the ability to regulate fertility, and that ability is positively related to income. In addition, it would seem less relevant to consider the absolute level of income than to consider the level with respect to what is considered to be a suitable standard for one's station in life.

Although there was only a minuscule upward movement in the mean number of children born to those women with at least two children, it does deserve attention because that particular measure had been declining for at least a century, and it was the prime source historically for the lowering of American fertility. Some demographers maintain that couples after the war inexplicably increased their demand for children in relation to goods. The principal support for this is Gallup poll information on the number of children desired or considered ideal, which did indeed increase as the level of fertility rose. Yet the wording of those questions contains no stipulation of the conditions under which the expressed number of children desired or considered ideal would indeed be the reproductive target; there is at least room for suspicion that such reports are a compound of the rationalization of past experience on the part of those whose childbearing is complete and fantasy on the part of those who have not yet faced the reality test of bearing and rearing children.

I think that a more important starting point for an explanation is the fact that between the prewar and postwar eras the mean age at which women had their second child declined from 27 to 24. This hastening of the process of family formation forecloses a woman's opportunity for nondomestic experience and increases the length of her exposure to the risk of an unwanted child.

The incidence of unwanted fertility was appreciable in the postwar period. The modal group of married women interviewed in the 1965 National Fertility Study was the group responsible for the baby boom. Of those who intended not to have any more children, a third admitted to having had at least one unwanted child; because of rationalization, concealment and further failures subsequent to the interview, this admission is probably an understatement of the eventual frequency of unintended births. It is my view that these unwanted babies came about from a combination of increased exposure to risk and a relaxation of the contraceptive vigilance required to prevent their occurrence. Contraceptive success, at least prior to the epoch of "the pill," depended much less on the intrinsic properties of the procedure employed than on the motivation of the user. In a time when the resources available to the average family seemed ample, at least by prewar standards, there may have been only a modicum of concern that an unwanted birth, if it occurred, would reduce the family fortunes below an acceptable scale of living.

Although it is too early to speak with confidence about the composition of the recent dramatic decline in fertility, there is an important clue from a question now included annually in the Current Population Survey conducted by the Bureau of the Census. Married women are asked the total number of children they expect to have. Among the younger cohorts in June, 1973, the proportion of women expecting to have at least two children is 81 percent (little changed from the 1956–1960 value) but the mean number of children for women with at least two children is only 2.8 (compared with 3.8 for the earlier period). In short, the composition of the recent decline (to the extent that these personal predictions come true in the aggregate) is precisely the opposite of the previous rise: we are witnessing a resumption of the long-standing decline in the births of an order higher than the second.

Perhaps some part has been played by the intensive publicity given to the perils of population growth, publicity keyed to the concept that more than two are too many. Perhaps there is also some effect of the reappraisal of the relations between men and women. Improved opportunities for women in both education and employment almost certainly have played some part in the currently later age at which the first two children are born, and they may also have contributed to a resolve to draw the line at that level. Delayed arrival of the second child increases exposure to alternatives to motherhood and decreases exposure to the risk of failure to prevent a third child. The principal explanation, however, is the substantial improvement in the ability to regulate fertility, by means that separate copulation from conception and accordingly reduce the requisite motivational level well below that necessary for successful employment of premodern techniques. Most couples use the pill, the termination of fertility by female and male sterilization has sharply increased and there is legal access to abortion. The way in which the population has responded in the past decade to the availability of these efficient means of avoiding excess fertility is strong testimony for the view that the baby boom was an unwitting phenomenon.

Although fertility in the U.S. is now the same as it is in other developed societies, this convergence is a recent development. In the U.S. (as well as in Canada, Australia and New Zealand) fertility began the postwar era at a moderately high level, rose further during the decade centered on the late 1950's and then declined sharply. In the nations of Western Europe the initial postwar level was much lower, and there was only a small increase (perhaps attributable entirely to a decline in the mean age of cohort fertility) somewhat later than the increase in the U.S.; the current level of fertility in these nations is lower than ever before in "normal" times. The most recent additions to the group of developed societies, Japan and the nations of Eastern Europe (including the European part of the U.S.S.R.), began the postwar period with comparatively high fertility; precipitous decline has been followed by stabilization at the level characteristic of the rest of the industrialized world [*see illustration on next page*].

It is remarkable that nations that once were so different in fertility level now constitute a homogeneous set in this respect. It is even more remarkable that the common low fertility has been accomplished by quite different strategies of fertility regulation. Fertility derives from the multiplication of three probabilities: that there is copulation, that copulation results in conception and that conception results in birth. Nuptiality control (permanent celibacy or delayed marriage) reduces the first probability; contraception and sterilization reduce the second; abortion reduces the third. The societal strategy for fertility regulation is the combination of these logical alternatives for achieving a low birth rate.

In the 19th century Western Europe was characterized by late marriage and high celibacy, Eastern Europe and the U.S. by early marriage and low celibacy, Japan by moderately late marriage and low celibacy. In the postwar period the nuptiality pattern in Western Europe has shifted strongly in the direction of that of Eastern Europe and the U.S.; Japan, on the other hand, now has even later marriage, although celibacy remains low. Permanent celibacy is currently of demographic significance only in those countries that adhere to a conservative form of Catholicism.

In the U.S. and Western Europe the principal kind of fertility regulation is contraception and sterilization, but the choices of contraceptive procedure differ widely. The commonest methods in Western Europe are the condom and *coitus interruptus;* in the U.S. the pill is dominant. Low fertility in Eastern Europe and Japan has been achieved primarily by resort to abortion. Although the moral opprobrium and criminal sanctions traditionally associated with abortion in the U.S. and Western Europe consigned it to a covert role, it is probable that abortion was a frequently employed second line of defense against the unwanted birth. The recent liberalization of abortion policy is an important part of the explanation of low fertility in such countries as Sweden, England and the U.S.

Thus the pursuit of diverse strategies of fertility regulation has led to the emergence of a common fertility level throughout the developed world. The similarity extends beyond the level to its composition by family size (both the large family and voluntary infertility are rare) and to its distribution by age (childbearing is concentrated in a brief span early in adult life). Within narrow limits one modern reproductive pattern prevails throughout contemporary developed societies.

In addition to its societal responsibility for producing new citizens (in adequate numbers) the conjugal family is obliged to provide its individual members with emotional support, an obligation that increases in salience with the level of economic development. In spite of the erosion of family functions associated with modernization, it is still the case that one spends almost the whole of one's life as a family member and in a household whose entire complement in the conjugal type of family is a husband, a wife and their preadult children (if any). Each individual is born into the junior generation of his or her family of orientation. The parents are expected to be evenhanded in their treatment of sons and daughters. Once adulthood is attained there may be a brief nonfamilial period. The decision to marry is solely that of the two persons most directly involved, and it is expected to be based at least in part on their love for each other. With marriage and parenthood a person becomes a member of the senior generation in his or her family of procreation. The responsibility for children is assigned exclusively to the couple who physically produce them. Ideally the family of procreation is completely independent of the respective families of orientation of the two spouses. The life cycle is terminated either by death or by another brief nonfamilial interval as a widow or widower.

The consequences of participation in the organized society give the conjugal family particular importance for individual well-being. The competitive and impersonal environment of an occupational structure (for the adult) or of an educational structure (for the child) is psychologically burdensome because it asks much of the individual in discipline and returns little in psychological security. The adequate functioning of individuals in the economic system, and thus of the system itself, requires effective maintenance of their emotional equilibrium. The conjugal family serves as an oasis for the replenishment of the person, providing the individual with stable, diffuse and largely unquestioning support, assuaging the bruises of defeat and otherwise repairing whatever damage may have been done in the achievement-oriented struggles of the outside world.

The network of relationships through which one could seek such acceptance without the test of satisfactory performance was once much larger; it encompassed the extended kinship structure and the community of residence. Although we still retain our links with our families of orientation and our friends, the requirement of spatial mobility (in the interests of labor-market efficiency) and the probability of social mobility (as individuals rise or fall through achievement) increase the distance between relatives and destabilize the community. With the erosion of these alternatives the importance of the immediate family as a source of dependable emotional support becomes enhanced.

The conjugal family is a relatively efficient design for supplying the kind of labor force a productive society needs and for providing comfort to the individual exposed to the consequences of participation in that system. The family has been the foundation of all systems of ascribing status on the basis of characteristics fixed at birth (such as race, sex, ethnic group and frequently social class). Its influence is antithetical to the exercise of productive rationality through equality of opportunity. Yet any attempt at further attenuation of family ties, in the interests of optimal allocation of human resources, would probably be self-defeating because of the high psychological cost to the individual. The family is an essentially authoritarian system persisting within an egalitarian environment. The growth of industrialism has been closely linked to the development of the ideology of individual liberty. Family political structure—the authority of male over female and of parent over child—has no immunity to the implications of this ideological change. Grave internal difficulties may therefore be expected.

Indeed, there are intrinsic problems in every role relationship within the conjugal family in a developed society. The major dimension of the family, at least empirically, is the husband-wife axis: mortality is now so low that one spends close to half of one's adulthood living with a spouse but no children. The husband is typically the major link between the family and the outside world. The specialization of an industrial society means that the family is separated from the job as well as the job from the family. The husband shuttles back and forth between two arenas that operate under contrasting sets of rules, and he experiences the strain of the continual transition. The wife has restricted opportunities to the extent that her function is a specialized domestic one. The education system, which typically exhibits less overt discrimination than either the home or the place of work, equips the young woman with capabilities for and interests in nonfamilial roles. If her aspirations are frustrated, she experiences discontent; if her aspirations are fulfilled, she experiences guilt.

The bonds between husband and wife are inherently fragile; emotionality alone is a quixotic foundation for an enduring arrangement. In the past those bonds were strengthened by the prescription of sexual exclusivity, a device in large part intended to ensure that no child would be without a father (as the consequence of a casual liaison). Now the availability of effective means of fertility regulation provides the opportunity for extensive nonmarital sexual experience without the implications of a long-term commitment to emotional exchange and economic community. Sexual competence, like other activities in the developed society, becomes subject to competitive testing.

Up to the present, at least, there is no

PERIOD TOTAL FERTILITY RATES of three developed regions are compared over the years 1948–1972. While the rates for Western Europe remained fairly constant throughout the period, the rate for the U.S. rose steeply and then fell steeply. The rates for Eastern Europe and Japan started out high and then declined. The net result is that all three areas now have about the same rate.

evidence that an increased toleration of sexual intimacy between individuals who are not married has led to a devaluation of marriage. There is, however, a substantial increase in the incidence of divorce in developed societies. If, in the judgment of the individuals the family is supposed to serve, it fails to perform adequately (if the husband or the wife fails to derive sufficient personal satisfaction from that particular marital pairing), then it is dissolved in favor of an alternative arrangement. In the U.S. the probability that a first marriage would end in divorce rose from 12 percent for women born in the years 1900–1904 to 29 percent for the cohort of 1940–1944. Recent data suggest a further increase in that probability: between 1967 and 1973 the crude divorce rate rose by 70 percent (from 2.6 to 4.4 per 1,000 population per year). This should not be taken as evidence that the marital institution is falling into disfavor. Couples today apparently consider it less undesirable to risk a poor marriage than to postpone marriage, and less undesirable to dissolve a poor marriage than to endure it. Only a trivial proportion of people eschew marriage altogether, and approximately 80 percent of those who get a divorce remarry, ordinarily rather promptly. Divorce is not so much evidence of the incidence of marital unhappiness as it is of the efficacy with which marital unhappiness can now be terminated.

The links between parent and child, unlike those between husband and wife, are forged during the long and intimate process of interaction required for child socialization. In spite of this solid foundation it is uncertain that those links will survive the child's transition to adulthood, because their structural supports, which are characteristic of a traditional society, have now largely vanished. The parents once controlled access to the land and provided most of the training necessary for the child's later work, but now land is not the prime base of production and technical education is acquired outside the family. The shift of the control of rewards and punishments from the family to the society has attenuated the traditional authority of the parent over the child. Deference, respect and gratitude alike have been diluted by the intrusion into the family structure of the alien ideology of individual rights and liberties.

Education, the basis for productivity (from an individual standpoint), is financed largely by the state and is ideally not the parents' prerogative to confer or withhold. The educational system is so-

ciety's agent, during that extended adolescent phase characteristic of the modern society, in releasing the individual from bondage to parents. In a society of specialization and change parents are no longer adequate role models for their children. Education raises aspirations, extends the child's vision beyond the limited bounds of the local community, differentiates the knowledge of the younger generation from that of the older generation and instills normative orientations alternative to those of the parents.

Modern young people experience the strain of demonstrating capability and achieving independence. They too shuttle back and forth between a universe of discourse keyed to achievement in an impersonal setting and one phrased in terms of assigned role definitions in the family. Whereas unsatisfactory husband-wife relationships can be dissolved by divorce, there is no comparable procedure for dissolving unsatisfactory parent-child relationships (other than the passage of time); the frequent consequence is rebellion. The most effective procedure for terminating emotional dependence on the family is for the individual to transfer that dependence to a new familial arrangement. Early marriage is the child's equivalent of divorce and remarriage.

The essential stipulation of the conjugal family design is that the family of procreation be independent of the family of orientation of either spouse. Although this arrangement is crucial to the rational allocation of human resources and valuable to the cause of individual liberty, it implies heavy counterpart costs for older people. With advancing age and declining productivity the husband is separated from the world of work (just as earlier the wife was separated from the world of motherhood); the resulting sense of a loss of purpose and meaning for others may be traumatic. The final stage of life, for the widow or widower, is a tragic culmination. No suitable solution now exists for this flaw in the conjugal design.

The key demographic question for the future is whether the achieved level of fertility in developed societies will tend to be greater or less than that required for population replacement (a value that, given low mortality, is approximated by a cohort total fertility rate of 2.1). Given the disparity of perspective between the individuals who determine how many children there are going to be and the societal aggregate that must live with the consequences of those

decisions, demographic equilibrium is an unlikely prospect.

The first consideration in assessing the prospects for fertility, although it is not necessarily the most consequential one, is the probability of continued improvement in methods of fertility regulation, such as long-term contraception, abortifacients to be administered quite soon after conception and the increased use of sterilization. Such developments would separate the acts of copulation and conception and diminish the role of nuptiality control in the strategy of regulation. They would also reduce the level of motivation required for success and accordingly increase the likelihood that infants would be born in the number and at the time wanted.

An enhanced ability to determine fertility implies greater sensitivity of response to instability in the political and economic environment and therefore an increase in the amplitude of future fertility fluctuations. If, as I have been suggesting, the size of a cohort is a significant influence on the level and time pattern of fertility, there may be a tendency toward a continual generational oscillation of the birth rate (as smaller cohort size gives rise to higher or earlier fertility, which implies larger cohort size, giving rise to lower or later fertility, and so on).

Should the means become available to enable couples to achieve their reproductive goals with considerable precision, then the principal source of future fertility variations will be changes in those goals. Granted that our understanding of this subject is imperfect and incomplete, it seems more likely that the direction of change will be downward rather than upward, in particular because the growing trend toward equality of opportunity for women in the occupational structure will make the alternatives to motherhood more attractive. I expect a continuing erosion of the proportion of families with more than two children, postponement of the first child to a somewhat higher age than at present and perhaps even the advent of a small cadre of women who will choose to remain infertile.

No society is likely to indefinitely tolerate a continuation of either negative or positive growth. Should individual reproductive decisions yield aggregate growth, the Government may respond in three directions, all of which are in one or another respect unsatisfactory. One type of proposal is legislation against the birth of a child of an order higher than the second. Although I am concerned about any abrogation of individual prerogatives, it is evident that such restraints on individual choice, in the interests of society, have long been accepted in other sectors of life—provided that they apply equally to all. The compelling case against this type of solution is derived from the arithmetic of replacement. Because some individuals will (voluntarily or involuntarily) have fewer than two children, replacement requires that some of those who want a third must be allowed to have it and the rest must be denied that privilege. The implicit choice here would be intolerable in a free society.

If the number of children to be borne remains an individual choice, the Government may reduce the attractiveness of parenthood by redistributing resources away from the more fertile and toward the less fertile. That would be a regressive move if fertility varied inversely with income, and it would be unjust: it would penalize the innocent children as well as the guilty parents. Alternatively the Government may attempt to make the alternatives to parenthood more attractive. In effect this policy would call for the creation of an institutional alternative to the family as a source of individual emotional support—a challenging assignment in the absence of any viable precedent in our history as a social species.

Provided my judgment is correct that free individual reproductive decisions will lead to subreplacement fertility, we shall not face the necessity of choice among these difficult alternatives. The bearing and rearing of children in a developed society are too expensive for the individual couple, and the rewards of parenthood are too uncertain within the conjugal family design. Some countries have recently reacted to warnings of an impending population decline by reducing access to the means of fertility regulation. This policy not only is an unacceptable limitation on human freedom but also is of dubious efficacy in the long run. The alternative direction of collective remedy seems meet and proper: given its stake in the production of sufficient numbers of children, the society has the obligation to reduce the costs of bearing and rearing children.

To summarize, my expectation is that individuals will show their intention and ability to prevent the birth of too many children, and societies will respond by subsidizing the reproductive endeavor to prevent the birth of too few children. Because society needs it and because the individual needs it the family will survive.

8

The Changing Status of Women in Developed Countries

The Changing Status of Women in Developed Countries

JUDITH BLAKE

The increasing number of women in the work force is reestablishing a balance between their economic and family activities. It remains unlikely that the majority will achieve occupational independence

The status of women has aroused widespread interest among students of population only recently. Investigators in the fields of economics, general sociology and political science have traditionally concentrated their attention on the status of men: on how men are ranked differentially in society, on their economic opportunities in life, on the deference they can command and on the power they attempt to wield. The great works on class, status and power rarely mention women. The reason for this neglect of women's social position is instructive: the status of women is derived. From the standpoint of their ranked position in Western societies women are expected to participate throughout their life cycle in terms of kinship attachments to men: early in life to a father and later to a husband.

Paradoxically, it is the derived nature of women's status that goes far toward explaining the demographer's special interest. The nature of women's position and the variations in its articulation with the status of men influence important variables with which students of population are concerned, in particular reproductive behavior and the size and quality of the labor force. For example, demographers have found that women, because of the linkage between their own lifetime position and the status of wife and mother, are typically well motivated to conform to social expectations regarding reproduction, such as the pressure to bear children until there are the desired number of living sons. Whether or not women participate in a secondary fashion in economic production in industrial societies—that is, whether or not they constitute "womanpower" on which a society can rely in addition to manpower—is closely connected to their primary status in the family. Thus in countries that have been chronically short of workers in recent years, such as France and Sweden, there is a lively interest in those aspects of women's position that impede their more extensive participation in the labor force.

Changes in certain demographic variables also have consequences for women's status. These too cannot fail to intrigue the demographer, who is as concerned with the impact of demographic trends on society as he is with the effects of social and economic structure on demographic behavior. The changes in migration, mortality and fertility that accompanied the Industrial Revolution appear to have profoundly disrupted the symmetry of the status of men and women. As a result, since the middle of the 19th century serious questions have been raised concerning the realism, as well as the legitimacy, of a continuing attempt in highly developed countries to prescribe one kind of position—a derived one—as being the primary status for *all* women.

Women's movements have appeared and reappeared in developed countries, each time focusing ever more closely on the central issue of women's derived status. As William L. O'Neill of Rutgers University has emphasized, "experience has demonstrated that the formal barriers to women's emancipation—votelessness, educational and occupational discriminations and the like—are less serious and more susceptible to change than the domestic, institutional and social customs that keep women in the home." Such movements advance the claim that all women should be afforded the opportunity to have their own nonderived, independent status without sacrificing a family life any more than men are required to do. Counterarguments that, whatever a woman may do on a secondary level, her primary place is as a wife and mother are, however, far from being silenced.

Against the background of these two polarized expectations, what is the position of women in highly developed countries today? Has it been changing significantly since World War II in the direction of an independent nonderived status? Or are alterations in many of women's activities merely superficial fluctuations superimposed on an underlying constant?

The highly developed countries to which I shall refer are the most economically advanced of those in Western Europe: Austria, Belgium, Denmark,

"GIRL BEFORE A MIRROR," the painting by Pablo Picasso reproduced on the opposite page, is widely regarded as a landmark in the evolution of modern art. Painted by Picasso in 1932, it is based on a traditional picture in which a vain young woman looking in a mirror sees not her own reflection but a reminder of mortality: a grinning skull. The head of the girl is seen both in profile and full face, a kind of imagery Picasso had been exploring since 1925. The figure of the girl is both clothed and nude; the visual shorthand is striped areas for clothing and flesh-colored ones for skin. The round form behind the girl's abdomen is her womb. The painting is in the collection of the Museum of Modern Art in New York.

England and Wales, Finland, France, the Netherlands, Norway, Sweden, Switzerland and West Germany. I shall also take up the New World countries of Australia, Canada, New Zealand and the U.S. Although the inclusion of Japan and the developed Communist countries would have added fascinating points of comparison, such a task would have been handicapped by major cultural disparities as well as by the unavailability of comparable statistics. Even as it is analysis of the countries considered here has been impeded because all the detailed tabulations from the 1970 censuses have not yet been published.

What happened during the industrializing process that gave rise to the strains over women's status that are as vital today as they were when the "woman's movement" first found expression in the 1830's? Put very schematically, the answer is as follows: Men became increasingly independent of the economic contributions of the family as a unit at the same time that women and children became more economically dependent on the extrafamilial occupations of husbands and fathers. This major change in the economic relationships of family members was associated with the migration of industrializing peoples out of

rural settings into the urban factories and bureaucracies of modernizing societies. This migration progressively removed work from the family milieu and put men in jobs away from home—jobs whose demands did not include participation by wives or offspring and whose criteria of performance emphasized each man's individual achievement. Conversely, the constraints of the household and the family made it extremely difficult for women to follow work into the outside world as it disappeared from the family unit, and their children could not readily participate in the highly rationalized and impersonal relationships of the adult world of work as it evolved. Thus, whereas in the rural ambience of family farms and enterprises husbands, wives and offspring had shared an economic dependence, gradually both wives and children became economic liabilities to the men. Although the families of poor, sick or deceased men worked in factories, in mines and in domestic service, such employment was associated with all the degradation of poverty. Except under the stress of dire necessity few married women would have left their families to work long hours at the onerous, exhausting jobs that characterized the industrializing process. Hence a significant

share of the social reforms of the 19th century and the early 20th consisted in the amelioration of economic conditions so that wives could remain at home to care for the family and older children could go to school. Step by step women's sphere shrank to the household only and men emerged (at least ideally) as the sole participators in economic life. The status of women was no longer simply derived; it became cumulatively skewed and diminished.

Not surprisingly, by the full bloom of the Victorian era industrializing societies capitalized into a virtue what appeared to be a necessity. They elaborated all kinds of rationalizations and legitimations for the wrenching change in the position of women that was accompanying the Industrial Revolution and the demographic transition. In particular they tried to justify it by asserting that women's personalities and behavior actually conformed by nature to the restrictions of their new way of life. Exit the sturdy partner, the practical helpmate who carried her share of the family's earning and living. Enter the romantic, inhibited, swooning Victorian whose fragility required cosseting (and corseting).

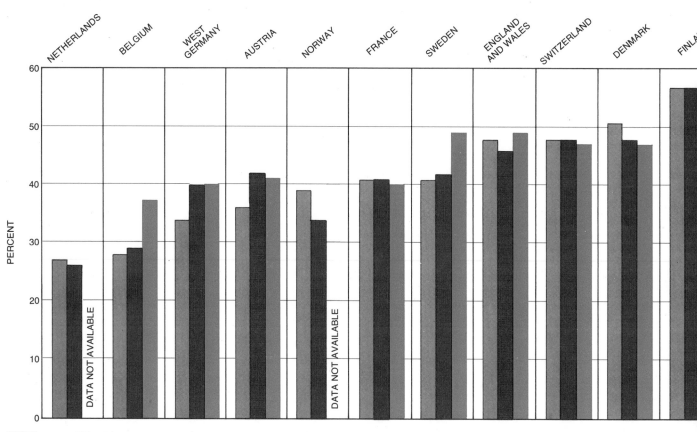

NONFARM WORK FORCE OF WOMEN, excluding unpaid family workers, is shown as a percentage of all women between ages 15 and 69 in the nonagricultural population. Estimates shown are for the dates 1950, 1960 and 1970 in 15 highly developed Western countries. In this illustration, as in those on pages 94 through 96, the author has divided the countries into two groups: the New World countries of Australia, Canada, New Zealand and the U.S., and the Old

Historians of "the woman's place" such as William O'Neill, Robert Smuts and William H. Chafe have made clear, however, that the domestic interment of women aroused protest even as it was taking place. Not only did at least some women balk at being removed from the flow of adult life and at having their derived status reduced to a total dependency; they also objected to the resulting inequities suffered by the many women who could not find or retain husbands. It was all very well for women to derive their status from men as long as those who could not marry, or who were widowed or deserted, could be absorbed into the kinship structure and attached to fathers, brothers, uncles or other male relatives. As family enterprises disappeared, however, such women had no economic role to play within the kinship group except perhaps as family servants—on sufferance simply for lack of a husband. Furthermore, as families migrated hither and yon in response to economic opportunity, family ties became attenuated and community opinion could no longer function to enforce kinship obligations. Unattached women—whether single, deserted or widowed—thus had to seek nonfamilial employment in a work world for which they were systematically unprepared and which, in turn, assumed that they were an anomaly. The "normal" course of events was for a woman to have a man to fend for her.

Yet in actual fact the proportion of women without husbands was very substantial during a good share of the industrializing period in many countries. For example, during the middle and late 19th century, at the very time when women were becoming acutely dependent on finding mates, the age at which women married and the proportion of those remaining unmarried were rising. John Hajnal has calculated that around 1900 in Belgium, Britain, Denmark, Finland, the Netherlands, Norway, Sweden and Switzerland between 40 and 50 percent of the women aged 25 to 29 were single and between 13 and 19 percent of those aged 45 to 49 were still so. Obviously as women became more dependent and their children became economically less useful, men had to be more circumspect before taking on such "hostages to fortune."

Moreover, even among those intrepid men who did marry many died early, well before their children had grown, leaving widows to fend for the family in a modern setting that had not yet come to terms with the still high probability of a husband's premature death. For the U.S. research by Peter R. Uhlenberg of the University of North Carolina has shown that among 1,000 white women born between 1890 and 1894 who survived to age 50, 100 never married, 225 were childless, 165 had fertile marriages that broke up (owing to death or intentional dissolution) and only 510—slightly more than half—experienced the "normal" pattern for a woman of having a fertile marriage that had not dissolved by the time she was middle-aged. In recent years the probability of the joint survival of a husband and a wife has increased in industrial societies, and spinsterhood and childlessness have declined, but the instability caused by death has been replaced by the personal instability of the marital relationship itself. Hence at no time so far during the modernizing process has it been realistic for all women to assume that they could rely on being wives and mothers as a lifetime status.

Even among those women who managed to catch and keep husbands the expectation that all wives would blithely submit to domestic encapsulation might have been more realistic if such domesticity had been congruent with the emerging constraints on family size. Paradoxically, however, even as women's status was being denuded of economic functions, many of the same forces were motivating couples to want fewer births, and the decline in infant and childhood mortality reinforced that motivation. For example, in the prototype case of England and Wales, E. A. Wrigley of the University of Cambridge has shown that live births declined from an average of 6.16 per woman to 3.30 among couples marrying in the decades 1860–1869 and 1900–1909 respectively. Among couples marrying in the period 1935–1939 there were on the average only 2.04 births per woman. With variations in timing and magnitude, this pattern of fertility reduction characterized all the highly industrialized countries of the West. Thus women's entire lifetime status was being geared ideologically to a function—reproduction—whose demands were diminishing in scope. Such a situation could not help but be unstable since, as far as the content of women's social position was concerned, they were rapidly becoming net losers.

Finally, the erosion of traditional acquired statuses among men in modernizing countries engendered a growing sense of illegitimacy about women's derived status. As the power of hereditary elites was vitiated and impersonal achievement criteria rather than family position were employed for according men differential status and rewards, the derived nature of women's status became more anomalous with respect to that of men. Whereas in traditional European society men had been comparatively fixed in their status by their social position at birth, modernization and economic and political liberalism had begun to give men at least a fighting chance to achieve according to their talents. Women, however, were left to achieve by finding men to succeed in their behalf.

Given this host of incongruities between women's prescribed status and the realities of the modernizing world, it is hardly surprising that the "woman problem" has erupted periodically in at least some industrial countries. Such recurrences have even followed periods such as that of the 1950's, when feminine discontent seemed to be in a state of total remission. By the middle and late 1960's a number of countries—most notably the U.S. and Denmark, Finland and Sweden—began experiencing an upwelling of protest concerning women's status, although some, such as West Germany and the Netherlands, seemed fairly secure in the notion that women "normally" belong in the home. In assessing what women's current status actually appears to be with respect to the polar norms of

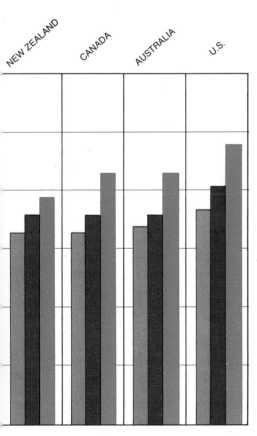

World countries of Europe. In 1950 the European countries had more women working than New World countries, but by 1970 the New World countries had caught up.

independence of men on the one hand and dependence on them on the other, I shall concentrate on women's participation in the occupational world since World War II.

In making such an assessment one is interested in women's participation apart from both agricultural and unpaid family work. Therefore my calculations eliminate farming and family labor. In 1950 the fraction of women working as a percentage of the total number of women in the nonagricultural population of the New World countries clustered around the one-third mark. The fraction of working European women varied widely from slightly more than one-fourth for the Belgians and the Dutch to one-half or more for the Danes and the Finns. Nonetheless, on the average 41 percent of European nonfarm women were economically active in contrast to an average of 34 percent for nonfarm women in the New World. Thus the Europeans had proportionately more women working at mid-century than was the case in the New World countries.

It is frequently assumed that the percentage of women working has risen strikingly in the postwar period. This assumption is not borne out by the censuses. Instead, although a consistent and substantial gain in women's economic activity in the New World countries had by 1970 put them more on a par with their European counterparts, the work rates of women in the Old World countries averaged only a 1 percent gain between 1950 and 1960 and a modest increase of 10 percent between 1960 and 1970. Hence by 1970, 45 percent of the nonfarm women in the highly developed European countries for which we have information and 43 percent of nonfarm women in the New World were in the labor force. These averages, of course, conceal some striking increases in specific countries such as Australia, Canada, the U.S., Belgium and Sweden. On the basis of these data, however, it would be hard to assert that since World War II there has been a revolution in the propensity of women to work.

The overall work rates for all the countries since World War II reflect two important countervailing tendencies in women's behavior. The first trend is that between 1950 and 1970 women married at increasingly youthful ages in all the countries except Australia, Canada and the U.S. They also married in higher proportions in every one of the countries. As of 1970 more women had married by the prime adult ages of 25 to 34 than was the case in 1950. Since at any point in time married women work less than unmarried ones, the marrying behavior of these women over the 20-year period operated to depress the work rates. At the same time, however, there was a second trend for more of the married women to work. Indeed, if over the years married women had not decided to work in higher proportions than they had in 1950, overall work rates in all the countries would have declined, and in some of the countries they would have declined appreciably more than they actually did. The reason female rates of participation in the work force actually rose in almost all countries between 1950 and 1970 is that the increased tendency of married women to work more than offset the greater proclivity of all women to marry.

One can thus see that the status of

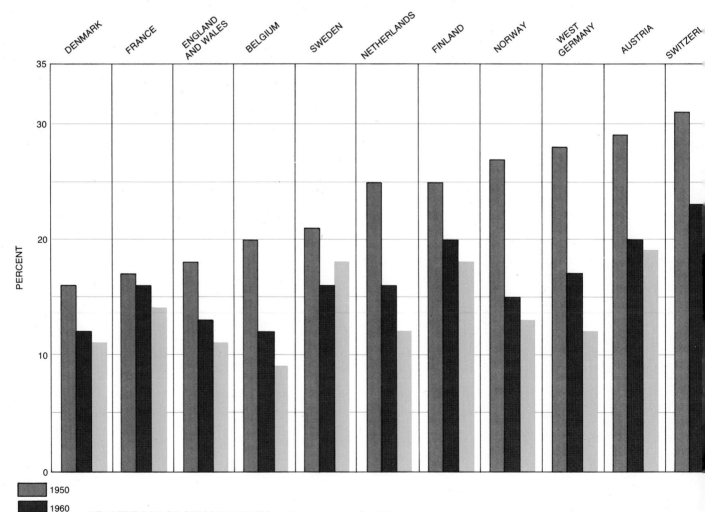

PERCENTAGE OF SINGLE WOMEN aged 25 to 34 has declined between 1950 and 1970, particularly in the Old World countries, indicating that there is an overall trend both for a higher proportion of women to marry and for them to

women in highly developed countries has taken a novel turn in the 20-year period from 1950 to 1970. More young women have married (indeed, very few remain unmarried), but increased work activity has broadened the character of the derived status for at least a share of married women. In most of the countries included in my analysis it is no longer true that only a small minority of married women are active in modern sectors of the economy. Yet it still remains true that, no matter whether one looks at the proportion of married women working, the pattern of women's participation in the labor force with respect to age, the types of occupations in which women are engaged, the relative earnings of women or feminine attitudes toward the primacy of work, one finds that women typically participate in economic activity only as a secondary supplement to their primary status inside the home. It is true that the augmented work behavior of married women is bringing their derived status back into balance, the balance it had lost in the industrializing process. Nevertheless, this labor-force activity does not indicate, at least so far, that many women

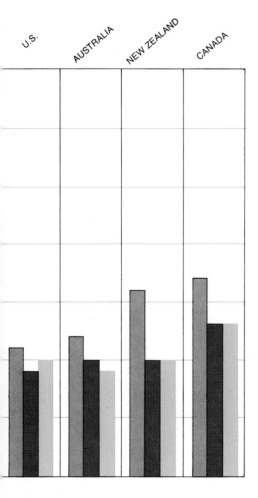

have achieved an independent occupational status.

To document the variation in the work rates of women according to age and decade for the countries considered here I plotted female work rates against age for each of the countries in 1950, 1960 and 1970 and then grouped the curves that were similar into five average types. (Austria, Finland, France and Norway were excluded because of the large role played in them by agriculture.) The five types took account of the magnitude of the peak in work rates during youth, the amount of the subsequent decline and the shape and level of the remainder of the work/age curve.

The results show that even at the highest levels of participation women's engagement in work differs dramatically over the course of their life cycle from the work rates of men. Furthermore, even at the most active ages female work rates do not approximate those of men until the men approach retirement. Thus not only do women show a sharp tendency to drop out of the labor force while they engage in family responsibilities but also at every stage of their life cycle women's work rates are at substantially lower levels than men's. The data from two countries in the 1970 period, however, exhibit a smaller decline in women's work rates after age 25 and a rapid recovery rate in the early thirties to levels approximating those of youth. This more continuous work rate is a new pattern for women in highly developed countries. It reflects a rising participation in the labor force by youthful married women, in some cases married women with young children.

Women's work experience differs from men's qualitatively as well as quantitatively, an important point in evaluating whether or not women have made significant changes in achieving an independent, nonderived status. For example, the International Labor Office estimates that part-time employment is widespread in Australia, Britain, Canada, West Germany, the Netherlands, the Scandinavian countries and the U.S. In Canada in 1961 nearly a fifth of the female labor force worked fewer than 35 hours per week. In Britain the figure was almost a sixth and in the U.S. in 1973 it was a fourth.

Women also concentrate markedly in particular occupational categories such as clerical, sales and service, and are excluded from management as well as those parts of the industrial and service sectors where highly skilled blue-collar jobs are found. This skewed occupation-

al distribution is further evidence that most women have not yet come close to achieving a nonderived status.

The relatively high proportion of women in the professional and technical category is misleading. Women cluster in the low-level professions, the majority of professional women being schoolteachers, nurses, librarians and social workers. For example, in 1970 teaching and nursing accounted for 80 percent of the professional women in New Zealand and 63 percent of those in the U.S. (The figure for the U.S. has dropped significantly from 71 percent in 1960.)

Valerie Kincade Oppenheimer of the University of California at Los Angeles has found that for the U.S. the large increase in the demand for women workers since World War II has been a joint product of the sex-typing of jobs (that is, the earmarking of certain kinds of jobs as "female" occupations) and the fact that these particular kinds of jobs are located in the expanding service sector of the economy. Oppenheimer's analysis of the sources of the U.S. demand for female labor is paralleled in all the countries considered here, among which Canada, Belgium, England and Wales, the Netherlands and Sweden have already become full-fledged service economies (having more than half of their labor force in the service sector).

Although among those countries the women's occupations are similar in broad outline, it is important to note in the context of this discussion that there is some variation at the most prestigious professional levels. Marjorie Galenson of Cornell University has shown that for highly industrial countries there is a substantial variation from one country to the next in the proportion of physicians who are women. In the mid-1960's the proportion ranged between 16 and 23 percent in Denmark, Finland, Sweden, West Germany and Britain, but it was only 7 percent in the U.S. The comparative proportions of women dentists for 1960 are even more striking: a little more than 1 percent of the dentists in the U.S. were women, whereas in Norway the figure was a fifth, in Denmark and Sweden it was a fourth and in Finland it was more than three-fourths. Apart from the health professions, however, women do not figure significantly in high-level occupations in the countries considered here.

Nonetheless, there have been some noteworthy changes in the U.S. between 1960 and 1970. I have calculated that among physicians the number of women increased by 62 percent, raising their representation in this category from 7 percent to 9 percent. Women gained

149 percent among lawyers, increasing their representation from 2.4 percent to 4.7 percent. They advanced between 159 and 200 percent in engineering, architecture and college and university teaching, and among life scientists and physical scientists they rose 106 percent. In these fields too the increases for women were substantially greater than they were for men, and women now have a somewhat larger share of each category. In some of these high-level categories, however, women are known to concentrate at the lower echelons. For example, although 28 percent of the college and university teachers are women, most of them are on low rungs of the academic ladder.

In the light of the typically modest occupational status of women in highly developed countries, it is to be expected that they earn less than men even when the comparison is confined to full-time, year-round employment. Studies suggest that the complex causes for the difference are related less to wage discrimination per se than to the concentration of women in low-paying occupations and to the secondary role of work in their lives; men normally have greater continuity of employment, work longer hours and get more job training. Even so, with the sex differential in hourly wages being as high as 40 percent in a country such as the U.S. (a differential much larger than that between blacks and whites) the ordinary working woman is clearly still some distance from having an independent primary status.

Is it likely that the primary status of proportionately more women in highly developed countries will expand to include a vocation? In attempting to answer this question one must consider factors affecting both the supply of women wanting to work and the demand for their services in the economy. With regard to the supply, more women may feel free to work, more may need to work and more may be attracted by work. Opposing forces, however, are also operating. Let us examine the situation in more detail.

More women may feel free to work because their families are remaining relatively small. Surveys in most of the countries considered here give no evidence that women want larger families than they are currently having; in fact, if anything, the evidence indicates that the trend is toward even fewer children. Furthermore, married women are no longer bucking strong disapproval when they enter the labor force. For example, in the U.S. at the end of World War II the Gallup organization asked: "Do you approve of a woman earning money in business or industry if she has a husband capable of supporting her?" In 1945 the survey found that only 18 percent of the population approved. Almost two-thirds actively disapproved and 16 percent offered qualifications, such as that they would approve if there were no children. During the past six years I have commissioned the same question on a number of Gallup surveys. The results have been striking. By October, 1973, 65 percent approved of a married woman's working; moreover, among those under age 30, 83 percent were in favor of it.

More women may need to work because of inflationary trends in the economy, high rates of divorce and the fact that their children leave school to support themselves at a later age than they did a generation ago. With rapid rates of economic inflation gripping the highly developed countries, there is great pressure on families to maintain their living levels by increasing the family income. This effort to forestall the erosion of consumption may push some women into the work force who would never have taken this step to simply augment

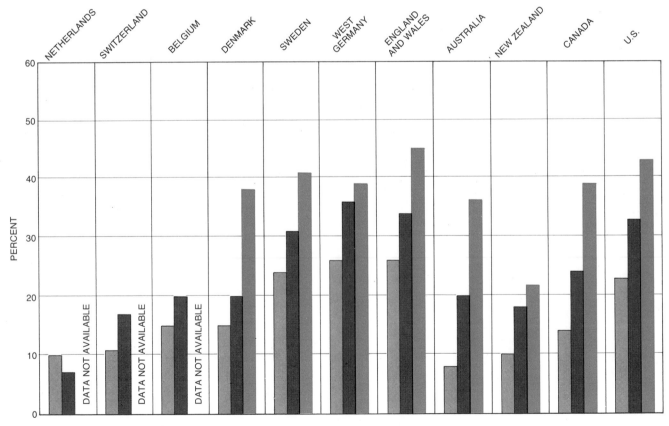

MARRIED WOMEN WHO WORK are portrayed as a percentage of all married women aged 15 to 64. The figures show that in spite of the fact that more married women were working in 1970 than in 1950, the labor-force activity among married women is still relatively low. Rates include agricultural and unpaid farm labor, although Austria, Finland, France and Norway are excluded because a high proportion of their labor force is engaged in agricultural work.

the level of spending by their family.

Trends in divorce have similar effects. The divorce rate has risen rather sharply since at least the middle of the 1960's in almost all the countries considered here. Thus more women may need to work both because more are divorced and because more go through the early nest-building stage of two or more marriages instead of one.

In addition, as higher education increasingly becomes an expectation instead of a luxury and the age at which children leave school to support themselves continues to rise, more families are faced with the "life-cycle squeeze." Using census data for the U.S., Oppenheimer has demonstrated that only at relatively high occupational levels do the average earnings of men peak at the same time that the needs of their families are also peaking, that is, when the children are adolescent and of college age. In occupations where the pay is moderate or low the average earnings peak at youthful ages, with the consequence that men at an age when family costs are heaviest are earning little more on the average than younger men, and in some occupations they are actually earning less. Hence the families of such men risk a deterioration in their standard of living unless extra income is brought into the household. The life-cycle squeeze appears to be a powerful motive for many middle-aged women to enter or reenter the labor force.

More women may also be attracted to work because they are more educated than their predecessors, because hours are becoming more flexible and because job benefits are greater. In almost all the countries being considered the proportion of women receiving the equivalent of a baccalaureate degree has been increasing and better-educated women are drawn by the job market more than their less educated contemporaries. In addition, if the incipient trend toward flexible working hours accelerates, data from surveys indicate that a substantial reserve of women await part-time opportunities. There are efforts in many countries to eliminate discrimination in fringe benefits and promotions for women. For example, Belgium has instituted major social-security reforms allowing a married woman to receive unemployment insurance, cash sickness benefits and a waiver of the qualifying period for medical care in the event that she leaves her job to have a child and then is reemployed.

Such compelling positive incentives for women to work are offset by some powerful depressants. Perhaps the most important is the overall assumption by both men and women that the primary obligation of a woman is to her home and family. In the U.S., Karen Oppenheim Mason of the University of Michigan and Larry L. Bumpass of the University of Wisconsin analyzed the answers to questions on sex roles in the 1970 National Fertility Study that were asked of women under the age of 45 who were married or had been married. The attitudes toward the primary status of women they found are congruent with the results from European surveys and with women's observed secondary commitment to work. Almost 80 percent of the 6,740 women interviewed in this national sample agreed with the statement "It is much better for everyone involved if the man is the achiever outside the home and the woman takes care of the home and family." Fewer than half of the respondents agreed with the statement "A working mother can establish just as warm and secure a relationship with her children as a mother who does not work." And more than two-thirds agreed with the statement "A preschool child is likely to suffer if his mother works." No significant differences appeared with respect to the age of the women interviewed.

Since these surveys show that it is so clearly normative for women to give primacy to their derived status if they marry and have children, few highly developed societies attempt to offer much supplementary help to married women who work. Even in countries such as France and Sweden where child-care assistance to working mothers is accepted as a social responsibility, facilities are often inadequate in both quality and number. In all advanced Western countries moderately priced, well-cooked takeout meals are typically a rarity. Working married women are thus very dependent on husbandly help, which, surveys have shown, is more likely to be forthcoming if the wife is employed but is usually insufficient in amount. As a result working women with families tend to be very hard-pressed.

In 1965 and 1966 Alexander Szalai and his colleagues conducted a monumental study of how people budget their time in urban areas of 10 Western and Eastern European countries as well as the U.S. and Peru. They demonstrated that, regardless of the country, employed married women work longer hours than either employed men or housewives. Moreover, on weekends (particularly on Sundays), when many housewives cut

back on their household tasks, employed women typically double the amount of time they spend on housework in an evident effort to catch up. Szalai and his colleagues point out: "The plight of the employed woman pervades all of our time-budget records.... After her day's obligations are done, she finds herself with an hour or two less time than anyone else.... The cramped nature of her time is reflected by marked constrictions in all leisure activities, particularly those relatively passive and recuperative ones such as sitting down to pass time reading a newspaper."

The results of this research conform to independent work done previously in France, the U.S.S.R., Sweden, Finland and Denmark. Indeed, it is significant that the Scandinavian "sex role" movement that began in the early 1960's has emphasized the importance of augmenting the household and child-rearing obligations of men. This change is regarded as mandatory if women are to experience an increase in opportunity to work outside the home and if, in the words of Eva Moberg (a leader in the Swedish woman's movement), they are to have more than just "conditional emancipation." Surveys on both sides of the Atlantic, however, indicate that men are typically willing to accord women broad political, civil and economic "rights," but only if they fulfill their household and family obligations too. Women are thus faced with a rather inflexibly structured choice: too much work or too much leisure. It would not be surprising if many women did not elect to be overworked.

The possibilities for greatly expanded work opportunities for women seem even less rosy when we look at the demand for their services. Projections of expanded demand for female labor all assume that there will be high rates of economic growth—rates that may be quite problematic over the next 25 years. Furthermore, the higher educational levels of women may be a mixed blessing unless the better-educated move out of traditional feminine occupations. The supply of female labor is becoming overeducated for the jobs that have been typed as feminine. Compounding the problem is the fact that major recent declines in the birth rates of some countries suggest that demand is actually contracting in the most important "female" profession: schoolteaching. Just how much these negative factors will be offset by a continuing shift of advanced economies to the service sector, where the demand for women has been highest, has not yet been investigated.

All these negative factors imply that,

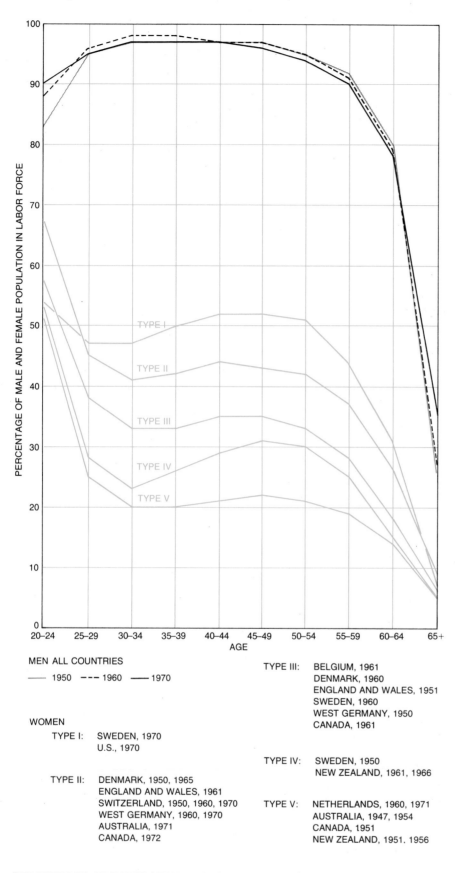

MEN ALL COUNTRIES

—— 1950   --- 1960   —— 1970

WOMEN
   TYPE I: SWEDEN, 1970
              U.S., 1970

   TYPE II: DENMARK, 1950, 1965
              ENGLAND AND WALES, 1961
              SWITZERLAND, 1950, 1960, 1970
              WEST GERMANY, 1960, 1970
              AUSTRALIA, 1971
              CANADA, 1972

   TYPE III: BELGIUM, 1961
              DENMARK, 1960
              ENGLAND AND WALES, 1951
              SWEDEN, 1960
              WEST GERMANY, 1950
              CANADA, 1961

   TYPE IV: SWEDEN, 1950
              NEW ZEALAND, 1961, 1966

   TYPE V: NETHERLANDS, 1960, 1971
              AUSTRALIA, 1947, 1954
              CANADA, 1951
              NEW ZEALAND, 1951. 1956

PERCENTAGE OF POPULATION WORKING at any given age is shown both for men (*top three curves*) and for women (*bottom five curves*). The overall work rates for women vary greatly over the life cycle and are quite different from the work rates of men. Moreover, age-specific work rates of women vary from one country to another as well as from one decade to another. They can be grouped into five average types, with Type I representing the highest level of participation and Type V the lowest. Type I curve, composed of two countries in the 1970 period, reflects a new pattern of rising participation among youthful married women in labor force in highly developed countries, with smaller decline after age 25 and rapid recovery rate in early thirties to levels approximating the rates in youth.

all other things being equal, there may be an upper limit in the highly developed countries on the demand for women at occupational levels attractive to them. This upper limit may be a major reason why countries such as Switzerland have ended up importing large supplies of foreign labor. The immigrants have done the jobs spurned by Swiss of either sex. The same pattern has prevailed in France and other developed countries that have had a large influx of immigrants since World War II.

From the evidence up to this point it seems almost academic to consider whether or not large proportions of women are on the verge of achieving a non-derived lifetime status in the highly developed countries. Indeed, survey data relating specifically to this issue reinforce the improbability of such an outcome. Studies in most of the highly developed countries show that significant proportions of women who work do not want to; also, among those women who are not working typically half or more either do not want to be employed or want only part-time jobs. In fact, the strongest preference among women appears to be for a part-time job: in effect a work situation that does not interfere with their primary status.

Women also do not seem to evince a widespread rejection of their derived status. For example, in 1972 a Harris survey asked a national sample of American women how often they felt that "having a loving husband who is able to take care of me is much more important to me than making it on my own" and "bringing up children properly takes as much intelligence and drive as holding a top position in business or government." Even among women under the age of 30 half said they "frequently" felt that having a loving husband was more important than an independent status, and an additional fifth admitted to having this feeling "occasionally." Only a fourth said they "hardly ever" felt that way. Among older women the importance of a loving husband was even greater. Similarly, more than 60 percent of all the women, even the young ones, said they frequently felt that being a mother is as challenging as having a high occupational position. Finally, few women (only a little more than 20 percent) indicated that they frequently hoped that their daughters would have "more interesting careers outside the home" than they had had. Half "hardly ever" entertained such a feeling. Survey data in other highly developed countries show no vast discontent among women. When they are asked, they typically seem to be as satisfied with life as men. Consequently it seems unlikely that high proportions of women will be impelled to swim upstream in these societies as they are currently constituted.

What does seem probable is that for some years to come a small but rising proportion of women will attempt to achieve an independent status. Factors that may encourage these women are the increasing moral support provided by the women's movement, some modification of sex-typed socialization and schooling, greater educational and career opportunities for women and a blurring of the difference in the way of life between being married and being unmarried.

As for the women's movement, although most women claim to be satisfied with a derived status, a growing and influential minority in many highly developed countries are actively dissatisfied with the popular expectation that all women should occupy that position. If Western societies are so committed to assuring men equal opportunity to develop their different talents, why should the diverse capabilities of women be expected to conform tranquilly to one mold? The incongruity of such an expectation, in addition to the resulting waste of talent and drive, has fueled women's movements with a constantly renewable source of energy. To be sure, surveys find that most women in the developed countries are unsympathetic to the tactics of women's movements. Yet there is a widespread sympathy for many of the goals, particularly for those relating to fair educational and occupational practices. Support has mushroomed for such cadres as the National Organization for Women in the U.S., and such groups are becoming increasingly able to provide moral backing and lobbying for the interests of those women who do want to make it on their own.

Will the minority find recruits among younger women as new cohorts come along? Some social scientists, I among them, believe they will unless the highly developed countries continue with their rigidly sex-typed socialization practices. Evidence concerning the socialization of women from birth onward indicates that there are extremely powerful pressures from all sources to select personality traits and behavior patterns that are believed to be congruent with the status of wife and mother. Among those who have conducted investigations in this area are Mirra Komarovsky of Barnard College, Alice S. Rossi of the University of Massachusetts, Eleanor E.

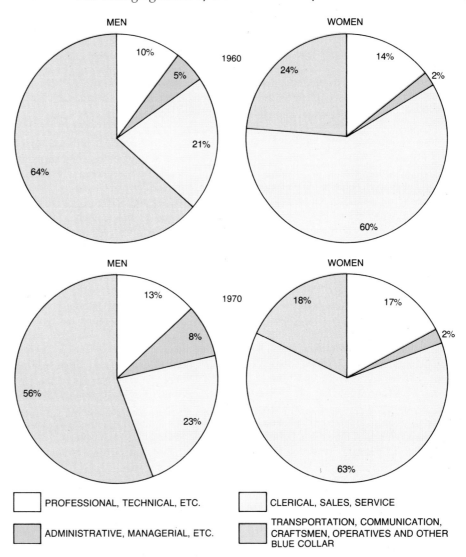

PERCENTAGE OF MEN AND WOMEN IN OCCUPATIONS in 1960 and 1970 demonstrates that qualitatively as well as quantitatively women's work experience differs from that of men. All occupations are civilian and nonagricultural. Relatively high proportions of women in professional and technical category are misleading, since women tend to be concentrated in lower-level professions such as teaching, nursing, librarianship and social work.

Maccoby of Stanford University, Lois W. Hoffman of the University of Michigan, Inge Broverman and her colleagues at Worcester State Hospital and Matina Horner, now president of Radcliffe College. Their general finding is that American women are socialized for defeat in those same goals and tasks where men are socialized for success. Indeed, the degree to which seemingly "emancipated" industrial societies engage in sex-differentiated practices of child-rearing and indoctrination is just beginning to be understood. Writing in 1972 of her research on young people, Horner said:

"It is clear in our data that the young men and women tested over the past seven years still tend to evaluate themselves and to behave in ways consistent with the dominant stereotype that says competition, independence, competence, intellectual achievement and leadership

reflect positively on mental health and masculinity but are basically inconsistent or in conflict with femininity. Thus despite the fact that we have a culture and an educational system that ostensibly encourage and prepare men and women identically for careers, the data indicate that social and, even more importantly, internal psychological barriers rooted in this image really limit the opportunities to men."

None of this research makes one sanguine about the possibility of revolutionary changes in the socialization of young girls. As the "implicits" of a society become explicit, however, they are at least available for scrutiny. Parents may gradually have a more informed choice in the way they rear their offspring and can thus become more aware of the stimuli and environments they wish to select. For example, analyses of the content of children's books show biases that some parents, once they become conscious of them, may reject as inappropriate for their children. Lenore J. Weitzman and her colleagues at the University of California at Davis have done a content analysis of the books winning the Caldecott Medal (a leading prize for children's books) during the late 1960's and early 1970's. A principal characteristic of these volumes is the invisibility of female characters, even when animals are included. In the sample of 18 Caldecott winners Weitzman and her colleagues found 261 pictures of males as against 23 pictures of females. Featured in the titles was a ratio of eight males to three females. In close to one-third of the books there were no women at all, and when they did appear they were typically inconspicuous. Not one woman in these books had a job or a profession. In the few cases where they did have leadership roles they were fairies or other mythical characters. A similar content analysis of children's books conducted in Sweden by Rita Liljestrom showed boys in situations emphasizing knowledge, action and intrigue, whereas girls were characterized as being devoted to clothing and personal appearance.

Are the current patterns of socialization appropriate even for women who will be primarily wives and mothers? Or are many aspects of such patterns relics of Victorian fantasy and Freudian theorizing? Broverman and her colleagues asked a sample of psychologists, psychiatrists and social workers, all in clinical practice, to assign traits to a mature healthy man, a mature healthy woman and a mature healthy adult of unspecified sex. The traits assigned to the man and the sex-unspecified adult were quite similar, but there was a significant difference between the concepts of health for sex-unspecified adults and for women. Broverman concludes: "Clinicians are likely to suggest that healthy women [are] more submissive, less independent, less adventurous, more easily influenced, less aggressive, less competitive, more excitable in minor crises, [have] their feelings more easily hurt, [are] more emotional, more conceited about their appearance, less objective, and [dislike] math and science. This constellation seems a most unusual way of describing any mature, healthy individual."

If some changes in the patterns of socialization are accompanied by greater educational opportunities for women, as seems to be the case in almost all highly developed countries, more women may move into fields of study leading to remunerative and prestigious occupations. In fact, as we have seen, this seems to be happening on a small scale in the U.S. Furthermore, in many of the highly developed countries such as Scandinavia, England and Wales, and the U.S., career opportunities are increasingly open to women.

Will this minority of highly-selected women typically have to forgo marriage and children in order to achieve? Probably not: they will merely have to be willing to run the risk. And this risk may seem less awesome in a world where the lines between marriage and nonmarriage, having children and not having them are becoming more blurred than in the past. Less rigid confinement of sexual relations to marriage means less of a penalty for late marriage or nonmarriage. The high risk of divorce, even for women with no career, also blurs the line between the married and the unmarried. Small families, even for full-time housewives, make the career woman with one or two children less of an anomaly. Both kinds of women will spend most of their lives without children around.

Why then will not high proportions of women become "emancipated" in this fashion? Why assume, as I have done, that only a minority will respond to changing socialization and opportunity? The answer is that even if one could assume that such changes will be sweep-

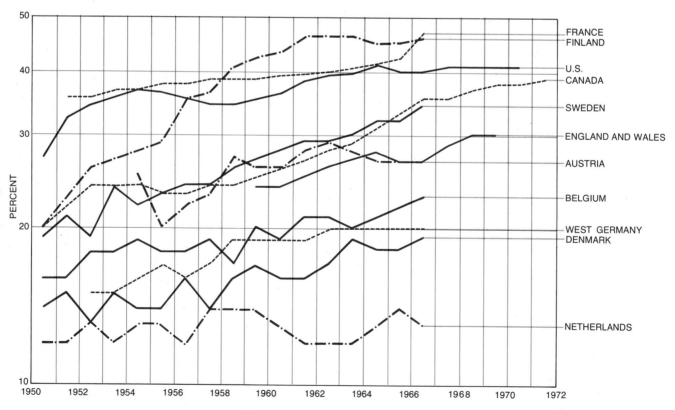

PERCENTAGE OF DEGREES AWARDED TO WOMEN from 1950 to 1972 shows a general upward trend in almost all the developed countries. The degrees roughly approximate the baccalaureate awarded at the end of four years of college in the U.S.

ing, there are still underlying constraints over and above the ones I have already discussed. We must not, for example, confuse equality of opportunity with equality of outcome. Given a range of choice, we must expect women's achievements to be variable, just as the achievements of men are variable. In addition, educational and occupational achievement will inevitably expose the achieving women to risks of nonmarriage and childlessness. While her peers are pursuing husbands the achieving woman is losing time from this activity, even though the number of men that she might want or who might want her is likely to be more limited than it is for other women. Exacerbating this risk is the paucity of occupations so fulfilling as to lead many women to risk impairing their marital opportunities.

Perhaps the most compelling fact of all is that women's derived status stands to benefit greatly from the opening up of genuine alternatives. For the first time women who want to be primarily wives and mothers will be in relatively short supply, as others are drained off into new opportunities and an additional "swing vote" hovers on the brink of decision. Given such a market situation men will have to make concessions concerning important features of women's derived status, concessions that no amount of exhortation by presidential and royal commissions has been able to bring about. Whatever these may be, whether they are more sharing of household and child-rearing tasks, greater economic equality and security of tenure or the elimination of double standards of morality, they will make the status of wife and mother more varied and advantaged than it is currently. Upgrading women's derived status inevitably places the alternatives to that status at a relative disadvantage. It means that women probably will choose the alternatives primarily for positive reasons such as satisfying their best talents and drives, rather than for negative reasons such as not wanting to be "a mere housewife."

It is idle to speculate what the various levels of derived status and nonderived status might become in some kind of equilibrium state. The main point is that two significant changes will have occurred. First, in Western societies there will be an opportunity for women to respond in a variety of ways to the selection of a lifelong position. Second, women's derived status will have regained at the very least the balance it lost during the Industrial Revolution and the demographic transition.

9

The Populations of
the Underdeveloped Countries

The Populations of the Underdeveloped Countries

PAUL DEMENY

These populations, accounting for nearly three-fourths of the human species, will continue their rapid growth for the rest of the century. Control will eventually come through development or catastrophe

During the 100 years before the outbreak of World War I nearly 30 million Europeans crossed the Atlantic to find a new home in North America. During the five months ending December 31, 1974, about the same number of people will have been added to the population of the three vast areas (Latin America, Africa and Asia, excluding Japan and the U.S.S.R.) that are called underdeveloped.

The juxtaposition of the two statistics emphasizes the extraordinary magnitude of the demographic expansion that is taking place south of the sharp dividing line that separates the relatively rich countries from the relatively poor ones. The expansion, which is the combined result of a high rate of growth and a high population base to which growth accrues, has no meaningful historical parallel. Nonetheless, the basic demographic facts needed to understand the dynamics of the expansion can best be considered in a historical perspective.

A few landmarks show the scope of the increase in the number of human beings. The world's population, having doubled in the previous 100 years, reached 2.5 billion in 1950. It will pass four billion in 1975. The net increase in the period from 1950 to 1975 will be almost twice the size of the population of the entire world in 1750.

It is instructive to trace this grand historic trend separately for the developed countries and the underdeveloped ones. To do so one must employ a fixed classification rather than one that shifts according to changes in the stage of development. The classification adopted here preserves broad continental boundaries relatively intact by grouping all Latin America with the underdeveloped countries and putting Australia and all Oceania with the developed countries. Three salient points emerge.

First, the rate of the world's population growth has been accelerating from less than .5 percent per year between 1750 and 1850 to 1.9 percent per year between 1950 and 1975 [*see illustration on page 108*]. Underlying these average figures, however, are sharply contrasting trends: from 1750 to 1850 the underdeveloped countries grew at an annual rate of .4 percent and the developed countries at a rate of .5 percent; from 1850 to 1950 the rates were respectively .6 and .9, and from 1950 to 1975 they were 2.3 and 1.1. Further detail would indicate a peak rate of 1.2 percent per year for the developed countries in the 1950's and a peak rate of 2.4 percent per year for underdeveloped countries during the past 10 years.

Second, the proportion of the world's population living in underdeveloped countries has undergone pronounced changes as a result of the shifting relative rates of growth. Taking the population of the world as 100 at successive dates, the following division is observed: in 1750 the underdeveloped countries had 75 and the developed countries 25; in 1850 the proportions were 73 and 27; in 1950 they were 66 and 34, and in 1975 they will be 73 and 27 again. In other words, a trend of long duration has been reversed in recent decades.

Third, both the acceleration of growth and the contrast between underdeveloped and developed countries are most striking in terms of absolute magnitudes. The average annual increase shows the following trend, expressed in millions of people: 1750 to 1850, three in the underdeveloped countries and 1.5 in the developed countries; 1850 to 1950, 7.5 and five, and 1950 to 1975, 50 and 10. Each year during the past quarter of a century a population as large as the population of France has been added to the underdeveloped world. The absolute yearly increase in the underdeveloped countries was five times as large as it was in the developed countries. In the underdeveloped countries the current annual increment is well over 60 million people.

Let us now examine the distribution and the main components of the remarkable growth in the underdeveloped world. A logical first step is to consider the underdeveloped countries by broad geographic regions and to break down the increase of population as a difference between births and deaths. (Net migratory balance, which is a potentially important element in population change, can safely be ignored at this level of analysis; its role as a factor affecting growth is negligible.)

The most striking fact that emerges from the comparative figures on current

RELIEF FIGURES in the photograph on the opposite page, made at a temple at Angkor Wat in Cambodia, reflect the high level of development that many countries now called underdeveloped attained when their populations were small. Demographic trends now absorb much of social energy and material that could be devoted to qualitative improvement.

population size is the numerical predominance of Asia's population in the world total [*see illustration on page 109*]. Underdeveloped Asia, which has a land mass smaller than Africa, contains almost 55 percent of the world's population. Of the somewhat fewer than 2.9 billion people in all the underdeveloped world some 75 percent live in Asia: 28 percent in China, 33 percent in South and West Asia and 14 percent in Southeast Asia. Latin America's share is 11 percent and Africa's is 14 percent.

The figures on births, deaths and the resulting natural increase, which are the components of population dynamics, also show a broadly similar regional balance. In fact, the current relative magnitudes of absolute population increase in the underdeveloped regions closely match the total population. Therefore growth rates are relatively uniform among the underdeveloped regions. The population of China is an exception: it

may be growing at a rate of 1.7 percent per year. The rates for the other four regions, however, fall within the remarkably narrow range of from 2.4 to 2.7 percent per year.

These figures are extraordinarily high, particularly if one considers that they are averages characterizing large continental populations. In spite of imprecisions in the underlying statistics there can be no doubt that the present rates are at or near their all-time high in each region, again with the possible exception of China. The implications of the figures for population trends in the years ahead, however, are not at all clear. Is growth still accelerating? If so, how fast and to what level? Are the rates of increase leveling off or even declining? If a decline is under way or imminent, how rapid is it likely to be?

Unfortunately the present state of knowledge allows no unequivocal answers to these questions, crucial though

the answers would be for a realistic assessment of the demographic future of the underdeveloped world and its social and economic prospects. The first steps toward an answer can be made on the relatively firm terrain of descriptive demography. Beyond that attempts at interpretation and prediction lead quickly to more speculative grounds.

A significant step toward understanding growth prospects in the underdeveloped world is the realization that the nearly identical growth rates of the major regions are the result of substantial compensating differences in birth and death rates. For example, in Latin America the number of births per 1,000 population (the crude birth rate) was 37 in the early 1970's, and the number of deaths per 1,000 population (the crude death rate) was 10, yielding an annual increase of 27 people per 1,000, or 2.7 percent. In Africa the similar growth rate of 2.6 percent resulted from much higher

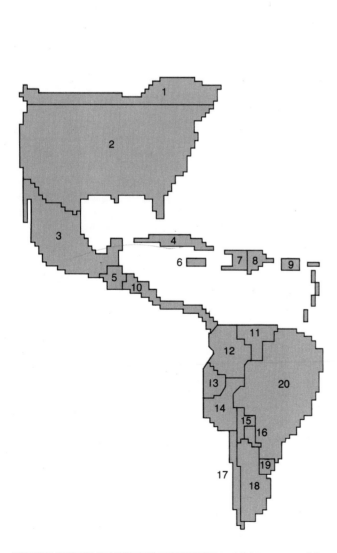
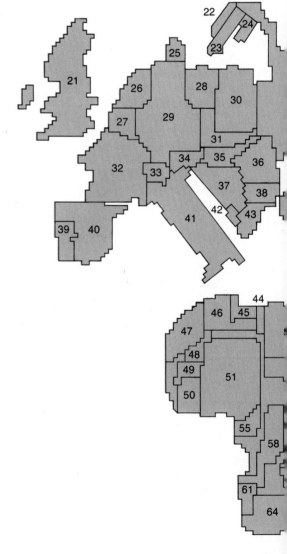

WORLD POPULATION DISTRIBUTION in 1974 is portrayed by countries in a scheme that makes the area of a region proportional to the size of its population while retaining the familiar geographic forms. As the jagged boundary lines suggest, the map is built up from small squares, each of which represents a population of 200,000. The proportional sizes of Europe and Asia, with the ex-

birth and death rates (46 and 20 respectively). Underdeveloped Asia outside China had a growth rate of 2.4 percent, resulting from a birth rate of 39 and a death rate of 15.

Given such contrasts even among the broad continental averages, it is not surprising that the national figures (from which the regional figures are built up) show a much greater variability. Even within the 10 largest countries of the underdeveloped world, which contain more than half of the world's population and more than 70 percent of the population of all underdeveloped countries, birth rates range from a low of 31 per 1,000 to a high of 49. Deaths vary from eight per 1,000 to 25. A broader sample of underdeveloped countries, which still excludes the smallest political units, extends the range of birth rates from the low 20's to about 50 and the range of death rates from five to nearly 30.

Demographers seek to sort out this

1. CANADA	36. ROMANIA	71. ISRAEL
2. U.S.	37. YUGOSLAVIA	72. SYRIA
3. MEXICO	38. BULGARIA	73. IRAQ
4. CUBA	39. PORTUGAL	74. SAUDI ARABIA
5. GUATEMALA	40. SPAIN	75. YEMEN
6. JAMAICA	41. ITALY	76. IRAN
7. HAITI	42. ALBANIA	77. AFGHANISTAN
8. DOMINICAN REPUBLIC	43. GREECE	78. PAKISTAN
9. PUERTO RICO	44. LIBYA	79. INDIA
10. CENTRAL AMERICA	45. TUNISIA	80. NEPAL
11. VENEZUELA	46. ALGERIA	81. SRI LANKA
12. COLOMBIA	47. MOROCCO	82. MONGOLIA
13. ECUADOR	48. MALI	83. CHINA
14. PERU	49. UPPER VOLTA	84. BANGLADESH
15. BOLIVIA	50. GHANA	85. BURMA
16. PARAGUAY	51. NIGERIA	86. THAILAND
17. CHILE	52. EGYPT	87. MALAYSIA
18. ARGENTINA	53. SUDAN	88. SINGAPORE
19. URUGUAY	54. ETHIOPIA	89. SUMATRA
20. BRAZIL	55. CAMEROON	90. JAVA
21. UNITED KINGDOM	56. UGANDA	91. REST OF INDONESIA
22. NORWAY	57. KENYA	92. LAOS
23. SWEDEN	58. ZAIRE	93. CAMBODIA
24. FINLAND	59. ZAMBIA	94. NORTH VIETNAM
25. DENMARK	60. TANZANIA	95. SOUTH VIETNAM
26. NETHERLANDS	61. ANGOLA	96. HONG KONG
27. BELGIUM	62. SOUTHERN RHODESIA	97. NORTH KOREA
28. EAST GERMANY	63. MOZAMBIQUE	98. SOUTH KOREA
29. WEST GERMANY	64. SOUTH AFRICA	99. JAPAN
30. POLAND	65. MALAGASY REPUBLIC	100. TAIWAN
31. CZECHOSLOVAKIA	66. MAURITIUS	101. PHILIPPINES
32. FRANCE	67. RÉUNION	102. ISLAND RESIDUALS
33. SWITZERLAND	68. U.S.S.R.	103. PAPUA NEW GUINEA
34. AUSTRIA	69. TURKEY	104. AUSTRALIA
35. HUNGARY	70. LEBANON	105. NEW ZEALAND

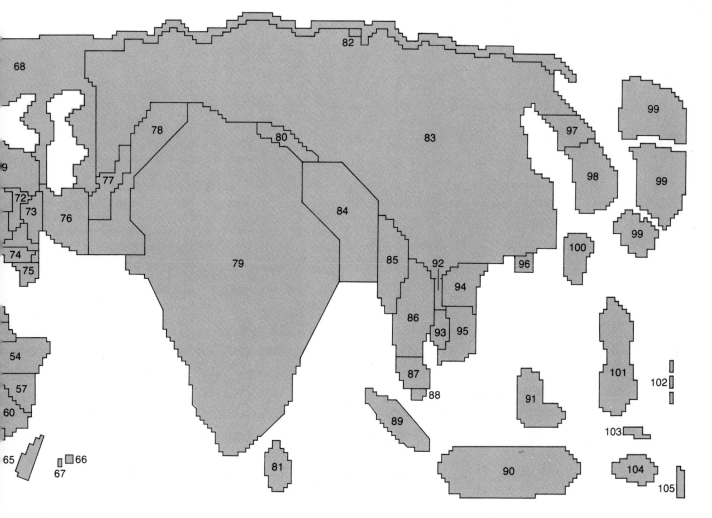

ception of Soviet Asia, are much greater in this map than in conventional maps because of the large populations in those regions. Africa and the Americas are smaller, reflecting the relatively low population densities in those continents. Several smaller countries in certain regions, such as Central America, are shown merged. The underdeveloped nations appear in color in the key to the map.

bewildering variation by means of the conceptual framework called the demographic transition. Niceties apart, the framework rests on two pillars of solid fact. First, mortality in premodern, preindustrial societies was high and so therefore were death rates. Populations that survived must necessarily have maintained high levels of fertility, that is, high birth rates. Second, in advanced industrial societies both mortality and fertility are low, without exception. The demographic transition is the process whereby societies move from the stage of high mortality and high fertility to the stage of low mortality and low fertility. All underdeveloped countries are now in such a transition. The wide differences in their birth and death rates show simply that they have traveled different distances along the route and that the relative timing and speed of their transitions in fertility and mortality are not uniform.

It seems clear that past distributions of birth and death rates for the underdeveloped areas were far more tightly clustered around their mean level than they are today. As recently as two decades ago the birth rates were with few exceptions in the range from 40 to 50 per 1,000. One can surmise that only a half-century earlier death rates below 30 per 1,000 must have been rare.

The difference in the time at which a loosening of the pretransition clusters of birth and death rates becomes manifest suggests another generalization that can be made about the demographic transition: The onset of the decline of fertility tends to follow the decline in mortality with a lag. Indeed, the spectacular acceleration of population growth in the modern era is largely a manifestation of the lag. The frequent references to "soaring" birth rates in popular interpretations of contemporary demographic changes in the underdeveloped world have little factual basis and in many instances no basis at all. Rapid population growth is mainly a result of falling death rates unaccompanied by adjustments in birth rates.

The underlying asymmetry in demographic behavior is readily understandable. Longer life is a universally recognized good. Mortality levels therefore closely reflect a society's capacity to control death. As that capacity increases mortality tends to fall.

The age-old attitude toward high fertility was always rather similar to the attitude toward longer life: high fertility was considered a blessing. The attitude may have stemmed from the necessity of coping with low rates of survival, but it was, and is, hardly rooted in that factor alone. Reducing fertility from traditional high levels that are buttressed by customs and social norms is not a process constrained only by what is feasible, as is the case with reducing mortality. Effective methods of fertility control have always been known and available in all societies. Fertility transition implies profound social changes rather than merely a change in technology.

What are the salient features of the transition that is transforming the demographic landscape in the underdeveloped world? Improvements in control over death, with periodic reverses, characterize the entire modern period. The phenomenon is emphasized by the fact that the total population of the underdeveloped countries nearly tripled between 1750 and 1950.

Such growth was much more rapid than was shown in the long-term trend before the era of intensive European contact and colonization. The growth appears to be attributable mainly to gradual (but not universal) improvements in levels of living resulting from improvements in economic organization, agricultural technology and transportation and distribution facilities. Recent decades have shown an often dramatic acceleration of the downward trend in mortality because of an increasing application of advances in the technology of health and environmental sanitation.

Although the impact of mortality on population growth is mediated by the crude death rate, the ratio of deaths to population is a poor index of mortality. The risk of dying is strongly influenced by age. The number of deaths in a population in any year is therefore a function not only of the overall mortality level but also of the age distribution.

To bypass this difficulty by presenting estimates for all ages separately is cumbersome. A more convenient measure of comparative levels of mortality, either over time or among different populations, is the expectation of life at birth. This measure is defined as the number

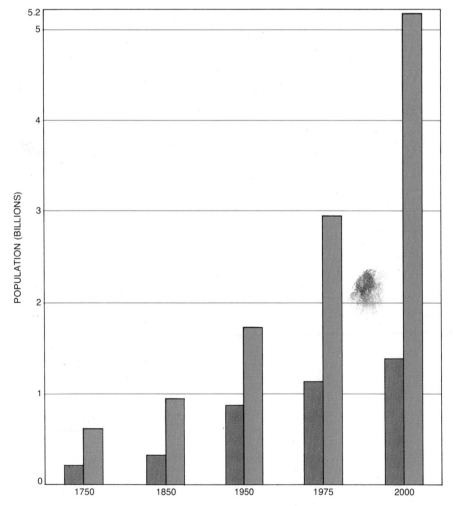

WORLD POPULATION INCREASE since 1750 is charted for developed countries (*gray*) and underdeveloped countries (*color*). Classification as developed or underdeveloped is according to economic and demographic differences now prevailing. Data for the year 2000 are based on a United Nations projection that assumes slowly ebbing growth rates.

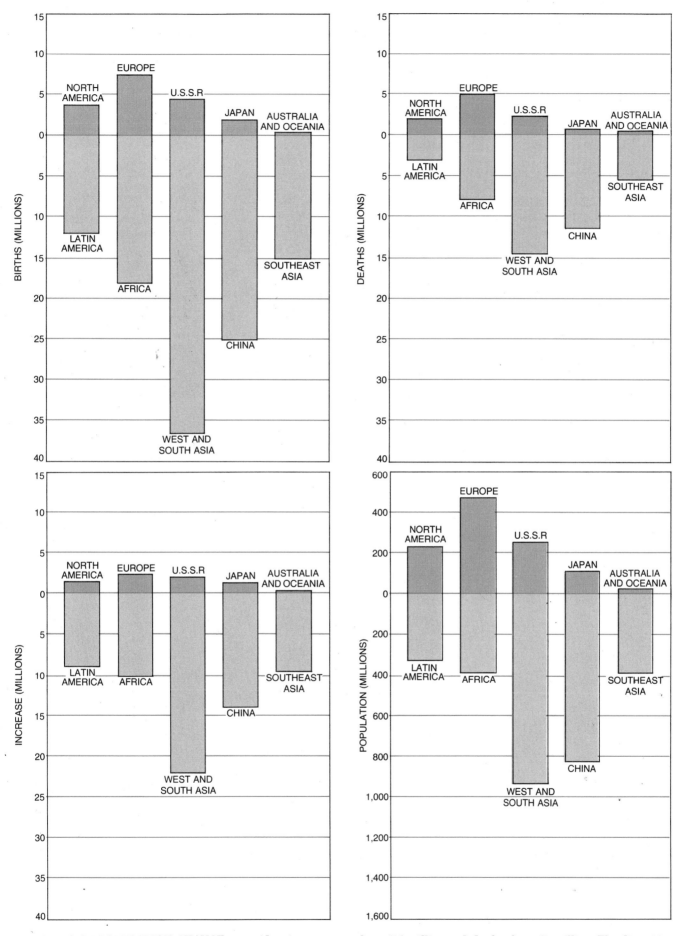

DYNAMICS OF POPULATION CHANGE are evident in a portrayal that puts the developed regions, which are mostly northerly, above the dividing line (*0*) and the underdeveloped regions below the line. The data are for 1974, during which births will total about 125 million and deaths about 52 million. The disparities between north and south are much greater in terms of such events than in terms of population size, reflecting the combined result of population size and the level of birth and death rates.

of years newborn children would live on the average if they were subjected during their entire life to the risk of dying at each age as observed in the year for which the index is constructed.

The pitfalls of attempting to compare levels of mortality by means of crude death rates are often anything but negligible. For example, the current death rate in Taiwan is five per 1,000 population and the expectation of life is somewhat less than 70 years. The current death rate in East Germany is 14 per 1,000, even though the expectation of life at birth exceeds 70 years.

As of early in the 1970's the expectation of life in underdeveloped countries was roughly 53 years. The figure represents the population-weighted average of the separate estimates for the more than 140 countries and territories that make up the underdeveloped world. In the developed countries the expectation

of life at birth was 71 years, which is close to the current level in the U.S.

Although the overall level of mortality in the underdeveloped countries is high in comparison with the level in the developed countries, it represents an extraordinary achievement by any other standard, most notably in relation to developmental status. It is a level that even in the leading European countries was not reached until the beginning of the 20th century. In the U.S. and much of Western Europe it was reached only during the period between the two world wars, and in the U.S.S.R. it was not reached until after World War II. The speed with which mortality has been reduced has also been much more rapid in the underdeveloped countries than it was in the developed ones.

Thus the historical relation of mortality level to developmental status, which was never excessively rigid, has

been substantially altered in the underdeveloped countries. The application of readily imported health technology provides the major explanation for the shift. It would be incorrect to assume, however, that the fundamental nature of the relation has also been modified. Both the willingness and the ability to apply the technology that will raise life expectancy still tend to reflect achieved levels of development [see top illustration on opposite page].

With the caution that prediction is risky, the following propositions that have a strong bearing on the prospects for population growth in the underdeveloped countries appear to be supported by the evidence. (1) Further substantial gains in longevity are likely to be achieved in most countries if per capita gains in consumption continue the upward course that has persisted since World War II. (2) A combination

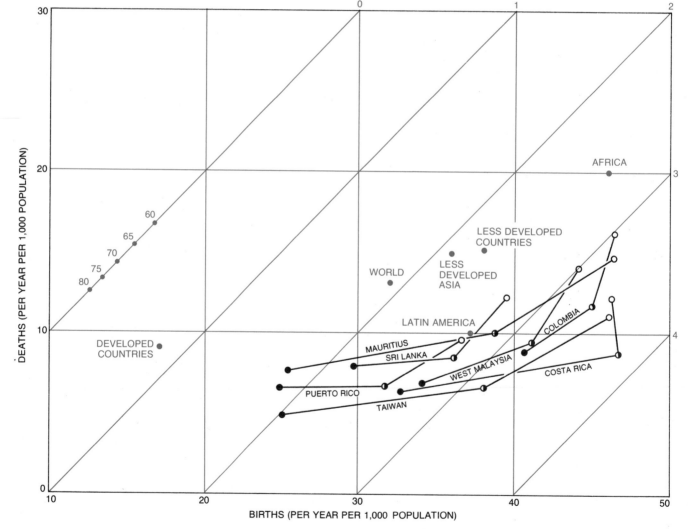

DEMOGRAPHIC TRANSITION of birth and death rates from high to low levels is charted for several countries on the basis of data for 1950–1952 (open circles), 1960–1962 (half-filled circles) and 1970–1972 (filled circles). For reference the chart also shows the level of current birth, death and growth rates for the world and for certain major regions. The diagonal colored grid repre-sents population growth rates ranging from 0 to 4 percent per year. Numbers on zero-growth line show eventual birth and death rates in a stationary population under varying assumptions about the expectation of life at birth, ranging from 60 to 80 years. A life ex-pectancy of 80 would entail stable birth and death rates of 12.5 per 1,000 population. For 60 the birth and death rates would be 16.7.

of moderate economic growth with a strong bias toward allocating resources to measures that reduce mortality, including particular attention to increasing the economic well-being of the poorest third of the population, could bring life expectancy in the underdeveloped countries close to 70 years by the end of the century.

The scope for further improvement in mortality is relatively modest in Latin America and in a number of countries elsewhere where fairly low levels of mortality have already been achieved, such as in Taiwan, Sri Lanka, Thailand, South Korea and Malaysia. The growth-generating potential is still high in much of Africa and, most significantly, in many of the countries with the largest populations, including India, Indonesia, Bangladesh, Pakistan, Egypt and probably China. Thus in many countries, including some of the most populous ones, the crest of the population wave may be yet to come, since initial fertility declines are unlikely to be strong enough to compensate for the effects of improving mortality. Where the wave will be ebbing, the deceleration for some time is likely to be held back by the still feasible gains in human survival.

The other crucial element (and most likely the deciding one) in the demographic equation is fertility. In the early 1970's the average birth rate in the underdeveloped world as a whole can be estimated as 38 per 1,000. Of the 37 countries with a population of 10 million or more in 1973 (representing some 90 percent of the total in terms of population size), 10 countries had birth rates below 40 per 1,000; in five of these the rates were between 35 and 40. In all underdeveloped countries with birth rates below 40 per 1,000 fertility has been declining, in some cases rapidly. It is possible that a decline is also under way in a number of the 27 countries with birth rates of 40 or more, although the inadequacy of the statistics makes the matter uncertain.

In trying to forecast the trend of fertility in these countries special interest attaches to the underdeveloped countries where a recent onset of fertility decline has been clearly established and where the tempo of the change can be measured with reasonable precision. Four countries among those with a population above 10 million are in this category: Taiwan, Sri Lanka, West Malaysia and Colombia. The pattern of their demographic transition during the past two decades is traced in the accompanying illustration [*opposite page*], together

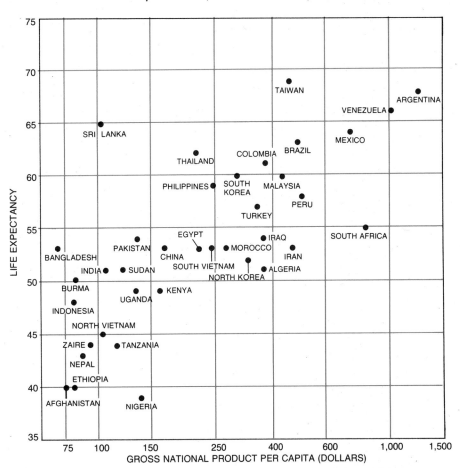

DEVELOPMENT LEVEL shows a relation to the expectation of life at birth. Here the life expectancy in the underdeveloped countries with a population of 10 million or more is plotted against average income per capita per year, shown on a logarithmic or ratio scale.

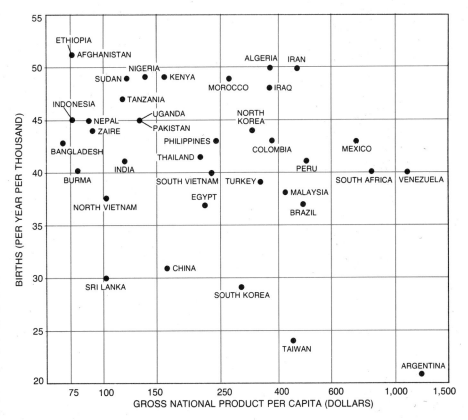

ABSENCE OF CLEAR RELATION appears between the birth rate and the level of development in the underdeveloped countries with more than 10 million population. Recent data suggest that a decline in birth rates has begun in a number of these nations.

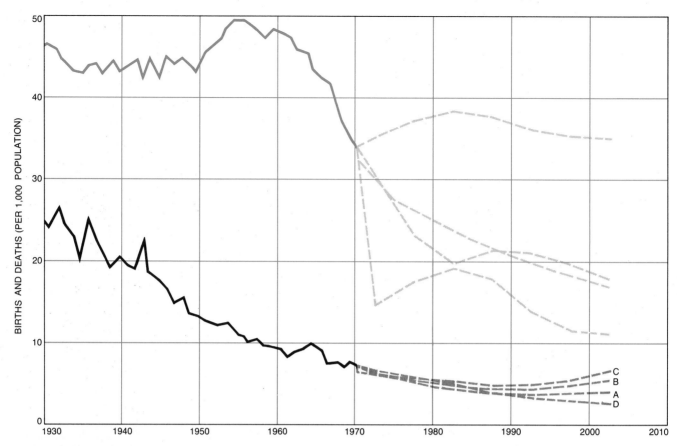

TYPICAL TRENDS in underdeveloped countries are exemplified by Costa Rica. Here the crude birth rate (*color*) and the crude death rate (*black*) are plotted from 1930 to 1970, with four projections from 1970 on. Projection *A* assumes that fertility remains at the 1970 level and *B* assumes a rapid fertility decline. *C* embodies the extreme assumption that after 1970 no parents have more than two children, and *D* assumes that the absolute number of births remains constant after 1970. Growth continues to the year 2000 under each assumption. The effects of the various possibilities on total population size appear in the illustration below.

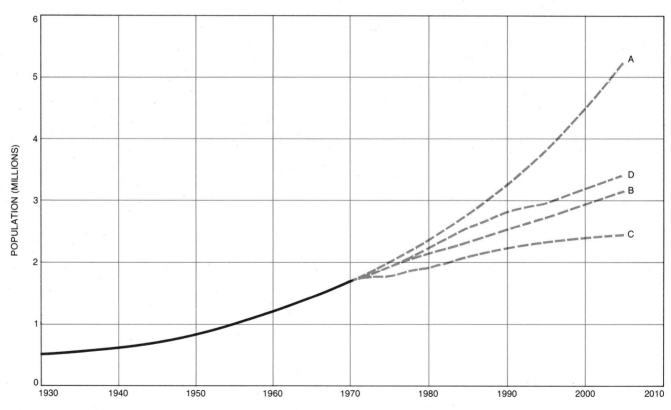

POPULATION TRENDS in Costa Rica from 1930 to 1970 and under varying assumptions from 1970 on are plotted. Assumption *A* implies a steady-state growth that would increase the population more than 22 times in a century. Assumptions *B* and *D* imply a population growth of zero by the year 2050, with the population respectively 2.1 and 2.5 percent larger than it is at present. Projection *C* implies a peak population in 2015 that would be 45 percent higher than the present population, with a steady decline thereafter.

with the pattern in three smaller countries (Mauritius, Costa Rica and Puerto Rico) that are broadly representative of a larger group, including notably Singapore, Barbados, Jamaica and Trinidad and Tobago.

The relative smallness of the population of the underdeveloped countries where substantial fertility declines can be documented and the numerous special economic, geographic and social features that characterize these populations should caution against generalizing from their experience as to the demographic prospects in the rest of the underdeveloped world. In fact, a clear lesson that emerges from an examination of contemporary demographic trends is that past transition experience gives only limited guidance in pinpointing the expected onset and the speed of the decline of birth rates.

This is not to suggest a lack of understanding of what causes such a decline. A significant drop in the birth rate can be explained persuasively by developmental changes that modify human behavior in such a way that the age of marriage tends to rise and the number of children per couple tends to fall. The developmental changes include increased schooling, greater social mobility, urbanization and increased participation of women in the labor force. In such circumstances the perception by couples of the cost and benefits of children may shift.

The behavioral motor force of the demographic transition can be summarized in a single sentence: In demographic matters, as in others, people tend to act in accordance with their interests as they best see them. What those interests are and how people see them are to a large extent determined by the objective environment. Nonetheless, the presence of a subjective component in the equation suggests the likelihood of varying fertility responses to broadly similar developmental circumstances, not only among individuals but also among countries. In particular, how changes in objective economic and social circumstances are reflected in the human consciousness may be powerfully affected by "cultural" factors. Thus, for example, what is seen as being "adequate" shelter, education or nutrition for one's children—a judgment that is bound to influence the level of fertility profoundly—is as much in the eye of the beholder as a matter objectively determined, at least above a critical minimum level. Indeed, the evidence shows that the response to similar changes in the

pattern of economic opportunities can differ greatly from population to population. Hence there is no reason to expect a close inverse relation between the level of fertility and any particular index of development, such as income per capita, or to assume that attainment of certain identifiable threshold values of development represents a generally valid precondition for achieving low fertility.

These considerations suggest that the potential range of variation in fertility trends among underdeveloped countries is wide. It is therefore of interest to explore the demographic implications of contrasting trends in fertility. At one extreme is the familiar upper-boundary assumption of continued high fertility with mortality approaching the level that has been achieved in the developed countries. The case need not be elaborated here—not necessarily because the assumption is implausible but because the implications of compound-interest growth are clear.

It is more interesting to examine trends that might be generated by exceptionally rapid and far-reaching patterns of transition in fertility. The calculations demonstrate that continued population growth is implied, even if fertility declines rapidly, whenever the demographic conditions resemble the ones in the underdeveloped countries. The conditions include an age distribution skewed toward the young, mortality that is relatively low or declining and high fertility or fertility that may have been declining but only over the past 10 years or so.

A typical example is Costa Rica [*see illustrations on opposite page*]. There the achievement as early as 1980 of a replacement-level fertility, that is, a level that, if it were maintained, would eventually generate "zero population growth," would not prevent the population from doubling within 50 years. At that time the population would still be growing at a rate of .5 percent per year.

An alternative and equally extreme assumption is that starting from the situation in 1970 no family would have more than two children. Such a fertility regime is drastically below replacement level; in the example illustrated it implies an eventual decrease of 23 percent between generations. Such is the momentum built into the existing age distribution, however, that growth would continue for more than four decades. The population in 2000 would be nearly 40 percent higher than in 1970. Although negative growth would set in by 2015, after extraordinary transformations in the age structure, the population in 2060

would still exceed the level observed in 1970.

Clearly an early stabilization of population through fertility decline, given typical conditions in an underdeveloped country, is an extremely remote possibility. The virtual certainty of continued rapid growth among the underdeveloped countries for many decades suggests that in most such countries a strong social interest should attach to the achievement of an exceptionally early and steep decline in fertility. This is not the place to review the economic arguments that lend force to the suggestion. It is enough to say that the arguments lead to the conclusion that rapid population growth results in a lower per capita income than is associated with lower rates of population growth.

One wonders therefore what the prospects are for an early and rapid decline in fertility in underdeveloped countries. Although a demographer can explain why fertility declines when it does and can specify conditions that are sufficient for fertility to decline, such knowledge does not add up to a useful predictive theory. The answer can therefore be at best only tentative.

Part of the answer is suggested by the likely course of development. Since a rapid growth of population slows down development, a high fertility (other things being equal) will delay the achievement of the objective conditions that make a decline in fertility possible. This relation could create a vicious circle in which poverty and high fertility sustain each other. Measured by most criteria, however, economic and social change in the underdeveloped countries during the past decades has on the average exceeded the rate of change in population size. If this difference persists (a somewhat optimistic assumption), it cannot fail to eventually create conditions that are more favorable to a decline in fertility. If the demographic response to development is similar to past patterns, however, the rate of progress in most instances will be too low to bring about a rapid completion of the demographic transition.

It is possible that the demographic response will not be the same as it has been in the past because of qualitative differences between contemporary development and past development and because of subjective factors. Decisions leading to lower fertility can be regarded as originating in two types of individual desire. One is to seize opportunities that open up in the process of development. Examples include the drive to acquire new consumer goods (epitomized by the bicycle-motorcycle-automobile sequence), the costs of which tend to outstrip rising incomes; the desire to expand a privately owned enterprise by acquiring capital goods; the desire to provide a better education and upbringing to children already born, and an interest in upward social mobility. The chance of success in such endeavors is often powerfully increased by restricting the size of one's family. The effect is reinforced by the decreasing economic benefit that parents derive from children as development progresses.

A second psychological factor that pulls in the same direction is the pervasive disinclination to accept a lowering of one's accustomed standard of living. Both of these motives played a role in past fertility transitions and now exert a downward influence on fertility in many underdeveloped countries. Moreover, it is likely that the exposure to consumer goods and styles of living that conflict with a large family is more intensive now than it was in the past.

The impact of such factors on fertility can be quite strong, particularly if at the same time the society's institutions allow access to social and occupational mobility, if the income distribution is sufficiently compressed so that in any social stratum imitating and catching up with the consumption patterns prevailing in the next-highest stratum appear to be realistic possibilities, and if existing social arrangements give wide scope to individual initiative in improving one's

economic and social status and impose much of the cost of improvement on those who benefit from it. Much of the rapid decline in fertility that has been documented so far in underdeveloped countries is explained by the fact that the countries involved had the kind of conditions I have described. Such conditions are increasingly present or are appearing in a number of other underdeveloped countries, thus holding out the prospect for a spontaneous and rapid fertility decline. In other countries, however, including probably those containing the majority of the population of the underdeveloped world, development-induced changes in the perceived costs and benefits of children to parents are unlikely to be strong enough to elicit a similar reaction in the foreseeable future. In such instances the grimmer alternative mechanism—resistance to a lowering of absolute levels of living due to adverse economic developments—may still play a catalytic role.

A new and possibly major element affecting demographic prospects is the scope of government activity in shaping economic and social development. In recent years the governments in many underdeveloped countries have introduced policies designed to hasten a decline in fertility. The step is without historical precedent.

The fundamental justification for intervention by a government in the choices that individual couples make on childbearing rests on what can be

termed spillover effects, meaning that the consequences of individual decisions on fertility are not fully borne by the people making them but impinge on the interest of others. In such situations it is at least possible that collective action arranged through the government can improve social welfare. Whether such a possibility does indeed exist must be tested through the accepted rules of collective decision making in any given society. As always, a clear diagnosis of a social problem is not enough; the available remedies may be deemed worse than the disease.

Up to now the practice of underdeveloped countries in the field of fertility policy has seemed to reflect both a desire to avoid measures that have high political costs and a lack of effective policy tools that promise to reduce fertility. Accordingly the main line of attack has been the introduction of family-planning programs, which help couples who already want to avoid having more children. Sound arguments exist for supporting the subsidized provision of family-planning services quite apart from demographic considerations. Indeed, access to modern methods of birth control is an element in social development. The power of family-planning programs to achieve more than limited demographic objectives, however, is questionable. Since people can be expected to find the means to control fertility if they want to, and since without such a desire the availability of inexpensive and effective contraceptive technology is inconse-

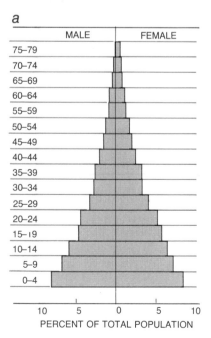

a

| MALE | FEMALE |

75–79
70–74
65–69
60–64
55–59
50–54
45–49
40–44
35–39
30–34
25–29
20–24
15–19
10–14
5–9
0–4

10   5   0   5   10
PERCENT OF TOTAL POPULATION

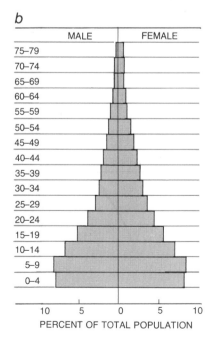

b

| MALE | FEMALE |

75–79
70–74
65–69
60–64
55–59
50–54
45–49
40–44
35–39
30–34
25–29
20–24
15–19
10–14
5–9
0–4

10   5   0   5   10
PERCENT OF TOTAL POPULATION

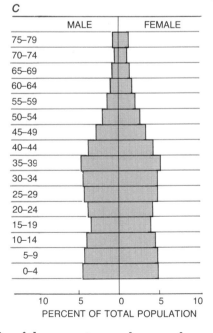

c

| MALE | FEMALE |

75–79
70–74
65–69
60–64
55–59
50–54
45–49
40–44
35–39
30–34
25–29
20–24
15–19
10–14
5–9
0–4

10   5   0   5   10
PERCENT OF TOTAL POPULATION

AGE DISTRIBUTION in Costa Rica is plotted and projected. In 1950 (a) it showed the pattern that still characterizes most underdeveloped countries. In 1970 (b) it was broadly similar, with more than 45 percent of the population under 15 and fewer than 5 percent aged 60 or more. The size of the youngest group, however, shows the onset of a decline in fertility. Intermediate age distributions that might be observed in the year 2000 are shown at c and d for two of the projections displayed in the illustrations on page 112,

quential, it is unlikely that family planning can do much more than accelerate a process that would occur in any case. Still, in most countries even this limited potential is far from having been exhausted.

In several countries family planning has been combined with another policy, which is often called population education. Apart from providing information, the policy seeks to modify desired family size by persuasion and by inculcating behavioral norms that are more in harmony with the collective interest. If the social costs of such an effort are deemed acceptable, and if the instruments for changing preferences can be perfected, population education may become a powerful device for achieving lower fertility. For the near future, however, its potential seems to be limited except in highly integrated societies with strong and respected leaders.

Beyond family planning and population education is one additional tool of policy with significant potential. It involves the modification of the objective signals that shape parental decisions on childbearing. A superficially appealing approach is to speed up the development process, since "development" does lead to lower fertility. This prescription, however, confuses ends and means. If it were not for dissatisfaction with the progress of the development process itself, the case for government interference with fertility would not arise in the first place. Such interference is a cost rather than an objective that is desirable in its own right.

A more realistic possibility is to rearrange developmental priorities in such a way as to strengthen the features of the socioeconomic fabric that help in reducing fertility. The rearrangement must be sufficient to provide a net positive return for the sacrifice of deviating from otherwise preferred developmental patterns. Two broad approaches can be described.

One strategy is to influence such factors as literacy, infant mortality, income distribution and the status of women, which in turn indirectly influence fertility choices. The obvious attraction of such a line of action is that it can promote policies that are also desirable on other grounds. Given the poor predictive power of existing fertility theory, however, it is doubtful that indirect effects alone would provide an adequate case for modifying social policies that would be adopted in the absence of the demographic argument.

The other strategy would operate directly on the costs borne and the benefits received by the people who make fertility decisions. The aim would be to eliminate or at least mitigate harmful spillover effects. Just as the system of national states largely decentralizes what is often referred to, rather misleadingly, as the world population problem (nations by and large reap the benefits and bear the costs of their demographic behavior), such a strategy in effect would seek to decentralize the national problem of finding the optimal pattern of fertility behavior to smaller units within the nation. The key element in the solution would require that the units be small enough so that informal decision making and flexible methods of bargaining on the desirable level of fertility would still be feasible. The individual family constitutes a plausible unit, but larger groups, such as village communities, are also possible candidates. If the signals on which such decentralized decisions are based correctly reflect the private and social costs of fertility, the outcome of the decisions could be accepted not only as an expression of individual or small-group preferences with which society has no reason to quarrel but also as being optimal for the society as a whole.

To transfer the burden of fertility to those generating it is, of course, not a costless policy. Nineteenth-century Europe practiced it to a significant degree, but most tendencies of social policy in underdeveloped countries go against the grain of the prescription. (China is an apparent exception, although the case is not well documented.) Nonetheless, if such a policy is combined with measures that soften its harshness but preserve its bite, it may provide the most humane and equitable solution to a problem with which the underdeveloped world should come to grips.

It is difficult to predict the extent to which an effective social technology for controlling population growth will be perfected and employed. As far as Latin America, Africa and the less populous nations of Asia are concerned, the most realistic guess is that they will muddle through a more or less classic (although probably accelerated) process of fertility transition in which pressures generated by "natural" development reduce fertility, and family-planning programs speed up the process somewhat. The forecast implies that the unprecedented population spurt now being experienced by those countries will continue through the 20th century. By the same token it implies a significant worsening of their long-term welfare prospects in comparison with what would have been possible with a different demographic picture.

It is less certain that such an option is still open to some of the largest countries in the southern half of Asia. There the costs of failing to achieve an early and dramatic reduction of fertility are likely to be prohibitively high. The increasing recognition of that fact may lead in the coming decades to solutions that do not now seem feasible.

namely projections *B* and *C* respectively. The markedly irregular shapes of these age distributions suggest the magnitude of the social and economic problems that might result from such rapid change. Sustained rapid population growth, however, would be harder to cope with. A stationary population, portrayed at *e*, could be achieved in about a century.

10

Food and Population

Food and Population

ROGER REVELLE

The earth and technology can probably provide food for a population of 40 to 50 billion. Increases in food production would help to create the conditions that would stabilize the population at a lower level

Inhabitants of the developed countries tend to forget that the preoccupation of most of mankind is obtaining enough food. The underdeveloped countries are engaged in a desperate race to keep food supplies growing at least as fast as population. In global terms the record of the period from 1951 to 1971 was reasonably successful. World production of cereal grains, the principal staples of the world food supply, more than doubled, whereas the world's population increased by less than 50 percent. Thus cereal supplies per person rose substantially, by about 40 percent, over the 20-year period. The increase was not, however, shared equally by the world's population. More than half of it was absorbed by the richest 30 percent of mankind and less than half was spread unevenly among the poorest 70 percent: the 2.6 billion people of Asia, Africa and Latin America. In these lands between 1953 and 1971 the volume of food produced barely kept ahead of population; it grew by 2.9 percent per year while population increased by 2.6 percent per year, for a net increase in per capita production of .3 percent per year. Even this small gain was inequitably distributed. Latin America fared best with a per capita annual gain of .9 percent. In the non-Communist countries of Asia the annual gain was only .2 percent. And in Africa the volume of food production per capita actually declined by about 1.1 percent over the 18-year period.

The situation deteriorated in 1972 and 1973. In large part because of droughts in India, Africa and elsewhere and poor weather in the U.S.S.R., combined with a rising consumption of beef in the developed countries, world grain reserves have fallen to their lowest levels in two decades, equal to only about a 27-day supply. At the same time the rise in petroleum prices has created a worldwide shortage of nitrogen fertilizers and has lessened the ability of farmers in the underdeveloped countries to pump water for irrigation.

The U.S., the leading exporter of food for the rest of the world, has brought all its idle cropland into production, and unless serious droughts continue it will have larger crops over the next few years than it had in 1973. Most of the surplus, however, will be sold to the other developed countries at prices the underdeveloped ones cannot afford; at the same time food-aid shipments are being reduced. Mankind may be coming closer to a precipice where mass starvation occurs whenever drought or plant disease results in below-average crop production.

There is no simple and dramatic formula for drawing back from the precipice. An obvious, difficult but in the long run absolutely essential step is to reduce rates of population growth. Meanwhile food supplies can be increased through three lines of action: in the short run, creation of a world food bank; in the long run, modernization of agriculture

in the underdeveloped countries, and finally a sharp intensification of agricultural and food research.

Six hundred years ago the eminently practical Chinese officially recognized the close connection between food and population. T'ai Tsu, the first Ming emperor, decreed that a sacred Yellow Register be compiled every 10 years, giving the number of households in each district and the number of "mouths" to be fed in each household. A placard, called Hu T'ieh, was posted on the household gate, and the family was obliged to mark on it the number of mouths inside the gate. The census takers then simply counted the mouths recorded on the placards, enabling the emperor's men to estimate the amount of food required for each district.

The relation between population size and the need for food appears obvious: the larger the population is, the larger must be the total quantity of food. The relation is not simple, however. Human beings can survive on much less than an optimum amount of food, and even adequately nourished populations of the same size may use vastly different quantities of edible plant materials. Apparently few peoples anywhere and at any time have allowed themselves to live very long at the Malthusian level of "bare subsistence," if by that term we mean a food supply just sufficient to sustain life, obtained by the maximum work effort the population can exert.

In many respects food is more directly related to the quality of the population than to its size. Unless there is an extreme shortage most adult human beings do not die from an inadequate amount of food, although their vitality and health and their ability to work and play may be greatly diminished. Mortality among undernourished infants and young chil-

"THE THIN KITCHEN" AND "THE FAT KITCHEN," the two engravings made by Pieter Brueghel the Elder on the opposite page, depict the two extremes of human nutrition. The engravings, done by Brueghel in 1563, were accompanied by doggerel in French and Flemish. Freely translated, the verse with *The Thin Kitchen* reads: "Where Thin Man's cook there's meager fare and lots of diet trouble. / Fat kitchen is the place for me; I'm going there on the double." The verse with *The Fat Kitchen* is: "Beat it, Thin Man. Though you are hungry, you are wrong. / This is Fat Kitchen here, and here you don't belong." The prints from which reproductions were made are in the Metropolitan Museum of Art.

dren is relatively high, but the effects on the survivors are more serious for society. Such children are more susceptible to the diseases of childhood and the crippling aftereffects, and both their physical and mental development are stunted.

Some undernourished children are permanently blinded; others are apathetic and hard to educate. Populations that have lived for many generations on meager diets are usually light in weight and small in stature. The average Bengali man weighs 45 kilograms (100 pounds), about the same as a jockey.

As my colleague Rose E. Frisch has shown, nutrition may be related to human reproductive ability. Menarche (the age of first menstruation) is delayed in undernourished girls, and the age of adolescent sterility is prolonged. Severely undernourished women apparently menstruate only irregularly, if at all; undernourished nursing mothers do not menstruate or ovulate for many months after giving birth. Undernourished pregnant women are more likely to suffer a spontaneous abortion than well-nourished ones.

The life expectancy of young children is lowered by the combination of undernutrition and infection that prevails in many underdeveloped countries, whereas in the developed countries the life expectancy of adults is probably reduced by the high content of animal fat in their diet and by overeating.

Human physiological requirements for food are directly related to body weight, sex, age, level of physical activity and ability to absorb the food eaten. Men are heavier than women, and their metabolic rate per kilogram of body weight is higher. Hence they require, on the average, nearly 40 percent more food energy than women. Growing, active children require more food per kilogram of body weight than adults. Although a seven-year-old child weighs only two-fifths as much as an adult, he needs 70 percent as much food. Seventy-year-old men and women require only about 70 percent as much food energy as 20-year-olds. Because healthy adult Bengalis are much smaller than average American men and women, they require only about 75 percent as many kilocalories per day. (The "calorie" of nutritional parlance is actually a kilocalorie.) The U.S. average is 2,700 kilocalories per day. With their high proportion of children the people of Bangladesh would require fewer than 1,800 kilocalories per day, if they were able to absorb as much of their food intake as the average American or European does. The fact is that many people in Bangladesh suffer from damage to the intestinal walls caused by parasites and infection, and as a result they are unable to absorb all the food they eat. Hence their average daily

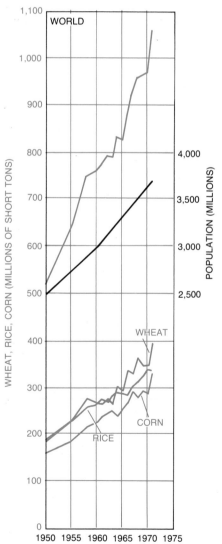

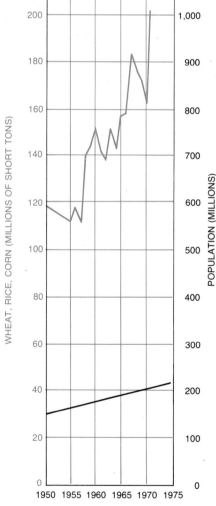

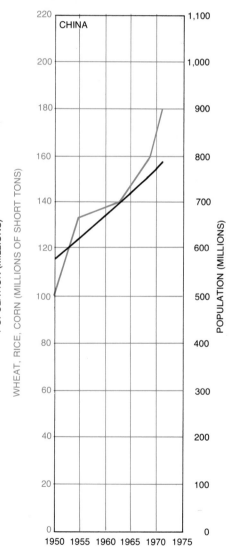

WORLD PRODUCTION of wheat, rice and corn (*top curve*) doubled between 1951 and 1971, whereas population (*black*) increased by less than 50 percent. Individual production of wheat, rice and corn is also shown.

U.S. AND CHINESE PRODUCTION of wheat, rice and corn are roughly comparable. Whereas virtually all the Chinese harvest is consumed directly by some 800 million humans, more than 60 percent of the U.S. grain output is required to feed 120 million head of cattle plus a huge population of hogs, sheep, chickens and other livestock, which yield only about one unit of food energy for humans for every four to seven units of caloric intake.

requirement for a normal level of physical activity is probably closer to 2,000 kilocalories.

Future physiological food requirements can be expected to rise faster than population size in the less developed countries, provided that diets can be improved. Better-nourished children will grow faster and larger. (In Japan since World War II the average weight of 15-year-olds has increased by three kilograms per decade.) And as birth rates come down the proportion of children to adults will diminish.

In discussing food we need to distinguish three terms: physiological requirements, demand and supply. Physiological requirements for calories, protein, vitamins and minor nutrients must be taken into account in the computation of the food supplies needed by different countries of the world. These requirements should not, however, be confused with the food demand of a given population, that is, the quality and quantity of the food actually consumed. This demand depends on food prices and on average incomes as well as on the size of the population. If the incomes of the majority rise faster than food prices in low-income countries, where many people are undernourished, the volume of the food demand per person will increase; conversely, if food prices rise faster than incomes, the demand will decrease even to a level where the diet of most poor people does not meet their normal physiological requirements.

The world demand for edible crops and animal products was about 2.6 billion tons in 1970, equal to nearly half the tonnage of all fossil fuels consumed that year and four times the weight of world steel production. The Food and Agriculture Organization of the United Nations (FAO) has estimated that world consumption will rise 40 percent by 1985, to 3.7 billion tons per year. For both years this works out to an average for the world's human population of about two kilograms (4.4 pounds) per person per day. Nearly half of the total tonnage of crops and three-fourths of the energy and protein content is in wheat, rice, maize and other cereal grains. A large fraction of these grains is eaten by domestic animals.

In high-income countries rising incomes or falling prices increase the demand for higher-quality, higher-priced food, although demand for total food calories at the individual level may not rise. The increase in food demand, expressed in money terms, is a small fraction, however, of the rise in incomes. In the U.S., for example, where we spend only about 13 percent of our disposable income on food for household use, a $1 increase in income will result in an additional expenditure on food of less than 13 cents at the supermarket, and the farmer will receive only about four cents more. In India the average person spends between 60 and 90 percent of his income on food, and a one-rupee rise in his income can correspond to an additional .7 rupee for food.

The discrepancy between developed and underdeveloped countries in the fraction of income spent on food reflects Adam Smith's insight that "the rich man consumes no more food than his poor neighbor. In quality, it may be very different, and to select and prepare it may require more labor and art, but in quantity it is very nearly the same.... The desire for food is limited in every man by the narrow capacity of the stomach."

In spite of their limited stomachs and low rates of population growth, all the developed countries have managed over the past 20 years to increase their food demands rapidly and substantially, in terms of both food costs and pressures on the volume of world crop production, by changing the character of their diet. With their rapidly rising incomes the Japanese have been eating more beef and less rice; similarly, Europeans are relying much less on cereals and potatoes to fill their stomachs and much more on meat, particularly beef. The consumption of beef per person in the U.S. more than doubled between 1940 and 1972, and total meat consumption per person increased by a third.

Although the average citizen of the developed countries spends a relatively small fraction of his income on food, that is a great deal more in absolute terms than the expenditure of the average Asian, African or Latin American. Compare the U.S. and India, the world's fourth- and second-largest countries in population size. Average household food supplies in the U.S. cost about $600 per person per year, whereas the value of the average Indian's diet is probably less than $45. Two-thirds of the cost of the American diet is for transportation, processing, packaging and marketing. Hence the value at the farm gate is about $200 per capita, still between four and five times the farm value of the Indian diet. For this difference in cost the American obtains about 50 percent more calories and protein and nearly seven times as much fat [*see illustrations on pages 124 and 125*]. He also eats between two and three times the quantity of green vegetables, four times as much fruit, nearly four times as much sugar and syrup but only about 40 percent the weight of ce-

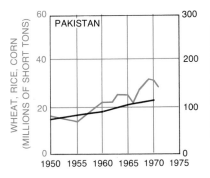

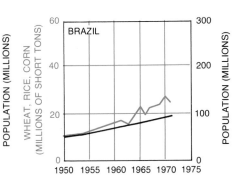

HARVESTS IN INDIA, PAKISTAN AND BRAZIL are compared with the population of each country. The fact that the Indian curve for wheat, rice and corn lies below the curve for population means the per capita production of these cereals is lower in India than it is in Pakistan and Brazil. India, however, has been raising its output rapidly. Since 1951 India has increased the area of land under cultivation by 20 percent, doubled the irrigated area and raised fertilizer use about thirtyfold. (India uses one-sixth as much fertilizer as the U.S.) The annual Indian harvest of rice, corn and wheat has been increased respectively by 105, 265 and 340 percent.

reals. He gets most of his protein and fat from meat (including fish), eggs and milk products, whereas most of the Indian's protein and 40 percent of his fat come from cereals, legumes and nuts. The average Indian's diet just about meets his physiological requirements of 2,100 kilocalories per day, whereas the food going into the average American's household exceeds his energy requirements by 20 percent. A large part of this excess is fat discarded in cooking and on the plate.

In terms of the world's food demand, the most important difference between American and Indian diets is the high proportion of meat, milk and other animal products in the American diet. Cattle, sheep and hogs require about seven calories of plant products for each calorie of protein and fat in meat. Chickens and cows eat about 4.5 calories of plant material per calorie contained in the eggs and milk they produce. Most of the plant calories eaten by domestic animals in the U.S. could also be eaten by human beings, so that Americans actually use, directly or indirectly, close to 10,000 kilocalories of humanly edible plant products per person per day. The average Indian feeds his domestic animals largely on humanly inedible materials,

and this, together with his low intake of meat, eggs and milk, means that he uses about 2,300 kilocalories of edible plant calories per day. In terms of the farm value of plant calories on the world market the cost per calorie of the average American diet is about the same as that of the average Indian diet.

In most underdeveloped countries there is a marked disparity in incomes between a few relatively well-off people and the great mass of the poor. Yet the poor, because of their numbers, consume most of the food. A rise in per capita incomes, resulting largely from an increase in the incomes of the well-to-do, will bring little increase in food demand for the country as a whole.

Between 1953 and 1971 the average volume of food consumption per capita in Africa, Latin America and the non-Communist countries of Asia, according to FAO estimates based on food production in those countries, grew by .3 percent per year. In the same period the average per capita incomes for the underdeveloped world (again omitting the Communist countries of Asia) rose 1.85 percent per year, ranging from 2.4 percent in Latin America to 1.8 percent in Asia and 1.5 percent in Africa. Only

about 16 percent of the average increase in per capita income was reflected in the increased volume of per capita food consumption estimated by the FAO, less than would be expected considering that the peoples of these countries typically spend 50 percent or more of their income on food.

Part of the discrepancy can be explained by uncertainties in the data and by the neglect of food imports in the FAO estimates of the volume of food consumed. Three other possible explanations could account for the remainder. First, there was probably some change from lower-priced to higher-priced foods in the diet of the people in the underdeveloped countries as their per capita income rose. Second, even without a change in diet the real cost per ton of food production may have risen. Finally, the rise in per capita income may have been unevenly distributed, with a small group of relatively well-off people getting most of it. The already well-off would not be expected to spend much of their additional income on food. The last explanation receives some support from the estimate by the FAO that food consumption per person rose two or three times as fast in the Asian Communist countries, which presumably have a nar-

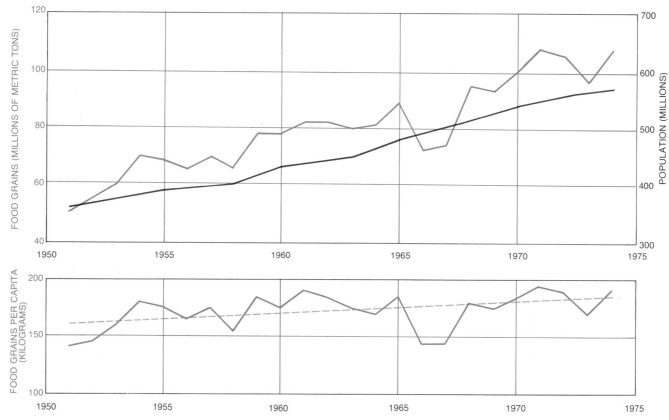

PRODUCTION OF ALL FOOD GRAINS IN INDIA (*colored curve in top graph*) has been moving upward, with some setbacks, for more than 20 years. In this illustration "food grains" includes millet, sorghum and the various legumes, such as beans, peas and peanuts, in addition to wheat, rice and corn. Together these foods supply more than 80 percent of the calories in the Indian diet. Since 1951 the annual per capita production of all food grains has increased by about 16 percent (*broken curve at bottom*). Perhaps more important, the Indian diet today contains a higher fraction of the grains that people prefer to eat than it did some 20 years ago.

rower range of incomes than the market-economy countries of Asia.

The total world food supply over a period of years depends largely on the crops and animal products produced by the world's farmers and to a much lesser extent on the world fish catch, but the supply in any individual country in a given year depends both on its agricultural and fish production and on the food reserves saved from previous years, together with its imports or exports of food. No country and no region in the modern world, except possibly some of the interior areas of New Guinea, is self-sufficient in food.

As we have seen, the worldwide doubling of cereal-grain production between 1951 and 1971 was divided nearly equally between the 1.1 billion people of the developed countries (Europe, North America, Oceania, the U.S.S.R. and Japan) and the 2.6 billion people of the underdeveloped countries (Asia, Africa and Latin America). Both groups of countries in 1970 produced approximately 600 million tons of cereals, but since the underdeveloped countries had a much larger population, their production per person was only about 40 percent of that in the developed countries. By the same token because the rate of population growth was more than twice as high in the underdeveloped countries the rate of increase of cereal production per person was far smaller.

There is a feedback relationship between food supply and demand in most of the underdeveloped countries. Since their economies are overwhelmingly agricultural, an increase in agricultural production that benefits the mass of the rural population will increase their real incomes and hence their demand for food.

The small production per head of staple food crops in the underdeveloped countries condemns most people to a monotonous, low-quality diet, consisting mainly of cereal grains or tubers and other starchy roots. For the poorest 20 percent of the population the diet falls below the physiological requirement for a normally active, healthy person. Low levels of production also cause food demand to tend to outrun supply in the underdeveloped countries. They are unable to produce much of a surplus of supply over demand in good years, which could be used as a reserve for lean years. As a result they are extremely vulnerable to fluctuations in weather conditions. That vulnerability is increased by the high sensitivity of traditional agriculture to the weather.

	MILLIONS OF KILOCALORIES (PER HECTARE)	(PER TON OF FOOD GRAINS)	RATIO OF MECHANICAL ENERGY USED TO FOOD ENERGY PRODUCED
IRRIGATION FROM WELLS	3.75	.585	.167
CHEMICAL FERTILIZERS	3.01	.469	.134
HIGH-YIELDING SEEDS	.15	.023	.002
PLANT PROTECTION	.05	.008	.002
FARM TOOLS AND MACHINERY	1.05	.164	.047
FUEL FOR MACHINERY	1.97	.311	.089
FUEL FOR DRYING CROPS	.30	.047	.013
TRANSPORTATION	.18	.028	.008
STORAGE AND MARKETING	.05	.008	.002
FOOD PROCESSING	1.25	.195	.056
TOTALS:	11.76	1.838	.525

FOOD-ENERGY YIELD V. MECHANICAL-ENERGY USE for a modernized, irrigated farming and food-processing system in India has been estimated by the author. The energy for food preparation in the home is not included. The table assumes a harvest of 6.4 tons of food grains per hectare (roughly 2.5 acres), equivalent to the average harvest of corn in Iowa. At present the average Indian farmer produces only about a ton of wheat or rice per hectare. Irrigation and fertilizers together account for about 65 percent of the energy that would be required directly on the farms to bring about the sixfold increase in yield.

During most of the past two decades the underdeveloped countries have been able to tide themselves over bad years, and to stretch their supplies in good years, by drawing from the surplus stocks of some of the developed countries, particularly the U.S. Before World War II the underdeveloped countries as a whole were net exporters of cereals, but they have since become net importers. Between 1949 and 1972 their gross imports of cereals rose from 12.4 million tons to 36 million. Before 1972 between a third and a half of this tonnage was obtained under U.S. and other food-aid programs. Although food aid has been justifiably criticized because it tended to hold back badly needed agricultural investments and incentives to farmers, there can be no doubt that it contributed substantially to the increase in per capita food supplies in the underdeveloped countries, and thus to the improved living conditions that were reflected in the dramatic rise in life expectancy of between five and 10 years per decade in many countries. Then in 1972 there was a crisis, and its effects still persist.

Food demand in the poor countries tends to be relatively insensitive to food prices because the need for food is the most urgent of all human needs. When food prices rise, poor families must forgo other wants in order to obtain food. At the same time if food reserves are low, the supply cannot be increased much during any given crop year by raising prices to provide greater incentives to the farmers. In the developed countries the same short-run constraints operate on supply; moreover, food expenditures are such a small part of total income that rising prices may have a relatively small effect on demand. Hence a slight decrease in world food supplies is likely to cause a sharp rise in prices.

Exactly this process operated during the crop year of 1972–1973. Droughts and poor weather conditions caused a drop in total world cereal production for the first time in more than 20 years. The decline from the 1971–1972 crop year was actually only 35 million tons, or less than 3 percent. Demand, however, continued to increase, partly because of the inexorably continuing rise in the world population and partly because of the continuing increase in meat consumption, particularly beef consumption in Europe, the U.S.S.R. and Japan. The world production of cereals, currently totaling about 1.2 billion tons, has to increase between 25 and 30 million tons per year if the rising demand is to be met. Thus the real shortfall in 1972–1973 was nearly 60 million tons, or roughly 5 percent. World cereal reserves have been drawn down to a dangerously low level, a supply of less than 30 days in the spring of 1974, and cereal prices rose steeply in 1972 and 1973. By December, 1973, the price of Thai rice was nearly four times the 1971 price and the price of wheat for export was more than three times as high. With the drawing down of reserves through export sales to the U.S.S.R., Japan and Western Europe, food-aid shipments from the U.S. and other rich countries were sharply reduced. The unprecedentedly high prices have been particularly hard on the poorer classes of the underdeveloped countries. Since 1973 the poor countries have been struck another heavy blow. The drastic increase in world oil prices not only has raised the cost of pumping ground water for irrigation but also has raised the cost of nitrogen fertilizer, which was already in short supply.

Many people have suggested that in order to avoid a repetition of the 1972–1973 situation there should be created an internationally managed world food bank, from which supplies in the underdeveloped countries could be augmented during years of poor crop production due to bad weather, insect plagues or widespread plant disease. Such a world food reserve would need to be operated carefully to avoid the undesirable effects of food aid in holding back agricultural improvements in the underdeveloped countries and to keep from unduly depressing farm prices. Without attempting to specify the characteristics of a world food bank in detail, it is possible to point out that such a bank should have several components: stores

of wheat and other cereals and of soybeans and other legumes; stores of fertilizers to enable crop production to expand quickly; reserves of land that can be put under the plow in emergencies; a store of information and technology that can be used to increase crop yields, and stores of crop genes to make it possible for seeds of new varieties to be quickly multiplied when the old varieties are stricken by pests or plant disease.

To even out the fluctuations in world production of cereals and legumes the capacity of the world food bank would have to be high, perhaps of the order of 5 percent of the average yearly production, worth at present prices between $10 billion and $15 billion. For example, from 1962 to 1966 there was a run of poor years in the world production of wheat, rice and maize, giving rise to a cumulative departure from the production trend line of 80 million tons by 1966, even though the total production of these major cereals rose from 790 million to 885 million tons over the five-year period.

Establishing a well-managed world food bank during the next three or four years could be helpful to farmers in the principal exporting countries. With nor-

mal weather the U.S. can expect a succession of bumper crops, with a resulting heavy downward pressure on prices. The prospect of wild price gyrations is made grimmer by the possibility of a recession in Europe and Japan resulting from inflated petroleum prices.

In the long run the solutions for the underdeveloped countries must be twofold: as fast a reduction as possible in their rates of population growth and a sharp upward turn in the trend of agricultural production. If a rapid and continuing increase in production can be directed toward a marked improvement in the lives of the poor rural masses, one of the essential conditions for lowering human fertility will be attained.

The physical possibilities for increasing agricultural production are great, in terms both of natural resources and of agricultural technology. When Thomas Malthus announced in 1798 his famous "Principle of Population" (that human populations were limited by the food supply because they grew "geometrically" whereas food production could be increased only "arithmetically"), he thought that the resources available for agriculture were primarily land, water and human and animal labor. For most

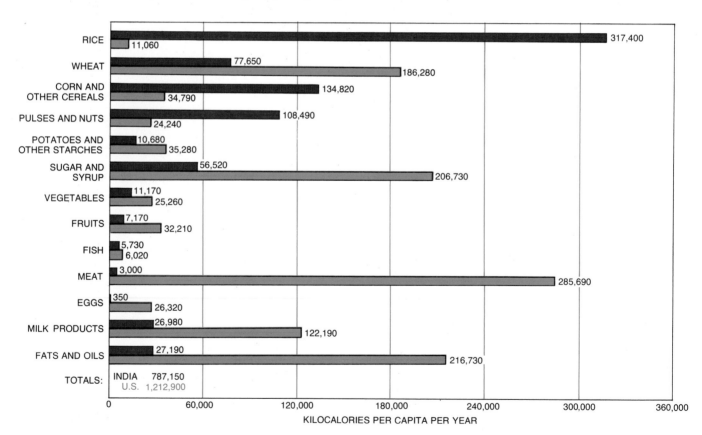

INDIAN AND U.S. "KITCHENS" are compared above and on the opposite page: gray bars for India, colored bars for the U.S. Whereas cereals, pulses and nuts supply 81 percent of the kilocalories in the average Indian diet, they supply barely 21 percent of the kilocalories in the average American diet. Meat, eggs and milk products supply 36 percent of the food energy in the U.S. diet (v. 4 percent in the Indian diet); sugar, syrup, fats and oils supply another 35 percent of the food energy in U.S. diet (v. 11 percent in the Indian diet). The "thin" Indian kitchen provides an average daily supply of 2,150 kilocalories per person, almost all of it consumed, whereas the "fat" U.S. kitchen supplies 3,300 kilocalories per person per day, of which roughly 600 are discarded or are left on the plate.

of the world that is still true. For human beings in the developed countries, however, agriculture and the procurement of food have decade by decade become progressively smaller components of the total economic activity. Today household food expenditures in the U.S. take less than 13 percent of disposable personal income in spite of an extravagant diet, and of this small amount the farmer receives only about a third. The transformation has been brought about mainly by the large-scale application in agriculture of two resources of which Malthus was hardly aware: mechanical energy from fossil fuels, and scientific and technical knowledge.

Mechanical energy is used, for example, in manufacturing and operating tractors and other farm equipment, making and applying fertilizers, pesticides and other farm chemicals, pumping water for irrigation and transporting the inputs and products of agriculture to and from the farm. The applications of science and technology to agriculture are equally diverse, from establishing the physics and chemistry of water and soils and the genetics, physiology and pathology of crop plants and domestic animals to the practical control of in-

sects, the engineering design of irrigation and drainage systems and the economic analysis of the alternative uses of agricultural resources.

To underscore the vast changes brought about by the new agriculture, let us compare the actual cultivated area on the earth with the area of farmland that would be needed to feed the present population if modern agricultural technology were used everywhere. The average harvest of corn in Iowa is about 100 bushels per acre, or 6.4 tons per hectare, corresponding to 60,000 kilocalories per day, enough to feed 24 people at a level of 2,500 kilocalories per day per person. With a present world population of 3.8 billion people, 158 million hectares would be required, assuming only one crop per year. Yet for the world as a whole at the present time 1.4 billion hectares are cultivated. This works out to one hectare of farmland for every 2.7 living people.

Several reasons explain why the actual cultivated land per person is nearly 10 times the hypothetical minimum. To begin with, the land actually harvested during any particular year is only about half to two-thirds of the total cultivated

land. The remainder is temporarily left fallow or used as meadowland for mowing or pastures or is not cropped for some other reason. When chemical fertilizers are not applied, much farmland must lie fallow for a year or more to recover its fertility. About 10 percent of the cropped area is devoted to raising nonfood crops: cotton, tobacco, rubber, coffee, tea, jute and so on. Another large fraction is needed to produce food for livestock and poultry. Some of the livestock are used as draft animals on farms. The products from the rest, including butter, eggs, milk and meat, are eaten by human beings. From a human standpoint domestic animals are only from 14 to 23 percent efficient, that is, they use from four to seven times as much food energy as the energy contained in their edible products. In addition from 10 to 20 percent of the food crops are destroyed by pests, and a small percentage is required for seed. The principal reason, however, 1.4 billion hectares of land now have to be cultivated is the low level of agricultural technology in most of the world. Instead of the more than six metric tons of cereal grain per cropped hectare that is obtained in high-technology farming, the average Indian or Pakistani

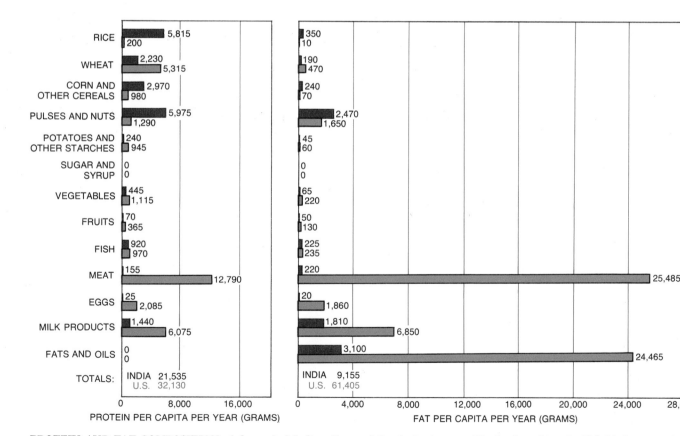

PROTEIN AND FAT COMPOSITION of the typical Indian diet (*gray*) and the typical American diet (*color*) exhibit striking contrasts. In these two charts the scales are adjusted to reflect the fact that fats provide about nine kilocalories per gram, whereas proteins supply only about five kilocalories per gram. Thus the two bars showing the protein and fat in meat equal in length the bar for kilocalories in meat. The food reaching the U.S. kitchen contains only about 50 percent more protein but nearly seven times as much fat as enters the Indian kitchen. Indians obtain 88 percent of their protein from vegetable sources and only 12 percent from animal sources, whereas Americans obtain 68 percent of their protein from animal sources and only 32 percent from vegetable sources.

farmer produces only about a ton of wheat or rice.

Because of the dispersed nature of solar energy and the low efficiency of photosynthetic energy conversion (about .4 percent in terms of human food energy) arable land remains a primary resource for agriculture. Large areas of the earth's surface are not now cultivated but could be if farmers and the necessary capital for development were available. The potentially arable area is limited by climate (the land must be free of frost during the growing season), the physical characteristics of the land surface and the water supply. Water must be available during the growing season in amounts approximately equal to or greater than the evaporation from the soil and the transpiration from plants.

In a 1967 report, *The World Food Problem,* President Johnson's Science Advisory Committee estimated that the world area of potentially arable land is 3.2 billion hectares. That is 24 percent of the land area of the earth, about 2.3 times the currently cultivated area and more than three times the area actually harvested in any given year. Unfortunately 500 million hectares of this total are in the humid Tropics, where precipitation exceeds evaporation throughout the year and no technology is currently available for intensive crop production (except in a few regions such as Java, where there are very deep volcanic soils). Crops could be grown on another 300 million hectares if water were available for irrigation. On the other hand, the potential gross cropped area, that is, the sum of potentially arable areas multiplied by the number of crops that with

a four-month growing season could be raised annually, is considerably larger than the net area. In many regions multiple cropping would require irrigation development.

In an attempt to estimate the limits set by water supply on the potential net and gross cropped areas I have examined the proportion of the flow of the world's rivers that could be used for irrigation. Only a small fraction of river runoff is now diverted to the world's farms, even though irrigation agriculture represents, even today, man's principal deliberate use of water. Less than 4 percent of the total river flow is employed to irrigate 160 million hectares, or about 1 percent of the land area of the earth.

The potential for irrigation development is thus very large, but it is limited by the uneven distribution of river runoff between the different continents and within different climatic zones on each continent. About a third of the total runoff comes from South America, which has less than 15 percent of the earth's land area, whereas Africa, which has 23 percent of the land, yields only 12 percent of the runoff. Runoff from Southwest Asia, North Africa, Mexico, the southwestern U.S., temperate South America and Australia is less than 5 percent of the total, yet these regions have 25 percent of the land area.

As a result of the uneven distribution of runoff, only slightly more than 30 percent of the land that is potentially arable with irrigation can actually be irrigated, and the potential increase of gross cropped area through irrigation development is limited to 1.1 billion hectares. Omitting the humid Tropics and taking account of the insufficiency of

water where it is needed, the total potentially arable land is reduced to 2.5 billion hectares (the present 1.4 billion plus 1.1 billion) and the potential gross cropped area reaches just under 4.1 billion hectares.

If 10 percent of this potential gross cropped area were set aside to grow fibers and other nonfood products, and if technology and purchased inputs of production (irrigation water, fertilizer, high-yielding seeds, plant protection, farm tools, farm machinery and farm practices based on scientific knowledge) equivalent to those used in Iowa corn farming were applied to the remainder, a diet based on 4,000 to 5,000 kilocalories of edible plant material could be provided for between 38 and 48 billion people, between 10 and 13 times the present population of the earth.

Much of the potentially arable land is of poor quality, and in general any major extension of the currently cultivated area, even for subsistence agriculture, would require a huge capital investment: of the order of between $500 and $1,000 per hectare. A more serious obstacle is the uneven distribution of potentially arable land with respect to the distribution of population. Seventy percent of the world's people live in Asia and Europe, where nearly all the potentially arable land is already cultivated; the remaining land in Asia could be brought under the plow only at the expense of large-scale irrigation development. The potential for increasing the net cultivated area is also relatively small in the U.S.S.R. Most of the uncultivated but potentially arable land lies in the more sparsely populated continents [*see illustration on these two pages*].

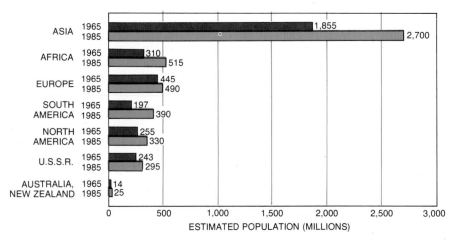
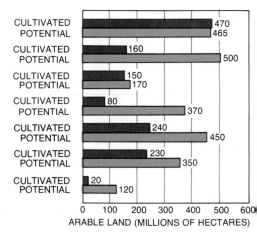

POPULATION AND CULTIVATED LAND on each continent are compared with the amount of potentially arable land outside the humid Tropics. The bars at the left show that the principal population increases between 1965 and 1985 will occur in Asia, Africa and South America. In Asia a small fraction of the land now under cultivation lies in the humid Tropics; hence the total present cultivated area (470 million hectares) actually exceeds the area that is potentially cultivable outside the humid Tropics. In both Africa and South America, however, the area that is potentially available for crops can be increased severalfold. For all continents the estimated population increase for the period 1965–1985 amounts to about 43 percent, whereas the potential increase in land avail-

Human diets in Asia are barely adequate today. If the Asian peoples are to have sufficient food in the future, it will be necessary to increase yields on currently cultivated land, that is, the weight of each crop per hectare. It will also be necessary wherever possible to grow two or three crops per year on each cultivated hectare. Such double or triple cropping will usually call for extensive irrigation development.

The largest areas of potentially arable land are in Africa and South America, which, except for the relatively small continents of Europe and Australia, have the smallest cultivated acreage. Outside the humid Tropics 630 million hectares with sufficient water remain uncultivated. The limiting factors in agricultural development on these continents are not natural resources but economic, institutional and sociopolitical constraints. In addition to the potentially arable land in Africa and South America, more than 300 million uncultivated arable hectares exist in North America and Australia.

The principal merit of the above calculations is their demonstration that the quantity of potentially arable land on the earth is so much larger than the area actually cultivated today, and the possibilities for increasing agricultural production on currently cultivated lands are so great, that the area of the earth's surface that will be devoted to agriculture in the future is chiefly an economic and social variable rather than a physical one.

In the less developed countries the basic requirement for a continuing advance in agricultural technology is the creation of better conditions for market agriculture as contrasted with subsistence agriculture, because high agricultural technology depends on the ability of the farmers to purchase, and of society to produce, many inputs from outside the farm. The modernization of agriculture depends on overall social and economic development in the poor countries as well as on the development and dissemination of new knowledge to the farmers. This will require much higher levels of industrialization and more effective public and private institutions.

Social and economic development that brings an increase in per capita income, and a more equitable income distribution is probably also a necessary condition for a continuing reduction of rates of population growth, and ultimately for a stationary world population. Here we are faced with a paradox: attainment of the earth's maximum carrying capacity for human beings would require a high level of agricultural technology, which in turn calls for a high level of social and economic development. Such development, however, would be likely to lead to a cessation of population growth long before the maximum carrying capacity is reached.

The underdeveloped countries are confronted with a more immediate circularity. In terms of both employment and production, agriculture is an overwhelmingly important component of their economy; agricultural modernization is essential for their overall economic development because it will create a consumer surplus that can be saved and invested in other economic sectors. At the same time, however, agricultural modernization depends on overall economic development because it requires many inputs from outside agriculture and a large and growing market for agricultural products.

Ecological deterioration caused by human agricultural activities is much more likely to occur through the expansion of traditional agriculture into unsuitable or easily damaged environments than through agricultural modernization, which from many points of view improves the environment (for example by the reduction of erosion). Nevertheless, agricultural modernization, particularly the use of wide-spectrum pesticides and excessive quantities of fertilizer and the elimination of potentially valuable components of plant and animal gene pools, has also been environmentally destructive. One of the kinds of knowledge that needs to be sought through research is the knowledge needed to minimize the deterioration of the environment.

The new consciousness of man's energy needs has generated alarm about the intensive use of fossil-fuel energy in modern agriculture. Some people have even called for a return to the old methods, when grinding human labor, assisted by the toil of horses and oxen, was the main form of energy used in farming. Apart from the manifest impossibility of maintaining traditional agricultural practices if the growing populations of Asia are to be able to feed themselves, this point of view has little basis in the realities of energy utilization.

John S. Steinhart of the University of Wisconsin and Carol E. Steinhart have recently pointed out in *Science* that American agriculture, in spite of its energy-intensive character, accounts for only about 3 percent of the total U.S. energy consumption. Our entire elaborate food system, including all processing, manufacture of food containers, transportation and distribution of foodstuffs, plus commercial and home refrigeration and cooking, requires less than 13 percent of the energy used in the U.S.

David Pimentel, Walter Lynn and their colleagues at Cornell University have estimated the quantity of fossil-fuel energy used in U.S. corn production, not only the energy applied directly in farming but also that used in manufacturing farm tools, machinery and chemical fertilizers, and in transportation to and from the farms. They find that the solar energy captured in the grains of corn, let alone that captured in the leaves, stalks and cobs, is two and a half times the total energy used by farmers, including their own labor. Corn farming can be thought of as a kind of breeder reactor in which much more energy-containing material is produced than is consumed. One of the reasons for the relatively small use of energy in U.S. corn production is that less than 4 percent of the area planted to corn is irrigated. Irrigation, particularly ground-water irrigation, is highly energy-intensive, but, as we have seen, it is essential in order to realize the full potential for multiple cropping in many underdeveloped countries.

Using the data compiled by Pimentel and Lynn, I have estimated the energy that would be required in a modernized, irrigated agriculture and food-processing system in India [*see illustration on page 123*]. Energy for the construction and operation of flour and sugar mills and cold-storage plants is included but not energy for cooking and food preparation in households. (Fuel for household purposes is a serious problem in India. The burning of cow dung, although an efficient method of energy conservation, does not provide an adequate supply of fuel.) My calculations show that the food

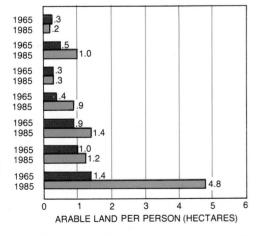

1965	.3	
1985	.2	
1965	.5	
1985	1.0	
1965	.3	
1985	.3	
1965	.4	
1985	.9	
1965	.9	
1985	1.4	
1965	1.0	
1985	1.2	
1965	1.4	
1985	4.8	

ARABLE LAND PER PERSON (HECTARES)

able for cultivation outside the humid Tropics is about 80 percent. The bars at the far right show the actual cultivated land area per person in 1965 (*gray*) and the potentially cultivable area per person for the estimated population of 1985 (*color*).

energy obtained would be about twice the mechanical energy utilized, in spite of the large amount of energy used to pump ground water for irrigation.

For the present average Indian diet of 2,150 kilocalories per day, 410,000 kilocalories of fossil-fuel energy per person would be required each year, equivalent to 55 kilograms of coal, costing, at 1974 prices, $2.50. That is about a fourth of the per capita use of fossil-fuel energy in India today. For a future diet of 3,700 kilocalories of primary plant materials and a population of 1.2 billion people, instead of the present 580 million the total energy requirement for agriculture would be the equivalent of 95 kilograms of coal per person, or a total of 114 million tons per year. Estimated reserves of fossil fuels in India are between 100 and 1,000 tons per person. Hence if India relied on her own fuel reserves, enough energy would be available for a modernized agriculture for several hundred years. As I have pointed out, however, agricultural modernization depends on overall social and economic development, and as this development proceeds total energy utilization can be expected to increase manyfold above the present level. Such an increase could not be sustained for very long with existing reserves of fossil fuels. Just as in the currently developed countries, the future welfare of India must depend on the development of nuclear and solar energy.

Since 1951 India's farmers have increased their production of food grains (mainly rice, wheat, corn, millet, sorghum, peanuts, beans and peas) by 86 percent and per capita production by 16 percent (.6 percent per year). They accomplished these impressive gains both by the traditional method that farmers have always followed—bringing more land under the plow—and by the beginning of a modernization of Indian agriculture. Over the two decades the area of India's cultivated land increased by about 20 percent, and the area on which more than one crop was grown per year and the area under irrigation both approximately doubled. The use of chemical fertilizers was increased thirtyfold. As a result yields per hectare of rice and wheat for all India rose by 60 percent and 83 percent respectively, and the total production of rice increased by 105 percent and of wheat by 340 percent. The total harvest of corn increased by 265 percent. The increase in these highly valued grains was much greater than that for millet, sorghum and the various legumes, which are less desired as foods. By expanding its own harvests India was able to reduce its imports of food grains

by some 60 percent. At today's prices this represents a saving in foreign exchange of some $800 million per year, much more than the annual costs of additional fertilizers and irrigation.

Both the need and the possibilities exist for a sharp acceleration in the rate of modernization of Indian agriculture. The Irrigation Commission of the Government of India has estimated that the irrigated area of 43 million gross cropped hectares in 1973–1974 could just about be doubled during the next 30 years, at a total cost of roughly $14 billion. This would be less than 1 percent of India's current gross national product.

If this projected irrigation development can be combined with an optimum utilization of fertilizers, with crop varieties that are highly responsive to fertilizers (the "miracle," or high-yield, varieties), with control of plant diseases and pests and with development of the knowledge, skill and human potential of Indian farmers, the problem of India's food supply could recede into the background for the foreseeable future. Assuming, for example, a population of 1.2 billion during the first half of the 21st century and yields equivalent to six tons of food grains and 500 kilograms of cotton per gross cropped hectare of irrigated land (yields of this magnitude have already been obtained in Egypt and some other underdeveloped countries), the total energy in edible crops would be the equivalent of about 3,700 kilocalories per person per day. This would allow a per capita consumption of about 25 grams of animal protein from milk, eggs and poultry and an average dietary energy content of 2,400 kilocalories. The socioeconomic changes resulting from such agricultural development could set in motion powerful forces for reductions in human fertility, and population growth could gradually be brought to a halt.

A more serious situation can be projected for Bangladesh. Careful studies by the World Bank and the Harvard Center for Population Studies have shown that with a total capital investment of nearly $2 billion annual rice and wheat production available for human consumption could be raised to about 20 million tons by 1993. Since rice and wheat constitute 82 percent of the energy content of the diet, 20 million tons would be barely enough to meet the average physiological requirement of the more than 130 million people anticipated at that time, meaning that the diet of half of the people would be below these requirements. Further modernization of agriculture might allow an eventual doubling to 40

million tons, but self-sufficiency in food production could not be long sustained in the face of continuing population growth. Thus Bangladesh is confronted with an urgent and potentially tragic problem. Both agricultural and industrial development for exports to pay for food will be necessary, possibly combined with out-migration on a large scale.

Much world concern has recently been focused on the Sahelian zone, the belt of semiarid steppe and brush-grass savanna that extends across Africa south of the Sahara. This belt is becoming narrowed on its northern side by the steady march of windblown sands, and its use by human beings and their cattle is limited on the south by the tsetse fly. A large fraction of the population of some 25 million are pastoral nomads; most of the remainder live on a meager subsistence agriculture. Human population densities are low, yet after several years of drought severe food deficiencies have become widespread. This is in spite of the fact that the possibilities for agricultural land and water development are great.

The problems here are in many ways opposite to those of India. Levels of living and the potentials for development are not constrained by the pressure of populations on natural resources but by the lack of human and technical resources and of capital for investment. Social, political and economic considerations all point toward the necessity of a rapid development of intensive irrigation agriculture, which could improve the condition of life and raise the aspirations of the people. Otherwise population growth will almost certainly keep up with increasing food supplies, and the final outcome would be a more desperate situation than the one that now exists. In the early stages capital and technical resources will have to be provided by the world community, particularly the developed countries, but the commitment of these countries to the underdeveloped ones has been diminishing for a decade.

Agricultural modernization in the underdeveloped countries is one of the great challenges facing mankind. For future human welfare such modernization must proceed much more rapidly than population growth, so that standards of living can be raised and opportunities for improvements in the conditions of life can be increased. If it does not take place quickly, it may not be possible at all. The developed countries have an essential role to play in the first stages of this modernization because they possess a large share of mankind's present ability to gain the needed knowledge through research.

11

The Transfer of Technology
to Underdeveloped Countries

The Transfer of Technology to Underdeveloped Countries

GUNNAR MYRDAL

The elimination of mass poverty is necessary to supply the motivation for fertility control in such countries. Other countries should assist in this process, not least because they have a moral obligation to do so

The proposition that the developed countries, in their dealings with the underdeveloped countries, should show a special concern for their welfare and economic development and should even undertake a collective responsibility for aiding them is an entirely new concept. It began to be articulated only at the end of World War II, with the dissolution of the colonial power structure. From the outset, perhaps inevitably, this novel and humane idea was suffused with expectations that were, as we can now see, excessively hopeful. Certainly this was true with regard to the prospects for the transfer of technology. In the developed countries, it was observed, there now existed a highly productive technology; the underdeveloped countries could simply take over that technology and so could be spared the slow process of inventing it themselves. The difficulties confronting the underdeveloped countries here as in other quarters have only gradually become understood. Hard lessons have been learned, partly from what has happened to those countries over the past 25 years and partly from closer study of their problems.

In the first place it had to be learned that scientific-industrial technology, to be maximally useful in the underdeveloped countries, cannot simply be transferred but must be adapted to the conditions prevailing there. The tropical and subtropical zones where these countries are mostly located have a different climate, and the importance of climate among all the problems besetting their economic development has been, in my view, grossly underestimated. The factors of production, capital and labor, are locally available in quite different proportions. Educated, experienced and skilled managers, engineers and workers are relatively scarce. Domestic markets are small, depriving new industries of economies of scale unless they can rapidly find large export markets. The external economies provided by a diverse surrounding industrial system are, of course, also absent and take time to develop.

Technology transfer imposes its own by no means insignificant costs in royalty payments for licenses and know-how. According to the estimate of a United Nations agency, these costs amounted to $1.5 billion in 1968 and have been increasing steeply. The transfer of technology through joint ventures is often accompanied by extraordinary costs imposed by the overpricing of imported intermediate goods, the underpricing of final goods for export, tax subsidies, various forms of tax avoidance and so on, the cumulative cost of all of which it is impossible to estimate. Even when the transfer is effected on long-term credits from individual developed countries, the almost universal practice of tying such "aid" to imports from those same countries implies the payment of prices higher —by 20 to 40 percent—than if the choice of imports from abroad were altogether free.

Against all these costs it has nonetheless been argued that the transfer of technology carries a net advantage. Edward S. Mason of Harvard University pointed out in the 1950's that the underdeveloped countries "could hardly be at an absolute disadvantage as compared with the initiators of industrial development, since they always have the alternative of devising techniques themselves as did their predecessors in development." Yet is it realistic to assume that the underdeveloped countries have such an option?

In the 1950's it was also frequently pointed out—and one hears this hopeful thought voiced even today—that in the history of economic development in the West it was often advantageous to be a latecomer. Britain has continually paid a price for being the first country to undergo industrial revolution. Time and time again, in one industry after another, other Western countries have succeeded in catching up with and then surpassing her. Taking over and advancing a technology first developed in Britain was a recurring historical event.

The countries that accomplished this feat, however, were very different from the underdeveloped countries of today. They were all, like Britain, located in the Temperate Zone. They had access to a competitive capital market where they could borrow for as little as 3 percent and sometimes even less. And they did not have exploding populations.

More directly pertinent to their ability to absorb new technology from

EARLY IRON BRIDGE IN JAPAN is portrayed on the opposite page in a woodcut that is part of a larger engraving in the collection of Mrs. Gerard Piel. The Japanese ideograms over the archway identify the structure as the Azuma Bridge, which was built over the Sumida River in Tokyo in 1875 under the supervision of British engineers. The people in the black carriage are clearly Europeans, and the occasion is evidently a ceremonial one.

abroad, the western European and North American countries could boast almost general literacy in their populations. In regard to elementary education they had passed Britain, which lagged in this respect until fairly recently. The technology they already had was much higher and more diversified than that now possessed by underdeveloped countries. They had universities and technical colleges and were generally part of Western civilization. In all these respects they were much more favorably placed to benefit from the transfer of technology.

Moreover, the technology they acquired was very different from that of today. Most of the technical innovations of the late 18th and early 19th centuries were of a rather simple mechanical kind, whereas today they grow out of scientific discoveries concerning the nature of matter and energy. The entrepreneurs themselves, in textiles and other industries, took an active part in improving the machines in their factories. Charles H. Wilson has observed that technology then "involved no principles that an intelligent merchant could not grasp."

To this it should be added that technology in those days was much less capital-intensive and in general did not confer so much advantage of scale. Private enterprises, often small at least to start

with, had their field day, and they effectively carried out the transfer of technology. The state often subsidized and protected them but seldom found reason to direct them.

Technology today is much more intimately related to science. From this difference stem the many other differences that constrain its transferability compared with the simple technology of the earlier years of the scientific-industrial revolution. And the connection between scientific discovery and technological innovation becomes closer every day.

This brings us to what can be called the dynamic problem. The transfer of technology must now take place in a setting of more rapid advance in science and technology than ever before in history. As the American historian Henry Adams and others since have observed, this advance is accelerating, proceeding on an exponential curve; the pace of history is accelerating in parallel, and the driving force is scientific and technological advance.

It is not only that the underdeveloped countries must attempt to approach, by adoption and adaptation, a much higher level of science and technology but also that they must reach for science and

technology that are continually and rapidly moving to a higher level. The developed countries are the site of practically all this advance. It is financed by their governments, philanthropic foundations, universities and industries. It is almost exclusively directed to the interests of the developed countries, although it produces occasional spin-offs useful to the underdeveloped countries.

All the elements cited here in the relation between the dynamics of scientific and technological advance and the prospects of the underdeveloped countries have been analyzed and accounted for separately by others in topic-by-topic studies. The conclusion that they add up to a general disadvantage for these countries is not, however, commonly drawn.

Thus the contribution of technological advance to the deterioration of the trading position of South Asian countries is recognized in studies of trends in their traditional exports. Synthetic fibers have largely displaced hemp, for example, in ship cordage and other technically demanding uses, and plastic film has been displacing jute in sacking. According to a recent U.S. Congressional committee report, coffee, tea and cocoa may soon have competition from synthetics. Rich countries will continue to develop manufactured substitutes for imported natural

NAGARJUNASAGAR DAM on the Kistna River in India represents a combination of modern technology and the employment of thousands of native laborers. The dam was built primarily for generating power, which is a basic element in the economic infrastruc-

commodities. Not many of the commodities exported by the poor countries are as difficult to replace as the petroleum for which the few exporting countries in the Middle East, Africa and South America have recently succeeded in exacting a much higher price.

The dynamic advance of industrial technology also militates against the successful development of manufactured exports by underdeveloped countries. Industries in the developed countries hold their markets firmly by dint of product and market research that brings rapid response to changing market preferences and by the internal and external economies that are provided by a broad and diversified industrial foundation. For contest with such competitors, enterprises in underdeveloped countries are ill-equipped. Typically their managers are weak in business acumen and their production workers are weak in skills; they lack capital, and they have little experience in standardized, high-quality mass production. The inefficiency of both management and labor and the absence of a supporting industrial environment will often, in spite of lower wages, tend to raise unit costs and so negate, in part at least, the international comparative advantage of low wage scales.

To all these well-investigated disad-

ture that a developing country must acquire, but its waters are also put to other purposes.

vantages facing new industrial enterprises in underdeveloped countries, industries in the developed countries have added research departments devoted to the improvement of their products and production processes. The resources of any one of these laboratories are amplified by the country's entire scientific establishment. What a new industry in an underdeveloped country must face is not only that the technological competence of its established competitors is high but also that it is constantly rising. Even if a license to use a particular technology is available, the contract does not often license future improvements; when it does, the obstacles to catching up are great.

With these difficulties in the way of reaching out with exports into world markets, underdeveloped countries have commonly adopted import substitution as the strategy for pushing their industrialization. By import restriction they can create markets at home. By the same action they should also be able to save foreign exchange. This advantage, if it is won at all, is secured only in the fairly long run. New industries, even those set up for the home market, need capital equipment from abroad and a continuous supply of spare parts, intermediate products and sometimes raw materials. Efforts to set up supporting industries that can provide substitutes for these imports raise again the same type of new import needs.

Seen from a planning point of view, import restrictions are more often a necessity than a policy. Shortage of foreign exchange usually comes first, and the protection provided by import restrictions for nursling industries is incidental. How the restrictions are handled determines whether or not they contribute to planned development. Import restrictions must either stop or make very expensive the importation of less necessary goods. That is rational. But domestic production of these goods then enjoys the very highest protection, often sky-high, which is not rational. Because the governments have not usually proved themselves able or willing to soak up "too high" profits by excess-profit taxes, they are compelled to resort to a large variety of direct controls. These controls have not often succeeded in reducing such profits, much less in redirecting investments according to plan.

Underdeveloped countries, quite apart from what their constitutions proclaim, are commonly ruled by upper-class elites. These people hanker for luxury goods, are glad to see them produced at home when restrictions bar their importation from abroad and usually have nothing against high profits. Protection thus becomes either unplanned or badly planned. It tends to create noncompetitive, high-cost and high-profit industries. This result in turn negates the planners' efforts to encourage entrepreneurs to enter more primary industries or to tackle the difficulties of the export market described above.

Keeping all of this in mind, it is surprising to learn that a few countries, in Latin America and Southeast Asia, have broken through the market barrier in certain fields and come out as exporters of manufactured goods. This is a sign that in these cases the difficulties of the transfer of technology have been overcome. Many of these cases reflect active cooperation from industries in developed countries. An important role has often been played by multinational corporations—an item to their credit that must not be forgotten in assessing their role in the world economy.

From the early 1950's there has been considerable discussion of how technology transferred from the developed to the underdeveloped countries could be adapted to be more labor-intensive. Underdeveloped countries are regularly short of capital, whereas their labor forces are grossly underutilized and become ever more so owing to the rapid, and increasingly rapid, growth of the populations in the labor-force age range [see "The Populations of the Underdeveloped Countries," by Paul Demeny, page 105]. Some such adaptation of imported technology normally takes place without much difficulty or planning. The handling, packaging and shipping of raw materials and finished products can easily be, and for the most part are, conducted by labor-intensive methods. Lack of skill and sometimes of physical stamina, combined with low wages, makes it a rather normal thing that machines are run at a slower pace or with more workers tending them—except when an enterprise has found it advantageous to hire only literate workers and pay them salaries that enable them to improve their nutrition and general health.

When it comes, however, to the technology implied in the industrial processes and embodied in the machines, which is what is usually meant by the transfer of technology, there is little choice but to take it all without much change. For one thing, a different technology in this more fundamental sense would be likely to call for more technological creativity than underdeveloped countries command. The only capital equipment available, in any case, is what the developed countries are currently employing. That, along with the problem of finding spare parts, explains why underdeveloped countries have not equipped themselves with secondhand machinery from earlier years of technological advance, as some well-wishers have suggested they should. What is more, entrepreneurs are reluctant to accept "second best" equipment. That is often a rational attitude and not merely an oversensitive one. The most modern technology may in fact be optimal for promoting economic development. In many branches of industry the most up-to-date capital-intensive equipment is capital-saving in the important sense of consuming less capital per unit of output.

Careful studies have shown that the adoption on a major—and otherwise totally impractical—scale of more labor-intensive technologies in India would not have secured a substantial increase in the employment of labor. Modern industry forms, and for a long time to come will form, a very small part of the total economy there, and a still smaller part in other countries of South Asia.

When industrialization was first advanced as the road to development, it was thought that the growth of modern industry would draw off the underutilized labor force bottled up in agriculture and the loosely organized nonagricultural pursuits. A UN report in the early 1960's stated: "The reason for em-

phasizing industrialization is that industrial development would absorb rural underemployed persons." The plans of underdeveloped countries echoed this theme; throughout the 1950's and into the early 1960's and sometimes even now economists in both kinds of country have endorsed it. In the long view it is also entirely rational. If India and most other underdeveloped countries do not by the end of this century have a much larger portion of their labor force—which by then will have doubled in size—employed in industry, there will then be no hope of preserving even their present low average levels of living, no matter what improvements have meanwhile been accomplished in agriculture. The underdeveloped countries have serious

LODGING RICE has been a problem in the areas where rice is a staple food. At left Syntha, a traditional variety of tropical rice from Indonesia, is portrayed before maturity. It has long, weak stems and wide, drooping leaves. When the rice is fertilized, the plants produce heavy grain heads and so are likely to lodge, or fall over, at maturity (*right*). The grain may dip into the paddy water or be eaten by rodents. The wide leaves also interfere with photosynthesis by blocking sunlight that could fall on a number of leaves.

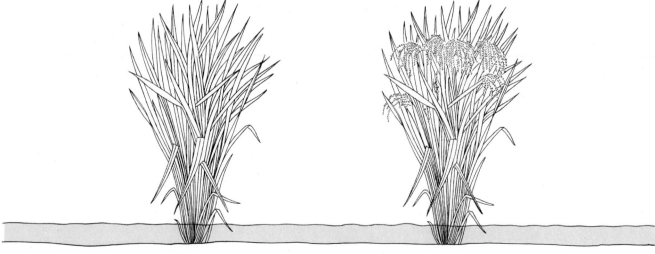

NONLODGING RICE was developed at the International Rice Research Institute. The varieties are semidwarfs with strong stems, which hold the plant upright when the grain heads mature. Narrow leaves also aid photosynthesis by letting more sunlight penetrate.

reason to press on with their industrialization.

For several decades ahead, however, the employment effects of industrialization cannot be expected to be very large. The impact on employment is a function not only of the rate of industrialization but also of the absolute size of industry. For some time the effects may in fact be negative, owing to "backlash" disemployment of people from traditional industries and crafts that are either competed out or modernized and so made less labor-intensive. This was the experience in the Soviet Central Asian republics of Uzbekistan, Kirghizia, Tadzhikistan and Turkmenia. In the throes of a rapid industrial expansion that began in the late 1920's, the proportion of the labor force employed in manufacturing (including crafts and traditional industry) actually decreased until fairly recently, when industrialization progressed to a much higher level. The statistics on "employment" and "underemployment" in underdeveloped countries—usually inadequate—do not contradict the judgment that industrialization, at its present level, does not create much additional employment, even allowing for its side effects on employment in the building of the "infrastructure" and in services.

In the same overoptimistic view of the employment-generating effects of industrialization, the influx of population to the cities was regarded during the 1950's as a response to the demand for labor in industry. In reality it must be recognized as a flight from agriculture. The cities in all the underdeveloped countries now have a much bigger labor force than can possibly be employed in industry, however fast it is growing. They are simply displaced rural people.

The transfer of technology to the agriculture of the underdeveloped countries presents a totally different problem. Apart from the highly commercialized plantations in some of these countries, which should more properly be reckoned with industry, yields are almost everywhere low. To the low yields correspond serious nutritional deficiencies, which at present are threatening to become worse. In most countries there is not much uncultivated land to put to the plow. The only hope for increased production is intensified cultivation aided by advanced technology.

Contrary to a common misconception agriculture in these countries is not labor-intensive; it is labor-extensive, even though an exceedingly large portion of the labor force is confined to agriculture. In many countries a part of that labor

force does no work at all; the nonworkers cannot all be classified as unemployed—members of the Brahman caste in Bengal do not work but hire workers. Most of the workers who do work do so only for short periods—per day, week, month or year—and not very intensively or efficiently. This is what, in false analogy to conditions in developed countries, is called "unemployment" or "underemployment."

The low yields per acre reflect the underutilization of the labor force. An increase in the input of labor and in labor efficiency would raise yields even without technological innovation or any additional investment except work. Much of any such increase in input should be directed to better use of existing technology—to improving the land, to constructing works for water conservation and distribution, to building more and

better roads and to generally improving the condition of the villages.

Technological innovations can improve yields still more. The new technology must, however, be highly labor-intensive. Otherwise it will swell the stream of migrants to the city slums. The agricultural technology of the developed countries—aimed almost from the beginning at the improvement of yields while the agricultural labor force was declining, first relatively and then absolutely—is not on the whole adaptable to conditions in the underdeveloped countries. Certain important exceptions can nonetheless make all the difference. These include the artificial insemination of livestock, new methods of preventing plant diseases and, of course, high-yielding seeds.

Properly adapted to local conditions, such techniques should be applied by labor-intensive methods for the double

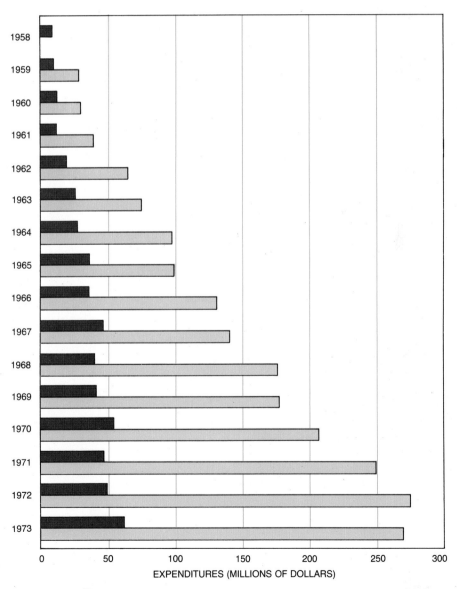

MULTILATERAL AID by the United Nations to developing countries is charted. The gray bars represent outlays by regular programs of UN agencies, and the colored bars show what has been advanced under the special UN Development Program of multilateral aid.

purpose of securing increases in both yields and employment. Whereas tractors have their place and may in some situations increase employment, mechanization in general disemploys human workers and would not contribute much to increased yields per hectare, which are better secured by labor-intensive methods. It is often maintained that the agriculture of the underdeveloped countries requires some "intermediary technology." This should not be understood to imply a technology that has become obsolete in developed countries. What should be transferred is a technology that engages the latest results of scientific research, adjusted to the highest possible utilization of the labor force.

There is thus a fundamental difference in the conditions that should rule the transfer of technology to the industrial and to the agricultural sectors in underdeveloped economies. In the former the use of modern technology makes it possible to establish new industries with minimal disturbance of the institutional framework and minimal diffusion of skills throughout the labor force. Industrial expansion may thus evade direct

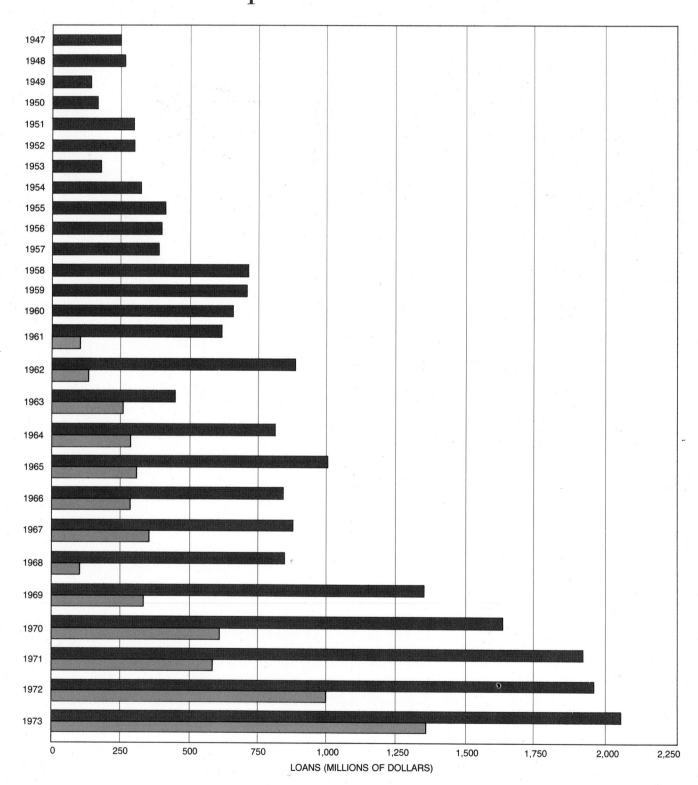

WORLD BANK LOANS to developing countries are another major source of multilateral aid. The bank's loans (*gray*) and operations of the International Development Association (*color*), which is the soft-loan arm of the bank, are shown. Multilateral aid will become a highly significant factor in development and the transfer of technology if it continues to increase at the recent rates.

confrontation with the social and institutional obstacles that have for so long inhibited economic development. The price paid for this strategy, however, is the perpetuation of the enclave industrial economy familiar from colonial experience. The "spread effects" of industrialization, that is, the generation of employment in ancillary industries and services and the percolation of productive skills and of the rational analytical attitude to the surrounding society, have proved very much smaller in many countries than was expected in earlier years and is still often assumed.

In contrast, the task of raising yields in agriculture through highly labor-intensive technology must confront the attitudes and institutions that have so long held these rural societies stagnant. Most important is to change "the relation between man and the land," creating the possibilities and the incentives for a man to work more, to work harder and more efficiently and to invest whatever he can lay his hands on to improve the land, in the first instance his own labor. This is the essence of the demand for a well-planned land and tenancy reform. Such reform has been on the agenda in all underdeveloped countries; with only a few exceptions it has been botched. As a result the auxiliary reforms often attempted in market organization, extension work and credits have been less effective. Hence, whereas industrialization can go forward without involving the masses, the successful transfer of technology to agriculture must change the people and all the social and economic relations there.

Once, on a visit to a famous agricultural school in a university in the American Middle West, I found myself talking with a large group of Indian and Pakistani students enrolled there. "What are you doing here?" I asked them. "What can you learn that can in any way help your people at home, toiling in fields around their mud huts?" Their answers showed they shared my misgivings.

Students so trained might just as well stay on in this country and swell the "brain drain." If they go home, they will either be unemployed or, thanks to their "connections," get administrative positions for which their education in the U.S. has not fitted them. For effective technology transfer it would be better to send teachers to the universities and schools in the underdeveloped countries. Some of them would at least get to understand what the practical problems there really are. Those who come to the developed countries for training should not be students, least of all undergraduate students, but people who are already established at home, for example physicians who want to learn a particular new technique or engineers who are out to master a new industrial process.

We in the developed countries should do whatever we can to enlarge and raise the standards of the universities and research institutions in the underdeveloped countries. Since many of them are bent on producing results that will impress us rather than solve their own practical problems, we have need of more knowledge about conditions in their countries and more imagination if we are to be of help to them. A very important part of our "aid" can be the redirection of our own research efforts to their problems. That should be done in collaboration with research institutions either already established or newly created in the underdeveloped countries. A model for such enterprise was provided by the work of the Rockefeller Foundation and later also by the Ford Foundation in the development of high-yielding strains of cereal grains. Another is the research conducted by the Population Council in the improvement of birth-control techniques and their adaptation to conditions in the underdeveloped countries, initiated at a time when the U.S. Government and public were not prepared to support such work. These are outstanding examples of what we should do on a large scale in many other fields.

It is evident that the transfer of technology must proceed on a much larger scale if increase in the production of material necessities is to overtake the increase in the population of the underdeveloped countries. The need for aid in the larger part of the underdeveloped world must therefore be recognized as substantial. Moreover, this need cannot be thought of as a short-term exigency; it will be long-lasting.

If my striving toward realism leads me to a darker view of the prospects for economic development than that still current among most of my fellow economists, this does not lead me to defeatism. On the contrary, my conclusion is that development requires increased and, in many respects, more radical efforts: speedier and more effective reforms in the underdeveloped countries and aid appropriations in the budgets of the developed countries that approach the amount those countries spend for other important national purposes, such as social security or education, not to mention armaments.

The Authors
Bibliographies
Index

The Authors

RONALD FREEDMAN and BERNARD BERELSON ("The Human Population") are respectively at the University of Michigan and the Population Council; Freedman is professor of sociology and associate director of the Population Studies Center and Berelson is president of the Population Council. Freedman was born in Canada and was brought to the U.S. as a child. He received his bachelor's and master's degrees at the University of Michigan in 1939 and 1940 respectively and his Ph.D. from the University of Chicago in 1947. He has been a member of the Michigan faculty since 1946. Berelson was graduated from Whitman College in 1934, obtaining his master's degree at the University of Washington in 1937 and his Ph.D. from the University of Chicago in 1941. He was on the Chicago faculty for a number of years, serving as professor of library science and of the social sciences and (from 1947 to 1951) as dean of the Graduate Library School. From 1951 to 1957 he was director of the behavioral sciences program for the Ford Foundation. He joined the Population Council in 1962 after two more years at Chicago and one year at Columbia University.

ANSLEY J. COALE ("The History of the Human Population") is director of the Office of Population Research at Princeton University and also William Church Osborn Professor of Public Affairs. All his degrees are from Princeton: his bachelor's degree in 1939, master's degree in 1941 and Ph.D. in 1947. For many years starting in 1947 he was on the economics faculty at Princeton, being appointed professor of economics in 1959 and receiving his present professorial appointment in 1964. He began his present association with the Office of

Population Research in 1955 and has been director since 1959. From 1961 to 1968 Coale served as U.S. representative to the Population Commission of the United Nations.

SHELDON J. SEGAL ("The Physiology of Human Reproduction") is vice-president of the Population Council and director of its biomedical division. Following his graduation from Dartmouth College in 1947 he did graduate work at the University of Geneva for a year and then took his advanced degrees at the State University of Iowa: his master's degree in 1951 and his Ph.D. (in embryology and biochemistry) in 1952. He was a member of the faculty there until 1956, when he joined the Population Council.

L. L. CAVALLI-SFORZA ("The Genetics of Human Populations") is professor of genetics at Stanford University, where he teaches in the human-biology curriculum and in the medical school. "Graduated in medicine at the University of Pavia, 1944," he writes. "For the first third of my scientific life I worked in bacterial genetics in Milan and Cambridge. For the second third I worked in the genetics of human populations (ranging from farmers of the upper Parma valley to pygmies of the African forest). With Walter Bodmer, now at the University of Oxford, I have written a fairly large volume by the same title. Having begun what should be, according to tables of life expectancy, the last third of my active life, I have become interested in behavioral genetics, cultural evolution and archaeology." Before Cavalli-Sforza went to Stanford he was professor of genetics and chairman of the department of genetics at Pavia.

KINGSLEY DAVIS ("The Migrations

of Human Populations") is Ford Professor of Sociology and Comparative Studies and director of International Population and Urban Research at the University of California at Berkeley. His appointment is in both the department of sociology and the Institute of International Studies. Davis was an English major in college, receiving his bachelor's degree from the University of Texas in 1930 and his first master's degree (in philosophy) there in 1932. He then went to Harvard University, where he obtained degrees in sociology: his master's degree in 1933 and his Ph.D. in 1936. His association with the University of California began in 1955; in 1956 he founded the International Population and Urban Research unit. From 1954 to 1961 he was the U.S. representative to the Population Commission of the United Nations; in 1959 he was president of the American Sociological Association, and in 1962–1963 he was president of the Population Association of America.

CHARLES F. WESTOFF ("The Populations of the Developed Countries") is Maurice P. During '22 Professor of Demographic Studies and professor of sociology at Princeton University and associate director of the university's Office of Population Research. He was graduated from Syracuse University in 1949 and received his master's degree there a year later; his Ph.D., which he obtained in 1953, is from the University of Pennsylvania. Westoff has been on the Princeton faculty since 1955; from 1958 to 1962 he also served as associate professor of sociology at New York University. From 1970 to 1972 he was in Washington as executive director of the Commission on Population Growth and the American Future. He describes himself as an "avid tennis and squash player."

NORMAN B. RYDER ("The Family in Developed Countries") is professor of sociology at Princeton University and a member of the staff of the Office of Population Research. Born in Canada, he was graduated from McMaster University in 1944 and received his master's degree at the University of Toronto in 1946. In 1949 he obtained his second master's degree at Princeton, receiving his Ph.D. there in 1951. Ryder was a demographer with the Canadian Bureau of Statistics in 1950–1951, a lecturer at Toronto from 1951 to 1954, a demographer with the Scripps Foundation in Oxford, Ohio, from 1954 to 1956, and a professor of sociology at the University of Wisconsin from 1956 until he returned to Princeton in 1971.

JUDITH BLAKE ("The Changing Status of Women in Developed Countries") is professor in the Graduate School of Public Policy of the University of California at Berkeley. For a number of years before receiving that appointment she was professor of demography, serving as chairman of the department of demography in the College of Letters and Science from 1967 to 1972. She was graduated from Columbia University in 1950 and obtained her Ph.D. there in 1961. "I have a continuing interest in international population research," she writes, "but during the past decade have spent a lot of time investigating the views of Americans on family size, birth control, abortion and similar issues of population policy. As for other interests, I have shared in rearing a daughter and a stepson. This activity, although it is highly educational and enjoyable, has taken precedence over my previous pastimes as a native New Yorker: theater, opera and museums. Our family loves to travel together. When we are home, my husband [Kingsley Davis] and I garden and take long walks."

PAUL DEMENY ("The Populations of the Underdeveloped Countries") is vice-president of the Population Council and director of its Demographic Division. Born in Hungary, he was graduated from the University of Budapest in 1955. After graduate work in Switzerland he went to Princeton University, where he received his Ph.D. (in economics) in 1961. Before joining the Population Council in 1973 he was for four years director of the East-West Population Institute at the East-West Center in Honolulu and professor of economics at the University of Hawaii. Earlier he had been professor of economics and associate director of the Population Studies Center at the University of Michigan and had been associated with the department of demography at the University of California at Berkeley and Princeton's Office of Population Research and department of economics. Demeny writes: "My father, a judge, collected books on statistics as a hobby, and by the age of 10 I had become fascinated with birth and death rates and the like. This prosaic interest has not faded, although for some years it competed with the ambition, never realized, to play bassoon in the Budapest Philharmonic."

ROGER REVELLE ("Food and Population") is Richard Saltonstall Professor of Population Policy at Harvard University and director of the Center for Population Studies at Harvard. He went to Harvard in 1964 after many years at the University of California, where from 1951 to 1964 he was director of the Scripps Institution of Oceanography. From 1958 to 1961 he was also director of the university's campus at La Jolla. Between 1961 and 1963 he was on leave of absence to serve as the first science adviser to the Secretary of the Interior. On his return to the University of California he became dean of research for all campuses. Revelle was graduated from Pomona College in 1929. He received his Ph.D. from the University of California in 1936.

GUNNAR MYRDAL ("The Transfer of Technology to Underdeveloped Countries") is about to begin an appointment as Morton Globus Visiting Distinguished Professor of Social Science at the City College of the City University of New York. He goes there from the Center for the Study of Democratic Institutions. Myrdal was for many years professor of international economics at the University of Stockholm. He is the founder and former director of the Institute for International Economic Studies at the university and also was until recently chairman of the Stockholm International Peace Research Institute. In Sweden he has served as a member of the Senate and as minister of commerce.

Bibliographies

Readers interested in further reading on the subjects covered by articles in this issue may find the lists below helpful.

THE HUMAN POPULATION

POPULATION GROWTH AND ECONOMIC DEVELOPMENT IN LOW-INCOME COUNTRIES. Ansley J. Coale and Edgar M. Hoover. Princeton University Press, 1958.

POPULATION: THE VITAL REVOLUTION. Edited by Ronald Freedman. Doubleday & Company / Anchor Books, 1964.

POPULATION STUDIES, No. 48: A CONCISE SUMMARY OF THE WORLD POPULATION SITUATION IN 1970. United Nations, 1971.

POPULATION AND FAMILY PLANNING PROGRAMS: A FACTBOOK. Dorothy Nortman in Reports on Population / Family Planning, No. 2; 1973.

POPULATION POLICY IN DEVELOPED COUNTRIES. Edited by Bernard Berelson. McGraw-Hill Book Co., 1974.

THE HISTORY OF THE HUMAN POPULATION

ECONOMIC PROBLEMS OF POPULATION CHANGE. Frank W. Notestein in Proceedings of the Eighth International Conference of Agricultural Economists. Oxford University Press, 1953.

HOW MANY PEOPLE HAVE EVER LIVED ON EARTH. Population Bulletin, Vol. 18, No. 1; February, 1962.

HISTORICAL OUTLINE OF WORLD POPULATION GROWTH. Goran Ohlin in Proceedings of the World Population Conference, 1965. United Nations Department of Economic and Social Affairs, 1967.

HISTORY OF HUMAN LIFE SPAN AND MORTALITY. G. Acsádi and J. Nemeskéri. International Publications Service, 1970.

MENSTRUAL CYCLES: FATNESS AS A DETERMINANT OF MINIMUM WEIGHT FOR HEIGHT NECESSARY FOR THEIR MAINTENANCE AND ONSET. R. E. Frisch and J. W. MacArthur in Science, in press.

THE PHYSIOLOGY OF HUMAN REPRODUCTION

GERM CELLS AND FERTILIZATION. Edited by C. R. Austin and R. V. Short. Cambridge University Press, 1972.

GONADOTROPINS. Edited by B. B. Saxena, C. G. Beling and H. M. Gandy. Wiley-Interscience, 1972.

HORMONES IN REPRODUCTION. Edited by C. R. Austin and R. V. Short. Cambridge University Press, 1972.

CONTRACEPTIVE RESEARCH: A MALE CHAUVINIST PLOT? Sheldon J. Segal in Family Planning Perspectives, Vol. 4, No. 3, pages 21–25; July, 1972.

THE REGULATION OF MAMMALIAN REPRODUCTION. Edited by Sheldon J. Segal, Ruth Crozier, Philip A. Corfman and Peter G. Condliffe. Charles C Thomas, Publisher, 1973.

THE GENETICS OF HUMAN POPULATIONS

THE GENETICS OF HUMAN POPULATIONS. L. L. Cavalli-Sforza and Walter F. Bodmer. W. H. Freeman and Company, 1971.

MEASURING THE RATE OF SPREAD OF EARLY FARMING IN EUROPE. A. J. Ammerman and L. L. Cavalli-Sforza in Man, Vol. 6, No. 4, pages 674–688; December, 1971.

ORIGIN AND DIFFERENTIATION OF HUMAN RACES–HUXLEY MEMORIAL LECTURE. L. L. Cavalli-Sforza in Proceedings of the Royal Anthropological Institute of Great Britain and Ireland, pages 15–25; 1973.

SOME CURRENT PROBLEMS OF HUMAN POPULATION GENETICS. L. L. Cavalli-Sforza in American Journal of Human Genetics, Vol. 25, pages 82–104; 1973.

A POPULATION MODEL FOR THE DIFFUSION OF EARLY FARMING IN EUROPE. A. J. Ammerman and L. L. Cavalli-Sforza in The Explanation of Cultural Change, edited by Colin Renfrew. University of Pittsburgh Press, 1974.

THE MIGRATIONS OF HUMAN POPULATIONS

EMIGRANT COMMUNITIES IN SOUTH CHINA. Ta Chen. Institute of Pacific Relations, 1940.

THE MYTH OF OPEN SPACES. W. D. Forsyth. Melbourne University Press in association with Oxford University Press, 1942.

EUROPE ON THE MOVE: WAR AND POPULATION CHANGES, 1917–1947. Eugene M. Kulischer. Columbia University Press, 1948.

THE REFUGEE IN THE WORLD: DISPLACEMENT AND INTEGRATION. Joseph B. Schechtman. A. S. Barnes and Company, 1963.

BRITAIN AND THE LABOR TRADE IN THE SOUTHWEST PACIFIC. Owen W. Parnaby. Duke University Press, 1964.

THE ATLANTIC SLAVE TRADE: A CENSUS. Philip D. Curtin. University of Wisconsin Press, 1969.

REFUGEES SOUTH OF THE SAHARA: AN AFRICAN DILEMMA. Edited by Hugh C. Brooks and Yassin El-Ayouty. Negro Universities Press, 1970.

THE UN AND THE PALESTINIAN REFUGEES. Edward H. Buehrig. Indiana University Press, 1971.

INTERNATIONAL MIGRATION LAW. Richard Plender. Humanities Press, Inc., 1972.

MIGRATION AND ECONOMIC GROWTH: A STUDY OF GREAT BRITAIN AND THE ATLANTIC ECONOMY. Brinley Thomas. Cambridge University Press, 1972.

THE MIGRATION OF WORKERS IN THE UNITED KINGDOM AND THE EUROPEAN COMMUNITY. W. R. Böhning. Oxford University Press, 1972.

INTERNATIONAL MIGRATION in The Determinants and Consequences of Pop-

ulation Trends: Vol. I. United Nations, 1973.

THE POPULATIONS OF
THE DEVELOPED COUNTRIES

U.S. POPULATION GROWTH IN INTERNATIONAL PERSPECTIVE. Michael S. Teitelbaum in *Toward the End of Growth: Population in America,* by Charles F. Westoff et al. Prentice-Hall, Inc., 1973.

FERTILITY AND FAMILY PLANNING IN EUROPE AROUND 1970: A COMPARATIVE STUDY OF 12 NATIONAL SURVEYS. Jerzy Berent. Population Association of America, 1974.

THE UNPRECEDENTED CURRENT DECLINE IN EUROPEAN BIRTHRATES. Jean Bourgeois-Pichât. Population Council Lecture at Princeton University, February 4, 1974.

BEYOND THE DEMOGRAPHIC TRANSITION. Arthur A. Campbell in *Demography,* in press.

THE FAMILY
IN DEVELOPED COUNTRIES

SOCIAL VALUES ABOUT FAMILY SIZE IN THE UNITED STATES. Ronald Freedman in *International Population Conference, Vienna.* International Union for the Scientific Study of Population, 1959.

WORLD REVOLUTION AND FAMILY PATTERNS. William J. Goode. The Free Press, 1963.

THE CHARACTER OF MODERN FERTILITY. Norman B. Ryder in *The Annals of the American Academy of Political and Social Science,* Vol. 369, pages 26–36; January, 1967.

THE AMERICAN FAMILY IN RELATION TO DEMOGRAPHIC CHANGE. Kingsley Davis in *U.S. Commission on Population Growth and the American Future Research Reports—Vol. I: Demographic and Social Aspects of Population Growth,* edited by Charles F. Westoff and Robert Parke, Jr. U.S. Government Printing Office, 1972.

THREE GENERATIONS OF PARENTS. Arthur A. Campbell in *Family Planning Perspectives,* Vol. 5, No. 2, pages 106–112; Spring, 1973.

THE CHANGING STATUS
OF WOMEN
IN DEVELOPED COUNTRIES

WOMEN IN THE MODERN WORLD. Mirra Komarovsky. Little, Brown and Co., 1953.

POPULATION STUDIES, No. 33: DEMOGRAPHIC ASPECTS OF MANPOWER, REPORT I—SEX AND AGE PATTERNS OF PARTICIPATION IN ECONOMIC ACTIVITIES. United Nations, 1962.

BARRIERS TO THE CAREER CHOICE OF ENGINEERING, MEDICINE, AND SCIENCE AMONG AMERICAN WOMEN in *Women and the Scientific Professions: Proceedings of the M.I.T. Symposium on American Women in Science and Engineering,* edited by Jacquelyn A. Mattfeld and Carol E. Van Aken. The M.I.T. Press, 1965.

THE FEMALE LABOR FORCE IN THE UNITED STATES. Valerie Kincade Oppenheimer. Institute of International Studies, University of California, Berkeley, 1970.

SEX ROLES AND SOCIAL STRUCTURE. Harriet Holter. Universitetsforlaget, Oslo, 1970.

THE CHANGING ROLES OF MEN AND WOMEN. Edited by Edmund Dahlström. Beacon Press, 1971.

THE WOMAN MOVEMENT. William L. O'Neill. Quadrangle Press, 1971.

THE AMERICAN WOMAN: HER CHANGING SOCIAL, ECONOMIC, AND POLITICAL ROLES, 1920–1970. William H. Chafe. Oxford University Press, 1972.

WOMEN AND WORK: AN INTERNATIONAL COMPARISON. Marjorie Galenson. New York State School of Industrial and Labor Relations, Cornell University, 1973.

THE POPULATIONS
OF THE
UNDERDEVELOPED COUNTRIES

THE MODERN EXPANSION OF WORLD POPULATION. John D. Durand in *Proceedings of the American Philosophical Society,* Vol. 111, No. 3, pages 136–159; June 22, 1967.

RAPID POPULATION GROWTH: CONSEQUENCES AND POLICY IMPLICATIONS. Edited by Roger Revelle. Published for the National Academy of Sciences by the Johns Hopkins University Press, 1971.

THE DEMOGRAPHIC TRANSITION RECONSIDERED. A. J. Coale in *International Population Conference, Liège.* International Union for the Scientific Study of Population, 1973.

THE FUTURE OF POPULATION GROWTH: ALTERNATIVE PATHS TO EQUILIBRIUM. Tomas Frejka. Wiley-Interscience, 1973.

POPULATION STUDIES, No. 50: THE DETERMINANTS AND CONSEQUENCES OF POPULATION TRENDS. United Nations, 1973.

WORLD POPULATION: STATUS REPORT 1974. Bernard Berelson in *Reports on Population / Family Planning,* No. 15; January, 1974.

FOOD AND POPULATION

TRANSFORMING TRADITIONAL AGRICULTURE. Theodore W. Schultz. Yale University Press, 1964.

THE WORLD FOOD PROBLEM. President's Science Advisory Committee. U.S. Government Printing Office, 1967.

SEEDS OF CHANGE: THE GREEN REVOLUTION AND DEVELOPMENT IN THE 1970's. Lester R. Brown. Praeger Publishers, Inc., 1970.

THE STATE OF FOOD AND AGRICULTURE. Food and Agriculture Organization, United Nations, Rome.

THE TRANSFER
OF TECHNOLOGY TO
UNDERDEVELOPED COUNTRIES

ASIAN DRAMA: AN INQUIRY INTO THE POVERTY OF NATIONS. Gunnar Myrdal. Pantheon Books, 1968.

Index